Catholicism and the World Today

Catholicism and the World Today

by

Dom Aelred Graham
Prior of St. Gregory's, Portsmouth,
Rhode Island

DAVID McKAY COMPANY, INC., NEW YORK

PERMISSU SUPERIORUM
CONGREGATIONIS ANGLIAE
ORDINIS SANCTI BENEDICTI

•

NIHIL OBSTAT:
THOMAS V. CASSIDY
CENSOR DEPUTATUS

IMPRIMI POTEST:
✠ RUFFILLUS JOSEPHUS MCVINNEY
EPISCOPUS PROVIDENTIENSIS
DIE 16 DECEMBRIS 1951

SECOND PRINTING

Preface

THIS book is neither an apologetic for Catholicism nor an exposition of its teaching. It was tempting to give it the subtitle "A Personal Essay," only that would have been misleading. The points chosen for discussion, the general line of thought, the emphases, omissions, criticisms, suggestions, are personal enough but the topics dealt with cannot, at this time of day, be greatly illuminated by purely subjective impressions. Too much that is worth while has already been thought and said about them. Accordingly the first person singular obtrudes itself but seldom. Two classes of readers have been in the author's mind throughout: those members of the Catholic Church who are concerned with the impact of their faith upon the modern world and those who, though owing no allegiance to Catholicism, find its claims sufficiently arresting to merit examination, if only to pronounce them exorbitant, specious, menacing, or merely absurd. No attempt has been made to reconcile the irreconcilable. The aim in view has been to explore those regions of thought where Catholicism impinges on Western civilization, influences it, and is in turn acted on by it. The negative virtues, to avoid special pleading and not force the argument, I have tried conscientiously to practise. If at the end there are any conclusions, the reader must draw them for himself.

One does not, however, plan and execute a work of this kind without a sense of conviction. Peter F. Drucker, in his well-known study *The End of Economic Man,* alluding to the Russian novelist Dostoevski, remarks shrewdly that "All his novels reflect but this one thesis: that only Christian man can make the modern world rational and sensible and can endure its reality." That is also the thesis implicit in this book. Or rather, as I should prefer to think, that is what emerges from an objective consideration of the facts. The problems that must necessarily present themselves are those that preoccupy the contemporary mind almost to the point of obsession. Communism, inevitably; though chiefly as the most disturbing symptom of a more general disorder that is slowly undermining the West. The conflict, real or apparent, between freedom and authority, individual and society, faith and reason. The relations between science and religion, institutionalism and mysticism, Christianity and Christ. What are the prospects for a *rapprochement* between "the Churches"—for the much canvassed "reunion" of Christendom? Giving form and backbone to the whole lies the central question: What is Catholicism's solution to the perplexities of our time? Each calls for a book in itself; but by concentrating only on the essential we should at least be able to establish our bearings. If it is too presumptuous to hope that what results will go far to meet the spiritual needs of the educated man and woman of today, certain pointers in that direction may yet lie hidden beneath the surface of such well-meaning intentions. Some slight mental effort and judicious selection should suffice to bring them to light.

That Catholicism should give some account of itself along precisely these lines is incidentally made opportune by the recent appearance of Paul Blanshard's *American Freedom and*

Catholic Power. This work—an interesting performance, despite its incomprehension of the subject with which it deals—covers much of the ground we have now to examine. The present book was well under way before Mr. Blanshard's study came into my hands. If it merits a detailed refutation, I gladly leave that polemical task to others. But it so happens that his inquiry and mine complement each other. He deals, as a non-Catholic, with the external and relatively superficial manifestations of the Church's "power"; I deal, as a Catholic, with the basic sanctions for the Church's exercise of *authority*. These sanctions, for argument's sake, may prove unwarranted; but that Mr. Blanshard takes no account of them is what largely falsifies his picture. As the same author in a later study developing his dubious theme, *Communism, Democracy, and Catholic Power*, has quoted me more than once, as being, by implication, both an "authoritative" expositor of Catholicism and an upholder of "undemocratic principles," what follows is not without its claim upon the attention of his readers. Mr. Blanshard writes of the Christian religion as a man who is tone deaf might discourse upon music. Nevertheless his industry has provided a useful series of headings for an examination of conscience by those who have the welfare of Catholicism at heart. It is a challenge to reconsider whether, in presenting the Church to the world, we always observe the right order of priorities; whether the Church's message is brought into sufficiently close touch with contemporary realities; whether much of present-day Catholic speaking and writing has been preceded by the requisite amount of Catholic thinking; whether, finally, we invariably take care to observe the virtues of intellectual integrity and justice, in default of which no effort of good will can save Catholicism from misrepresentation.

The following chapters have not been written in the manner of a theological treatise. Such a method would have been alien

to their purpose. They aim at engaging the attention of the
humanist as well as the theologian, or indeed of anyone who is
prepared for a little thinking. We shall be concerned to elucidate positions rather than to dogmatize about their validity.
Theology, however, is bound up with our theme, and with it
the author's firm belief that the Catholic Church is in fact what
she claims to be.

> Prince of the degradations, bought and sold,
> These verses, written in your crumbling sty,
> Proclaim the faith that I have held and hold
> And publish that in which I mean to die.

The same faith, not in Bellocian verses, nor, alas, in the vivaci-
ties of Bellocian prose, but in paragraphs written as best I may
is here likewise proclaimed and published. Mr. Belloc's characteristic robustness would be out of place: the playful trucu-
lence, for example, of "Heretics All," with its jovially defiant
"Caritas non conturbat me." The heretics, if not their heresies,
shall have some good words from me. But in religion, as in
other departments of life, there are no more misguided pro-
moters of mutual understanding than those who would ingemi-
nate "Peace, peace," when "there is no peace" (Jer. 6:14). To
take one's stand upon Catholicism, however, is not to overlook
the difficulties it presents to the detached spectator. Those
difficulties are, I believe, more formidable than Catholics commonly admit. Four hundred million adherents is an impressive
figure, but it says nothing whatever about the truth of their
beliefs. Psychologists can give their own account of why an
authoritarian religion, with its promise of mental security, has
its charms for so many. To institutions, however exalted, no
less than to individuals, the Socratic dictum applies in its full
force, "the unexamined life is not worth living."

No one is qualified to conduct an inquiry into the relations
between Catholicism and the modern world as a neutral. If his

intellectual sympathies are not engaged, he has no frame of reference for his facts. And it may be that a truer eye for the essential belongs to him who views the situation from within, as a life-long member of that Christian society which nursed our Western culture for at least a millennium, than to more learned observers who survey the scene with supposed detachment from without. Secularists share with believing Christians an incapacity to forgo their origins, to get outside their own skins. But if neutrality is not required, the same cannot be said of an overriding concern for objective truth, whether this be favorable or otherwise to one's predilections. No charge is more galling to the reflective Catholic than the reiterated insinuation that the Church is too preoccupied with furthering its interests to be overscrupulous about the truth. We recall T. H. Huxley's scathing epigram at the expense of the Catholic educators of Descartes. Descartes—"naturally endowed with a dialectic grasp and subtlety which even they could hardly improve, and with a passion for getting at the truth which even they could hardly impair." Or Augustine Birrell shedding crocodile tears over the fate of Newman, "Oh, Spirit of Truth, where wert thou, when the remorseless deep of superstition closed over the head of John Henry Newman, who surely deserved to be thy best-loved son?" To ascertain and state the truth is a more complex affair than is generally assumed, whether by scientists unconscious of their naïve epistemology, by philosophers absorbed in their own mental categories, or, for that matter, by theologians gravely pontificating *de haut en bas*. There are others who share the delusion with which Chesterton taxed Carlyle, that to tell the truth is as easy as playing blind hooky. But the ideal, at any rate, must control an inquiry such as this, however inadequate its fulfillment may turn out.

With the best will in the world, it may be objected, how can any professing Catholic give due weight to hostile criticism of his Church? Corporate loyalty, reinforced by the well-known Roman discipline, casts him for the role not of judge but of advocate. Besides, the discerning will have noticed, this book has been submitted to the normal processes of ecclesiastical censorship. These signs of an approved orthodoxy may be taken as a reassuring advertisement in Catholic circles, but as a recommendation of an author's work to liberal-minded non-Catholics, are they not, in Mr. Blanshard's picturesque phrase, a "kiss of death"? The impression conveyed to the uninitiated that here we have writing to order is so hard to resist that the point is worth explaining. The modest functions of a *censor deputatus* are seldom understood by those who have never been entrusted with them. Their character, though a legitimate exercise of the Church's teaching authority, is essentially negative. An *imprimatur* is not an official approbation of an author's opinions but an acknowledgment of his right to express them. The object in view is to insure that, where they are touched on, neither Catholicism nor its doctrine is misrepresented. As even an unintentional deviation at this point would be fatal to our present purpose, the interests of author and censors here clearly coincide. For the rest, there may be some things in this book which the censors would not themselves have written, things which they personally may have preferred that I had not written; but Catholicism, by definition, has no "party line." Within the limits of human reason a Catholic enjoys the privilege of the great tradition of the West, that of following the argument wheresoever it may lead.

Pope Pius XII, in his encyclical *Humani Generis,* which hasty critics have misconceived as an attack upon disinterested research, is at pains to point out that, when dealing with many of the topics we have now to discuss, there is no need for Catholic writers to invoke ecclesiastical authority. Readers of Douglas Hyde's recent exposure of Marxism will remember how, upon his reception into the Church, he expected to be given directives, analogous to those of the Politburo, from the editor of a Catholic weekly whose staff he had joined, even from the Cardinal Archbishop of Westminster. No such directives were forthcoming. The assurance may therefore be accepted that, for better or for worse, the author, as an entirely free agent, bears sole responsibility for every sentence in this book. If it seems somehow to serve the cause of Catholicism, may not that suggest a further inference? That Catholicism is itself in direct line with a unique declaration of no party commitments—"What I was born for, what I came into the world for, is to bear witness of the truth" (John 18:37).

AELRED GRAHAM

The Priory,
Portsmouth,
Rhode Island.

ACKNOWLEDGMENTS

THE AUTHOR gratefully acknowledges permission to quote extracts from the following copyrighted material which appears in this book: to Appleton-Century-Crofts, Inc., from "The Hound of Heaven" and "The Kingdom of God" in *Poems of Francis Thompson*, edited by Rev. Terence L. Connolly, copyright 1941; to Harcourt, Brace and Company, Inc., from *The Rock* by T. S. Eliot, copyright 1934; to The Macmillan Company from Dante's *Purgatorio*, translated by Laurence Binyon, copyright 1938; to Oxford University Press, Inc., from "The Blessed Virgin Compared to the Air We Breathe," in *Poems of Gerard Manley Hopkins*, copyright 1948; to Penguin Books, Ltd., from *Antigone*, translated by E. F. Watling, copyright 1947; and to Sheed and Ward, Inc., New York, from "Ballade to Our Lady of Czestochowa," in *Sonnets and Verse* by Hilaire Belloc, copyright 1939.

Contents

Catholicism and
the World Today

1

The Problem of Catholicism

NO one who chooses to think about the modern world will deny that Catholicism presents it with a problem—or rather, a series of problems. It is perhaps the most obvious problem of all to the Communists, being the chief obstacle to the achievement of their aims. Accordingly, they are now at work ridding society of so needless an encumbrance in the path of human progress. But it is not only Communists and their fellow travelers who have difficulties. The extent and complexity of these can best be measured by the fact that, hard pressed as are the defenders of our Western way of life, the majority of them regard Catholicism as, at best, a dubious ally in the cause. The totalitarianism of the Vatican may be less harsh than that of the Kremlin, but it is totalitarianism none the less. "The two patterns of power (Vatican and Kremlin)"— to quote Paul Blanshard's words as displayed on the jacket of his *Communism, Democracy, and Catholic Power* (Boston: Beacon Press, 1951)—"are as alike as the two poles of the earth. They occupy the opposite extremes of the moral universe, but they represent the same intellectual climate—the climate of authoritarian rule over the human mind." Is there not some element of truth in this facile antithesis?

1

No doubt there are many who will be tempted to argue that, just as the Marxist is precluded by his peculiar dialectic from understanding the viewpoint of his critics, so is the Catholic incapable of that effort of mental detachment which is necessary before he can see the Church as others see it. There is no little evidence, it must be admitted, to suggest that this is so. Why, if it comes to that, should he make such an effort? Is he not already in possession of that treasure beyond price—the truth? It is for others, then, to come and share it with him, not for him to dissipate his intellectual sympathies amid the aberrations of materialism and heresy. Yet history shows that there is another side to the story. The philosophical synthesis of the medieval Church—upon whose accumulated capital Catholicism has been drawing in lavish quantities ever since—was achieved in the thirteenth century by a man with precisely this gift of grasping and accurately stating the point of view of his opponents. St. Thomas Aquinas was capable of this in virtue of his conviction that a disinterested concern for truth was the highest form of service that could be rendered to the Church. He held that all truth is in the last analysis a unity, that therefore there can be no real conflict between truth and truth, and that consequently truth from whatsoever quarter is to be welcomed. The method of his famous *Summa Theologica* is first to give full weight to the case against the view he accepts and then, not unceremoniously to demolish, but to sort out the true from the false in the arguments of his critics. To share St. Thomas's theological presuppositions and to follow his method is not, as can easily be demonstrated, to acquire his largeness of spirit; but at least there should be some value in attempting an adaptation of his procedure, however sketchy the manner and modest the compass of the essay. Accordingly in this chapter we shall be concerned with a statement of the question—a focusing of attention on those impediments, genuine or otherwise, which seem to hinder Catholicism from making an effective contribution to the needs of modern society. Something more positive by way of answer, as well as an explicit countercriticism, will form the argument of the chapters that follow.

The counsel for the prosecution falls into two main groups: the secularists and the representatives of Protestant Christianity. Among secularists must be classed all those whose philosophy of life excludes religion—Marxists, some notable scientists, the more vocal Logical Positivists, sociologists and political thinkers who have no use for Christianity. Among Protestant Christians are those who take their stand unashamedly with Luther and those who, not being entirely happy about the Reformation, would claim to be "Catholics" while repudiating allegiance to Rome. To these must be added the upholders of the Western liberal tradition, humanists who can commit themselves neither to an unqualified secularism nor to Catholic orthodoxy. Such neat classifications, needless to say, are not to be too rigidly applied; there are no clearly marked boundaries between these various groups; but they correspond sufficiently with the facts to form a convenient basis for discussion.

With the contrast between the secularist and the Catholic outlook we shall be occupied throughout this inquiry. The nature of the opposition between Marxism and Christianity is well known and has had many exponents; its relevance to our present theme is too obvious to require emphasis; but it may be better to illustrate what is implied in this conflict as we proceed rather than go over ground that has been thoroughly explored by others. Scientific positivism, considered as a philosophy acknowledging no reality beyond phenomena and observable facts, is based on assumptions that leave no place for religion. Nor is it content with an appropriate neutrality; it attacks Catholicism for its "supernaturalism" and its allegedly obscurantist teaching on such "scientific" questions as the creation of the world and the origin and destiny of man. It demands, however, a specialized treatment which falls outside the scope of this essay. We shall confine ourselves to an attempt at a later stage to lay a finger on the nerve of the dispute.

Logical Positivism—now very much the fashion with what Berkeley might have called the "minute philosophers" of our day—has a theory of knowledge which makes short work of the *philosophia perennis* to which Catholicism appeals. It is more a system of logic, an assessment of the value of verbal propositions, than a philosophy that claims to add to the sum total of human knowledge; though it takes upon itself, if only in a critical and chiefly negative sense, a number of philosophy's hitherto accepted functions. The work of reason, it holds, is limited to rearranging the data supplied by sense experience and to pointing out to scientists and others what they really mean. There is only one kind of genuine knowledge, that which arises from common sense experience and can be verified by methods of observation and experiment. Human reason is incapable of formulating a synoptic view which would include the invisible world; its task is the more modest one of stating the interconnection between things as they appear to us in space and time. Since the teaching of the Catholic Church is irreducible to a series of "empirical" propositions (which alone form the basis for an advance in knowledge) it would seem that, according to Logical Positivism, the bulk of it can be dismissed as either "non-sense" propositions or tautologies. To this we shall briefly return on a later page.

Secularist sociology, since it advances a formidable critique of Catholic social teaching, calls for less summary treatment. Perhaps the case has been most effectively stated by Peter F. Drucker under the significant heading "The Failure of the Christian Churches." He writes in the year 1939, but it may be doubted whether his argument would take a very different form today.

The conspicuous and remarkable failure of the churches to provide the basis for a new society is obviously not due to the "godless spirit" of our age which is so often deplored from the pulpits. On the contrary, an age in which an elite can turn to the churches must have a very strong urge toward religion. In spite of this need and search, Christianity and the churches have been unable to provide a religious social solution. All they can do today is to give the individual a private haven and refuge in an individual religion. They cannot give a new society and a new community. Personal religious experience may be invaluable to the individual; it may restore his peace, may give him a personal God and a rational understanding of his own function and nature. But it cannot re-create society and cannot make social and community life sensible. Even the most devout Catholic is today in the religious position of an extreme Protestant like Kierkegaard, for whom God was a purely personal, untranslatable, and uncommunicable experience which only emphasized his own isolation and loneliness, and the utter irrationality of society.[1]

This judgment is held to be quite compatible with an acknowledgment of social responsibility on the part of more enlightened Catholics. Of G. K. Chesterton it can be said, "There is, for instance, little doubt that the driving force in Chesterton's Catholicism was the social end and not private religion. Yet the only social ideal which he was able to produce was significantly enough *The Return of Don Quixote*—the most asocial, most isolated figure in all literature, who lives entirely in his own personal imagination and finds so little use for the real world and for society that he ignores them altogether. And so does Chesterton's modern Don Quixote ignore or overlook all social realities—class war, machines, the decay of society—of which the journalist Chesterton was as keenly aware as any

[1] *The End of Economic Man* (New York: The John Day Co., 1939), pp. 101-2.

other man in the England of his time" (p. 101). The constructive attempts of an élite within the fold are not overlooked, but
they can come to nothing because the Church authorities themselves "emphasize in every conflict only the negative, reactionary
angle" (p. 100). "The impotence and inadequacy of the forces
of religion just at the time when they are most urgently needed
is perhaps the most disheartening feature of the European situation today" (p. 108).

The official social teaching of the Church, according to this
critic, appears as either "outright reactionary or as meaningless
fancies. The papal encyclicae on social questions might be successfully tried in a country like Portugal, which has none of the
problems of modern industrial society which the encyclicae set
out to solve. But, applied to an industrial country like Austria,
their teaching appeared as pseudo-romantic reaction or as non-
sensical theorizing, far removed from the hard facts" (p. 100).
Even the socially effective groups within the Church cannot
grasp the new meaning of the term "property." "Their concept
of property is that of an inalienable social right which the individual needs to fulfill his social duties and to discharge the social
functions in which his claim to social equality rests. This view
is radically and incompatibly opposed to what property has
become in the demon-ruled world: a completely irrational and
unreal, yet extremely powerful, fiction which carries with it
only privileges and no duties" (p. 107). The dismal conclusion
is that "The masses, who in their despair search for a new
rationalization and a new social order to banish the demons and
who must have such an order at once because they cannot face
the world in the utter isolation of the society-less individual,
can obtain their salvation as little from the churches as from
socialism" (pp. 110-11).

The reason why the Church cannot become a constructive
force in the changed situation of the modern world is because

it is inextricably tied to "the fundamental institutions of the old order—its community life, its schools, its politics, its social structure." The would-be reformer must inevitably fail since, despite himself, "his object is the fundamentally conservative one of preventing the break in historic continuity"; hence he is faced with the inherent contradiction created by the conflict "with the vested material and immaterial interests of his own church." To this conflict there are only two solutions: "the retreat to the socially ineffective position of 'personal religion' or the defence of the existing institutions, which is equally ineffective." "There is no solution which allows the preservation of the positions in the old society and the simultaneous creation of a new society" (pp. 108-9). A final quotation, as interesting as it is to the point, may conclude this formidable indictment.

This is a worse failure for any Christian church than even a complete loss of all believers. A church that is only a tiny, persecuted minority in a vast sea of atheists might still be strong and successful if it gave its adherents a real community. It would emerge triumphantly as soon as materialism had revealed itself as hollow. That happened in the French Revolution. It might well happen again in Soviet Russia in a generation or two, since the tiny minority who preserve and reform their church form a real community. But a Christian church which, though strong in number and quality of believers, cannot give them more than private religion and private satisfaction, ceases to be a church altogether—at least in the sense in which Europe understands the word (pp. 103-4).

No honest and well-informed Catholic, pausing to reflect, can write all this off as worthless; but such criticism should appear in a different light when the time comes to reconsider its implications. A further charge against Catholicism is that it is hostile to any form of political democracy. If the Church, taught by its bitter experience of Nazi and Communist totalitarianism, has lately learned to look more benignly upon representative institutions, this indicates only a tactical maneuver, not a change of heart. Catholic authoritarianism and the Church's hierarchic system of government take small account of any demands voiced by the people. This is the substance of Paul Blanshard's case as set out in his book *American Freedom and Catholic Power* (Boston: Beacon Press, 1949). The Pope, with legislative, executive, and judicial authority vested in his own person, and the bishops, his compliant appointees and agents, exercise an influence intolerable to those who have tasted the sweets of personal freedom. Like seeks fellowship with like, and Catholicism has, it seems, a fatal facility for making common cause with political regimes which most nearly approximate to its own form of autocracy. The Catholic Church may perhaps be allowed to perform the function of a bulwark against Marxist materialism, on the principle of opposing one form of totalitarianism by another, but the Vatican's policies and methods are in themselves scarcely less objectionable than those of the Kremlin. Christianity, with its invitation to the glorious liberty of God's children, is one thing; Catholicism, with its ecclesiastical dictatorship, quite another.

We must now listen to objections from another quarter. Not only the secularist and democrat but the liberal humanist also has his quarrel with the Church. Let us hear it as stated by a distinguished historian, well aware both of the supreme importance of Christianity and of Catholicism as its age-long embodiment; for the criticism of a sympathetic friend is always more disturbing than the attacks of a declared enemy. Arnold Toynbee has lately reminded us that "Two hundred and fifty years ago, the founders of our Modern Western Liberal faith left Christianity out deliberately when they were compounding this secular humanitarian ideology which still seemed so self-evidently satisfactory to our fathers." [2] That liberal faith is now

2 "Religion and the Rise of Western Culture," *Hibbert Journal,* Vol. XLIX, October, 1950.

itself breaking down; ". . . in our generation we have begun to find our fathers' self-complacent secularism spiritually more and more unsatisfying"; ". . . a secular Liberalism has been grievously failing us."

. . . we ourselves have lived to see great Western nations—nations that had been in the very fore-front of our Western World's achievement in the fields of technology and science and scholarship and literature—allowing themselves to be led astray by devilish leaders into committing, in cold blood and on a stupendous scale, all the seven deadly sins in our Modern Western table of secular commandments: the sin of cruelty, first and foremost, which is, I suppose, the one that we most genuinely abhor, and, along with that, the sins of militarism, tyranny, intolerance, the violation of consciences, the suppression of truth, the propagation of falsehood. And all this has been done by Western peoples in whose acts we are implicated because we and they have been hewn from the same block.

What adds to the interest of Toynbee's analysis is that he sees in Christianity the only effective barrier against the onrush of the Communist juggernaut. "Except the Lord build the house, their labour is but lost that build it; except the Lord keep the city, the watchman waketh but in vain."

This is a totalitarian question which Democracy cannot answer. But Christianity *can* answer it; and Christianity's answer to Juggernaut is that the individual and his claim to freedom do count for something more than collective humanity and its claim to power. The individual counts, according to the Christian catechism, because this mannikin who is of no account in the cold calculations of this idol Juggernaut is a child of the One True God and is infinitely precious in his Heavenly Father's eyes. And the individual's freedom matters too for just the same reason, according to the Christian belief; for Christians believe that Man's freedom has been given to him by God, not for the contemptible satisfaction of the individual's frivolous self-regarding purposes, but for the noble attainment of the true end of man, which is to glorify God and to enjoy him for ever.

But can Catholicism again become the constructive force molding Western society that it was in an earlier time? Modern man, taught by the lessons of history, may have his doubts. "Our thirteenth-century ancestors had the unforgettable experience of seeing the Papacy betray Mediaeval Western Christian ideals of which the Papacy itself had been the living embodiment." Western culture round about the year 1200 had attained, according to Toynbee, perhaps the highest point that we Westerners have yet managed to reach. The achievement was not the fortuitous result of unorganized good will; it was the deliberate product of a master plan, conceived and controlled in its execution by the medieval Papacy, "whose David is the eleventh-century Pope Gregory VII and whose Solomon is Pope Innocent III, who sat in Saint Peter's chair from 1198 to 1216." But the commonwealth of medieval Western Christendom did not endure; it collapsed because the Papacy forfeited its moral hold over Western Christian hearts—a collapse that was fatal to the social structure in which the Papacy's moral influence had been the keystone. "Was the Papacy's subsequent loss of this spiritual treasure as well deserved as the previous winning of it had been? As a non-Catholic Christian historian, trying to look into the past as objectively as I can—and no human being can ever be sure that he is not being blinded by prejudice—I should say that the medieval Papacy's downfall was deserved. The people of Western Christendom judged, and judged rightly, I believe, that the Papacy had failed grievously to live up to its own sublime ideals. It had betrayed its principles, first in order to fight for power, and then in order to raise the funds that are indispensable sinews of worldly warfare."

"Tantum religio potuit suadere malorum"; "Such were the lengths of wickedness to which Religion could persuade human nature to go." Lucretius' words come to the historian's mind as he surveys the moral decline and fall of the Papacy. "The

reputation left behind them by a Pope Innocent IV and a Boniface VIII account for Voltaire's war-cry *écrasez l'infâme*: 'Crush that monster, Religion, and set Western Man's spirit free for pursuing his glorious enterprise of raising his culture to Olympian heights.' " That enterprise has not proved an unqualified success. Modern man is no nearer to the summit of Olympus; he may even have reconciled himself to the thought that it is unattainable. But is he likely to retrace his steps? Can he be persuaded that the genius of Catholicism is still capable of assimilating the positive achievements of our post-Renaissance culture? That its latent energies are sufficient for the task of reinvigorating Western society? And more than this, that it can meet the chief contemporary need and provide an acceptable basis for the effort to rebuild, in a setting very different from that of the Middle Ages, a world-wide commonwealth of nations? This is the question with which we shall be engaged in the chapters that follow.

When we turn to the specifically Protestant grievances against Catholicism we find, in the work of Karl Barth and Emil Brunner, that they can be formulated no less effectively today than they were by Luther and Calvin. "Protestantism," says Barth, "protested not against but for the Church, and as a *Church* it is not only not less or weaker but more and stronger than the Roman Church." [3] Catholicism places a wrong stress on "reason" and "Nature," to the detriment of "faith" and the consideration of God as a "Person." Commenting on Catholic theologians who talk of "super-nature," of "life streaming through the sacraments," Barth observes "Where the concepts, Life, *Eros,* Being, Nature (even if it is 'super'-nature, divine nature) dominate, there dominates a Neuter," and not a Person,

---

[3] Karl Barth, *Die Theologie und die Kirche,* quoted from R. Birch Hoyle, *The Teaching of Karl Barth* (London: Student Christian Movement Press, 1930), p. 54.

such as meets us in His word. He laments the Catholic optimism with its refusal to take seriously the fact of sin, which is due to a mistaken doctrine of grace. "The Reformation is the re-establishment of the Church as a sinful Church, or rather a Church of sinners." "The Reformation was the re-establishment of the Church as the Church of the pity of God." Protestantism may admit the relative, delegated authority given to Peter, but this must be understood as under the authority of the written and preached words of the Bible.

Brunner, in his *Revelation and Reason*,[4] goes so far as to say that "the Roman Catholic misunderstanding" of how human reason is related to God's revelation—"the fundamental problem of all theology"—touches the question of "the basis of our Western civilization." He is concerned to counter "the over-valuation of the intellectual aspect of faith which hangs like a dark shadow over the whole history of the Church"; he charges a certain type of "authoritarian faith" with being "ethically neutral," "both religiously and ethically sterile . . . an unspiritual attitude." "No Church can guarantee the divine truth for me; if I want to have certainty, then I must get it from a more than human source. I can never believe something is true simply because a single person, or a particular group of people or an ecclesiastical hierarchy, assures me that he can 'guarantee' that this is true." And further, "There is no 'proof' for revelation. Now the Church has very often made the mistake of offering 'proofs' for revelation, which frequently provide easy targets for the attacks of rational criticism. A theology that allows itself to be drawn into producing proofs for its claim to revelation has already thrown up the sponge. It is the just punishment for the fact that it does not take its own subject and its own basis seriously. Either faith or proof; you cannot have both."

[4] Trans. Olive Wyon (London: Student Christian Movement Press, 1947).

Basically the same criticism, directed against any human agency claiming to "possess" God's revelation and hence to speak with His authority, is contained in a recent English statement of the Protestant case:

For the Christian Church and for the Christian believer ultimate and absolute authority in matters of faith can and must reside only in the Word of God, who was made flesh, died and rose again for our salvation, and abides for ever in His Church. In Him and through Him God has spoken to men; here only have we the unmistakable voice of God, unimpeded in its utterance by the weakness of sinful human nature and the fallibility of sinful human thought.[5]

The "Church's catholicity," says another exponent of this view, "can be found only by standing under the Word of God in Jesus Christ, as He is declared to us through the testimony of the Apostles." [6] "But we must insist that 'the structure of catholicism' must be understood in the sense we have defined, as expressing the criticism of the Lord of the Church upon the Church so that the Church makes manifest His Lordship and that alone. The Roman Church, because she is unable to distinguish between the action of Christ and the action of the hierarchy, is compelled to regard the maintenance of her own existence as an organization as her first concern, and is thus driven to tie herself in many countries to a social and political and cultural order which in no way make manifest the Lordship of Christ. Once more, it is the presence of Christ and that alone which ensures the Church's 'universality of appeal.' " [7]

The charge that Catholicism, not necessarily in its individual adherents, but precisely as a *Church,* a corporate institution,

[5] *The Catholicity of Protestantism.* Ed. R. Newton Flew and Rupert E. Davies (London: Lutterworth Press, 1950), pp. 115-16.

[6] Daniel T. Jenkins, *The Nature of Catholicity* (London: Faber and Faber, 1942), p. 162.

[7] *Ibid.,* pp. 131-2.

lacks the distinctive note of Christian humility is too persistent to be ignored. This defect arises, so it is repeatedly argued, from the Church's claim to be identical with the Kingdom of God. It is this claim which precludes the possibility of the Church standing in proper submission to God and His word, confers upon the ecclesiastical hierarchy an unwarranted authority, and eliminates all effective self-criticism from within the Church's borders.

In the Scriptures the people of God, the old Israel and the new, are revealed to us as the chosen instrument of God and yet as always under the judgment of God. This is just as true in the New Testament as in the Old. Peter is called, yet, lest Peter (or his "successor") should boast, Peter denies his Lord. The Twelve are chosen, but one betrays his Master. St. Paul calls the Church of Corinth the Body of Christ, but he also recalls the Divine judgments on God's ancient people as an admonition to the same Church. To the Church of Rome he gives a similar warning, "If God spared not the natural branches, neither will he spare thee" (Rom. 11:21). In a fine phrase of Dom Gregory Dix, "the Church is the Body, alike of Sin and Glory, at once the object and the instrument of the judgment and the salvation of God." It is the main count against the Church of Rome that she has failed to maintain the New Testament tension of thought. She has nobly explored the meaning of the phrase "the Body of Christ" and has enriched the whole Christian world with a wealth of prayer, devotion, and sacrificial living that fills us with thankful admiration. No one would wish to detract for one moment from that magnificent achievement. But she has forgotten that the Living Christ not only dwells in the Church but also reigns over it. Thus she has silenced the voice of prophecy within her borders and crushed the possibility of self-criticism. She has erected one kind of totalitarianism which we now see confronting another. She has too often sought increased worldly power for the ecclesiastical corporation and has believed that thereby she was advancing the Kingdom of God.[8]

[8] T. R. Milford and C. Kenneth Sansbury in a letter to the *Times,* November 16, 1949. Republished in *Catholicism To-day* (London: The Times Publishing Co., 1949).

A further charge, too well known to be passed over in silence, is that Catholicism, having linked its theology with the principles of a natural philosophy, is at the same time incapable of assimilating the agreed findings of modern Biblical scholarship. "The Roman Church, having committed itself in advance to the absolutizing of relative human language about God through the acceptance of an 'official' philosophy, is compelled —in practice, if not entirely in theory—to dogmatize about philosophical matters which are, very obviously, open questions. Even more strikingly, her erroneous conception of the nature of tradition and of inspiration drives her to assume not a wisely conservative but a merely timid and prosaic attitude in matters of Biblical criticism which prevents her from reaping the benefits of the immeasurably more inward and vivid understanding of the Scriptures which Biblical criticism, when seen in the right perspective, has helped us to achieve." [9] The same writer strikes a sharper note when he disparages the suggestion that recent Popes have given a "prophetic lead" to contemporary Europe, where he alludes to "modern Papal Encyclicals with their dreary platitudes and their complacent self-congratulation," and refuses, with a rather self-conscious emphasis, "to be overawed by the much-exploited 'glamour' of the See of Rome." [10]

Here it will be in place to recall the adverse comment upon the recent most spectacular action of the Roman See, that of defining as a dogma of faith the bodily Assumption of the Blessed Virgin Mary into heaven. The reactions in England and America to this event will still be remembered. They were paralleled by those on the continent of Europe. "Rome still feels herself strong enough," writes Pastor Etienne Mayer, "to impose

[9] D. T. Jenkins, *op. cit.,* p. 138.
[10] *Ibid.,* p. 86.

upon her faithful the dogma of the Assumption, right in the midst of a period of ecumenical promulgation." [11]

Pastor Pierre Maury, President of the National Council of the Reformed Church of France, observes that

. . . even to the most superficial observer it will appear highly significant that the first verity imposed *ex cathedra* upon the belief of the faithful, since the Pope centred upon his own person the right of the Church to speak without error, concerns not God, Christ, the Holy Ghost, or some ethical verity, but indeed Mary. It would appear that development of doctrine is to terminate in the placing of the Mother of the Saviour in an eminent position hitherto insufficiently radiant, and not Him who is the Saviour of all, including His mother . . . not only Roman piety, but also Roman faith are orientated upon an object and an intercession other than that of the one and sufficient Mediator.

In Germany the Bishops of the United Lutheran Church put out the following statement: "For the first time in history Christians hear a Pope, basing himself upon the infallibility decreed in 1870, define an article of faith. The opposition aroused in all the Christian churches by the proclamation of the dogma of papal infallibility, and which has caused the formation of the Old Catholic Church, receives today, in the moment when belief in the Assumption is erected as a dogma, an alarming and impressive justification. Indeed, this dogma is not only, as other ancient dogmas of the Roman Church, an erroneous interpretation of apostolic doctrine, it is without any scriptural foundation and signifies that the Bishop of Rome deliberately departs from faithfulness to the Apostles of our Lord Jesus Christ."

Such are the principles, and an instance of their application, which underlie the Reformation protest against Catholicism. When, finally, we come to consider the case for the prosecution

[11] This and the following two citations are taken from *Unitas,* ed. Charles Boyer, S.J. (Unitas Association of Rome), Vol. II, No. 4 (October-December, 1950), pp. 299, 301.

as it is stated by those who appear least unfavorably disposed to recognize the traditional Catholic claims, we find that, though more balanced and judicious, it embodies with an added precision much that we have already seen. It is perhaps most cogently formulated in a report entitled *Catholicity* (London: Dacre Press, 1947), presented to the Archbishop of Canterbury by a distinguished group of Anglican scholars. Here we are reminded that the close involution of ecclesiastical with social and political life in the Middle Ages left the Renaissance Papacy exposed to all the hazards of sixteenth and seventeenth century power politics. Despite the efforts of many churchmen to avoid the entanglement, the Hapsburg and Bourbon monarchies in turn all but succeeded in identifying Catholicism with their own political ascendancy. "It was quite impossible for the members of the reformed Churches to consider the Roman Church simply *as* a Church at all, when it appeared to be acting principally as the instrument of an overwhelming political menace" (p. 37).

Admittedly the vicious elements in this situation largely disappeared with the death of Louis XIV, but the alliance between throne and altar remained a living memory in the popular mind down to the French Revolution. "The divorce of Catholicism from the liberal tradition in the eighteenth century led the Church to identify itself increasingly with the *ancien régime,* an identification which continued, broadly speaking, throughout the nineteenth century. It is really only in the twentieth century, against a secular background which menaced all churches alike, that those outside the Roman Communion have been placed in a position to view the Roman Church simply as a Christian Church. The results of this, in the way of greater understanding, are already not small." Meanwhile the Council of Trent had reasserted and reformulated the Western tradition—"with its penetrating analyses, but also with its limitations, its gaps and its distortions" (p. 38)—against the Protestant negations. But the theologians at Trent, being on the defensive, could achieve no new enlargement of their vision; thus no fresh synthesis, no improvement of theological balance, was effected. "The elements which Protestantism and humanism had separated and opposed to one another, were still held together in Tridentine Catholicism: but they were only held together at more or less that stage of incipient division which they had reached during the later Middle Ages. In some cases they were really only clamped together by the declaration of ecclesiastical authority, without much attempt at fruitful harmonisation."

Tridentine theology appears to have retained the whole vast elaboration of the scholastic system of reasoning upon the *data* of Revelation. ". . . the codification of a huge syllogistic structure of reasoning, not only upon revealed truth but upon other deductions from revealed truths and their consequences, and the requirement of it all for orthodoxy, seems to end in the substitution of a human rationalism for the *pistis* of the New Testament, and in the obscuring of the grand central facts of Divine Redemption—even though it is directed solely to safeguarding and illuminating them." ". . . it is this great system of reasoning about Revelation, rather than the Biblical Revelation in itself, which is presented as that 'teaching of the Roman Church' that the convert is required to accept. It would be difficult to devise anything more likely to repulse the instructed Protestant at the outset" (p. 39).

A further difficulty is the "legalistic" aspect of Catholicism. Some system of canon law is admittedly an administrative necessity, but in the later Middle Ages this developed to an extent beyond all reasonable bounds. "It was not so much the Avignon Popes (most of whom were personally spiritual men) as the Avignon bureaucracy of rapacious officials and lawyers, who provided the real justification for the Protestant repudiation of 'legalism' in the administration of the things of God"; and "the evident survival of something of the same mentality in post-Tridentine Catholicism has appeared to most Protestants still to justify outright their forefathers' original protest." It is recognized that the position of the Papacy itself rests on far deeper foundations than those provided by canon law, that "the Primacy *jure divino,* and the Infallible *Magisterium* of the Successor of St. Peter in faith and morals, are made the theological basis of the whole claim that the Papal Communion, and it alone, constitutes in the eyes of God the entire Catholic Church of Christ" (p. 40). What is, however, the product of canon law is "the system of Curial bureaucracy, by which the administration of the whole Papal Communion is centralised, and through which what is called 'Papal absolutism' finds expression" (p. 39).

Further, the practical tendency to equate the Catholic Church as so conceived with the *Regnum Dei* is bound to make Roman Catholics fight for their Church as for God, and this fighting for God and the Church without any *distinguo* has some of its worst effects in situations where the Roman Catholics are self-consciously distinguishing themselves from other Christians: and certain of these effects are particularly and painfully evident in this country. Moreover, the force of the claim to be the entire Church was even in the Middle Ages greatly weakened by the existence altogether outside that Communion of the Orthodox Churches of the East, with their admittedly valid Orders and Sacraments, their faithful witness to some elements of the Patristic Tradition which the Western Church had lost, and their impressive organic life. Even in the West since the sixteenth century, the Papal Church has been forced by the realities of its situation to act again and again as one Church among many, despite its claim to universality (p. 40).

None of the material utilized in the preceding pages has been gathered from sources that can fairly be dismissed as negligible.

The indictment, as will later be shown, is in many particulars unjust; it reveals a number of fundamental misunderstandings; but, with one or two exceptions, there are no signs that either bigotry or ignorance has played much part in its formulation. These are the things that the educated man and woman of today sincerely thinks and says about the Catholic Church; they are important elements in the climate of opinion in which the Church lives and moves and has its being. Together they constitute what I have called the "Problem of Catholicism"—a problem which demands examination, not only by those outside the Church's fold, but more particularly by those within; by those at least who are concerned with the manner in which Catholicism makes its impact upon the modern world. The great debate has shifted from disputes about the meaning of any given Christian doctrine to a wider field, from the articles of faith to their underlying assumptions.

Can Catholicism offer its acknowledged strength and security only at the price of human freedom? If so, we shall certainly be told, they are not worth the having. What becomes of the personal aspirations of each individual when he is absorbed in a totalitarian religion? How account for the contrast between the simplicity of Christ's Gospel and the monumental complexity of the Catholic system? In what way does God's word make itself known to man? Does not institutionalism in any form crush the heart out of religion, which is the worship of God in spirit and in truth? These, surely, are now the *status quaestionis,* the framework in which the claims of the Church must be discussed. Our contemporaries may admit a sense of failure and frustration, make no secret of the fact that the prospect is bleak indeed; but until these questions are honestly faced they are likely to prefer those ills they have, for they are not unmixed with good, than fly to others that they know not of.

There shall always be the Church and the World
And the Heart of Man
Shivering and fluttering between them, choosing and chosen,
Valiant, ignoble, dark, and full of light
Swinging between Hell Gate and Heaven Gate.
And the Gates of Hell shall not prevail.
Darkness now, then
Light. [12]

[12] T. S. Eliot, *The Rock.*

2

The Basic Either / Or

AS we think so do we act. At the root of all our conscious actions lies a thought in our minds. Upon the strength of men's convictions depends the effectiveness of what they do. These truisms deserve closer attention than they commonly receive. We can lay no claim to wisdom unless we know what facts are certain, what may be taken as provisional, on what we should suspend judgment. To bring to birth just this state of mind is the chief aim of any education worthy of the name. Not to provide merely a mass of miscellaneous information; not to condition men's minds so that they think along predetermined lines—as do the Marxists and perhaps certain misguided religious pedagogues; not even to impose a world picture and a scale of values of whose rightness the teacher is himself convinced; but to make available the materials and the mental discipline which are the foundations of that intellectual discernment which in its turn is the only satisfactory basis for personal responsibility.

We of the West tend to be more impressed by the virtues of the open mind than with the importance of moral conviction. After all, we say, the other fellow may be right. Hence arise the tolerance, the give-and-take, the willingness to compromise that are felt to be the distinguishing marks of civilized intercourse. The English political tradition is anything but doctrinaire; it is distrustful of abstract ideas, of pushing principles to their logical conclusion. We treat written constitutions lightly, dislike utopian theories of government, avoid planned commitments, preferring to arrange matters by methods of unprejudiced discussion and practical experiment. Such principles as do in fact underlie parliamentary democracy, with its healthy tension between the stabilizing weight of tradition and the forces of progress, are tacitly agreed to rather than explicitly formulated. The same is true of what today is the characteristically English view of religion. Dogmatism and the imposition of creeds must be reduced to a minimum; the freest play should be allowed to the individual conscience, the members of the Christian community held together by a "comprehensiveness" whose content remains studiously undefined. Not only the sectarian fanaticism of enthusiasts, but the uncompromising affirmations of prophets and seers, may be countered with the plea for moderation and restraint: "I beseech you, in the bowels of Christ, think it possible you may be mistaken."

This liberal atmosphere is highly congenial to the cultivated Western mind. It brings with it the incontestable benefits of detachment, criticism and a sense of humor. Nor does it, as might have been supposed, affect us with that mental lassitude which is the enemy of action; our practical energies remain apparently unimpaired. Where thought does not trail off into airy speculation but is focused upon the concrete realities of this workaday world, there appears no danger of its being reduced to sterility and impotence. In the business of industrial enterprise or of defending ourselves against the opponents of liberty we have proved more than equal to the demands made upon us. But all this notwithstanding, there are signs that the citadel of freedom is none too secure in its foundations. Not only is it assailed from without, there is evidence of weakness within.

The substitution of a large measure of State control for the selective liberties of capitalist *laissez faire* is not necessarily a defeat for genuine freedom. It might conceivably be a gain. Liberty, as will be argued later at greater length, presupposes law; without such a sanction and framework the way lies open to the anarchy of an individualist go-as-you-please. But if the breakdown of nationalist self-sufficiency and the manifestly interrelated structure of world economy demand greater cohesion, in terms of increasing State supervision, among the members of the Western community, certain hitherto unresolved problems present themselves. The function of government, *de facto* if not *de jure,* is not now simply that of providing an arena in which man may live his own life and work out his personal destiny; it enters the scene of action itself and both supplies him with aims and objects and largely prescribes the means for their attainment. The process of State encroachment into private life may be modified by democratic safeguards but there are no signs of its future abatement. It is this situation which poses the problem of the tension between liberty and authority in its most acute form.

Where the impact of the central government upon its subjects is remote and indirect, as it may be in small, isolated and relatively self-sufficient communities, its exercise of authority need create few difficulties. The administration of justice, for example, which in an earlier age was the chief function of rulers, raises no more far-reaching issues than can be settled by equitable decisions based on the requisite knowledge—though even these questions receive a new and more complex setting in the structure of modern society. But when government enters such vital fields as education and the subsequent livelihood of its citizens— a step necessitated by any program to establish and maintain a "welfare state"—there can be no shirking its deeper implications.

It is not enough to keep before our minds the always pertinent question, *"Sed quis custodiet ipsos custodes?"*: "Who will take care of those who govern?" More is demanded of us than the eternal vigilance which is the price of freedom. What is required is not so much a re-examination of the methods of democratic government as a radical analysis of the nature of man himself, his legitimate aims, and, above all, the character and scope of that personal liberty which is his most cherished possession. These are the realities upon which, whether we like it or not, our legislative and administrative procedure now impinges. It is on account of a lack of agreed assumptions at this level that Western democracy fluctuates perilously between the extremes of a dictatorship by the majority in power and a purposeless inefficiency which is not the least among civilization's present dangers.

These perils cannot be met by policies of negation; by propagating the unquestionably sound view that government in any form has its attendant evils and drawbacks; by attempts to restore pre-industrial social conditions; by a die-hard resistance, in the name of the sanctity of the individual, to all forms of social legislation. Nothing is to be gained by a refusal to face the facts. The incapacity of the West to legislate for freedom in positive instead of negative terms is what creates cynical disillusionment within its own ranks and thus offers no effective barrier against its enemies. To be safeguarded from the suppression of free speech, from religious persecution, from want and fear (the catalogue of Franklin D. Roosevelt's "Four Freedoms") are among the greatest human blessings, but they do not disclose any profound understanding of liberty and point to nothing beyond themselves. Being essentially freedom *from* recognized evils, they provide no call to constructive action based on a vision of what is the goal of human society and the necessary conditions for its preservation.

Politics, let us admit with Bismarck, is not an exact science; it is the art of the possible; its concern is with the contingent, the fluid, the unpredictable. But when politics enter the inner recesses of each individual's life, when, too, as modern democracy necessitates, politics are everyone's affair, their underlying assumptions demand scrutiny in the light of some ultimate philosophy of man. The postive content in Western political values—freedom, justice, the rights of man, the rule of law— are a heritage from Christianity, so that the phrase "Christian civilization," hackneyed and somewhat hollow as it has become, is still not entirely without meaning. Post-Renaissance humanism, however, has wrested these values from their original context and in so doing has distorted and transformed them. Under the influence of secularist liberalism they have been deprived of their transcendental reference and so placed in a false dimension. Thus freedom, raised to the status of an end in itself, degenerates into an apotheosis of the individual; justice has no firmer basis than an uncertain weighing of claims and counterclaims; man's rights take precedence over his duties; and the rule of law can appeal to no higher sanction than the expedients of politics and diplomacy.

There is no need to short-circuit the argument by insisting that the sole cure for this state of things is to re-embody these ideas—they are nothing less than secularized theological concepts—in their appropriate Christian setting. That this is in fact the only solution can be seen by examining the causes for the lack of drive, inspiration, and sense of purpose which, in marked contrast to its Communist antagonist, characterize Western society. Briefly they can be summarized in our reluctance to face and answer precisely those ultimate questions about whose paramount importance the Marxists are in no manner of doubt. What we treat as matters of opinion, philosophical views and religious tenets which men may hold or reject according to their private conscience, areas of thought from which it is the precise business of democratic government to stand aloof, they perceive to be the key to the whole situation. From the answers given to these questions are derived the principles which determine the entire structure of the State, the function of its members, their manner of life, the aims and objects they shall pursue.

Is human destiny bounded by life on this earth?—or is it not? Are the resources within man's grasp sufficient for his well-being?—or are they not? Above all, does there exist a creator God whose providence extends "from end unto end mightily and orders all things graciously"?—or does there not? These are the basic alternatives, the ineluctable *either/ors*. Here there is no room—we may admit with Kierkegaard—for the noncommittal ambiguities of *both/and*. It is necessary to pose the problem in its ultimate form of alternatives which admit of no middle term; for it is at this level that it now confronts not only Western civilization but the world. Communism makes no attempt to hedge or suspend judgment on any one of these questions, indulges in no subterfuges of having it both ways; it replies with an unqualified yes or no to each. And on the answer that it gives it acts. Therein lies its consistency and strength. A philosophy of life and a program for action can be built up on either set of alternatives. But what if you refuse to decide? What of the position of those who take their stand on a perhaps, a question mark?

This is the pass to which our secularized Western culture has now been brought. Modern man, capable of dealing with everyday surface contingencies, assured and efficient within a limited practical sphere, is lost in uncertainty before the basic realities. The wide spaces upon which the sceptics have taught him to open his mind are turning to vacancy. Liberalism, venturing boldly upon uncharted seas with no guiding stars, has come to shipwreck on its voyage and founders in the shallows of agnosticism. The god of individual freedom turns out to be an idol rewarding its votaries with nothing more substantial than "the reign of Chaos and old Night." It will not do, as the Marxists again have clearly seen, for each individual to decide for himself with regard to these questions. The fundamental unity which must underlie the no less needful diversity in any civilization demands that the community as a whole should be persuaded to make its choice. This is especially required of the West, whose representative institutions can only work on a basis of agreed, if implicit, assumptions. Whether or not the fact be recognized, the policy of governments, the education of their citizens, the methods of generating public opinion, the ideas of what achievements are desirable, are proceeding on one or other answer to these vital problems. "Where there is no vision, the people perish." At least let us know where we stand.

Is the West, then, simply to take up an opposing position to the Marxists on the supreme issues now in debate? To do so is indeed to fall into line with the laws of its own development, to re-establish the links with the Christendom which it once seemed destined to embody and yet today so questionably represents. For Catholic Christianity remains on any showing the most powerful upholder of those values which Communism denies. But in this there is no ready-made solution. Not only is liberal thought alienated from Catholicism, Catholicism itself cannot be utilized as a plank in a political platform. The Church may countenance or support this or that political regime but essentially it transcends politics. In any event the case cannot be met by some up-to-date version of an alliance between throne and altar. If history imparts any lessons, not the least fruitful is the futility of enacting the present in terms of some facsimile of the past. Whatever the mortal weakness in post-Renaissance society, four centuries have not elapsed without vast gains being achieved, precariously though they may be held. What is called for in the first place is a fundamental re-thinking of the relations between religion and the secular order at a deeper level than either the past or the present. We need to focus attention on those timeless concepts which find a partial embodiment in both and are therefore valid for the future.

Here a word may be in place about the dangers of an uncritical anti-Communism. Only the purblind idealist can fail to see that the Communists, with their reliance on revolutionary force, must be frustrated by weapons of their own choosing, greater material resources and superior power. Dialectical materialism cannot be refuted by any arguments of sweet reasonableness. This is a bourgeois luxury in which no Marxist can afford to indulge. Propaganda and the removal of the pretexts for Communism have a vital part to play; but the normal condition for winning men's minds to what is right and just is that you first save their bodies from those who would enslave them. What is not sufficiently recognized, however, is that, treat the Communists as you will, Communism itself, like Christianity or democracy or any other philosophy of life, cannot be overcome by force. To suppose that in this case it can, on the grounds that Communism is sheer materialism, is to misconceive its true nature and commit the error of invoking Satan to cast out Satan. The only way to rid the mind of a false idea is to replace it with a true idea. Communism must be criticized and exposed as a sham; it cannot be bludgeoned out of existence. There are grounds for the conclusion that Communism's providential role is that of compelling the idea of a Christian civilization to realize itself, to descend from its former habitat in the minds of theorists and the ivory castles of vocational groups and seek concrete expression in the life of the everyday world. It is the historic challenge to the West to attain the maturity of full self-consciousness. The Western and Communist way of life deny each other's presuppositions; hence they admit of no effective theoretical discussion; the dispute must be conducted in "the light of common day." By raising the momentous questions as to the meaning of human existence, and providing their own answers in terms of life as it is lived, Communism has broken down the barriers behind which men seek to shield themselves from ultimate reality. For this service at least we may be grateful.

Is human destiny bounded by life on this earth? The Marxists reply with an unhesitating yes. A fullness of life hereafter—"pie in the sky when you die"—is an outworn illusion still being exploited by the lackeys of the bourgeoisie, the priests, to keep the workers in their place. It must be shown up for what it is; men will then be free to attend to their chief business, which is to co-operate in the establishment of paradise on earth—the classless society in which each will give according to his capacities and receive according to his needs. This may take generations to achieve and its birth pangs will be acute. You cannot carry out its preliminary stages—the dictatorship of the proletariat and assisting the State to "wither away"—without someone getting hurt. But what are the sufferings of individuals compared to the final well-being of mankind? To be deterred by such sentimental considerations is to make the mistake of ranking the individual before the community, promoting self-interest at the expense of man's obligations to society. So, quite consistently, the Marxist argues, and so he acts.

Catholicism's answer to the same question is equally definite. Man is destined for immortality. It is not merely that his mind rises above the level of time, that he has "those thoughts that wander through eternity"; he himself, body and spirit, will reach his full stature in an order of existence other than this.

The hints given him to this effect in self-conscious reflection, the intimations of philosophy, the witness of personal frustration and restlessness and suffering, reinforced by what he learns from Christian revelation of the resurrection-life, point to a moment when "God shall wipe away all tears" and man will at last be where he belongs. This world is "the vale of soul-making"—a truth which discloses in human life a tension between the temporal and the eternal not easy to hold in balance. Communism cuts the Gordian knot; Catholicism insists on untying it. There is a Christian otherworldliness which oversimplifies the problem: by stressing unduly the preparatory nature of our present existence it tends to sever the connecting links which bind heaven and earth together. It is as if man's final happiness came to him as an alien gift, like money, a reward for services rendered having only a symbolic relation to the work performed. Whereas there is a basic continuity; the transformation at death is not an exchange of new life for old, it is life itself reaching fruition. What we are striving painfully to be now is what we shall be then. We are being shaped to become fit dwellers in man's true home, our Father's house, not equipped for some strange adventure in a foreign land.

Christians, it may be, have still to bring to light the full implications of these truths. They are open to the criticism, if not of a self-regarding preoccupation with personal salvation, at least of cultivating a "fugitive and cloistered virtue" too little concerned with the present well-being of society. The charge that twentieth-century Christianity is disturbed by a bad conscience is not without point. We are compelled to the sad admission that if professing Christians had always been ready to live up to the Gospel, there would have been no room for the appearance of Marxian Communism. The lesson of our deficiency is being dearly bought. But as heresy is the occasion for

the Church to unfold the richness of its truth, so there are signs
that the greatest challenge it has yet had to face will be met,
not merely by fulfilling its time-honored role of denouncing
intellectual error, but by a response in terms of manifest good
works—a projection in space and time, at the level of practical
affairs, of its incomparable treasures of insight, generosity, and
constructive power. In thus acknowledging a renewed responsibility for this temporal scheme of things Catholicism will
demonstrate afresh the unique character of its saving task. The
Church's members, each in his own milieu, are called upon to
exemplify the mission of a Founder who, far from leaving His
contemporaries to compensate for present misfortune, with the
hope of future blessings, "went about doing good and healing all
that were oppressed" (Acts 10:38).

Are the resources within man's grasp sufficient for his well-
being? Substantially they are, say the Marxists. We have only
to apply ourselves to developing the earth's latent capacities,
to redistribute its existing wealth, to harness its methods of
production for the benefit of the people in order to satisfy every
human need. The claims of the spirit are not overlooked. The
arts and sciences may flourish, provided they give rise to no
deviations from the Marxist-Leninist pattern. The free play of
the mind, disinterested research with truth alone as its object,
are not in place. When you are concerned not to explain the
world but to *change* it—which is a dogma of Communist
philosophy—the concept of absolute truth is an irrelevancy. To
suppose that there are unchanging realities which man's mind
must discover and submit to is a mark of the reactionary. He
owes it to that misguided idealism which has bedeviled Western
thought since the days of Plato. If at times we are conscious
of a seeming inadequacy, weighed down by the problem of
human suffering, feel the need for light and strength from a
source outside ourselves, that is because we are unrealists. All

such unprogressive notions will melt before the realization of the world's available riches and the means that lie to hand for their development. The Marxists can make their own Swinburne's pathetic words, which somehow no longer appeal to us of the West: "Glory to Man in the highest! for Man is the master of things."

Catholicism gives a different answer. It knows of no such "glad confident morning." Try as we will, and as we should, to develop our material resources, to raise the standard of living, to regulate inequalities, there are limitations inherent in this process. The balance between the rights of the individual and the claims of the community is to be adjusted, not ruthlessly broken down. Human personality of its nature revolts against being totally expended in the acquirement and distribution of wealth. Catholicism, though it is often charged with the contrary, defends the liberty of the spirit. The Church imposes no alien restrictions on the arts and sciences; it encourages them to flourish freely according to their own laws. Catholicism insists, however, that man's mind is not the measure of all things. Essentially the intelligence discovers, it does not create, truth. Looking before and after, our minds open upon the universe, even glimpsing a transcendent order of goodness and beauty. But, paradoxically, the mind makes its conquests by an act of surrender, an admission of insufficiency, not by fashioning for itself a world of its own. Catholicism, by recognizing the gulf which in fact exists between what is and what should be, takes at its full seriousness the problem of suffering. No trumpetings to the march of progress, no organ tones of psychological suggestion and scientific propaganda, are allowed to drown "the still sad music of humanity." Authentic Christianity gives no countenance to Job's comforters or to the complacent advocacy of patience under trial; it urges present healing to every manner of distress. But its philosophy is too profound to suppose that pain can be eliminated from a world that revolves to the rhythm of birth and death, of coming and ceasing to be.

Thus we can at best lay claim to no more than a precarious and much qualified self-reliance. An accident, an epidemic, some cataclysmic disaster, the annihilation which science now enables us to precipitate upon ourselves may be waiting round the corner to provide the ironic comment on all programs for security.

> As flies to wanton boys, are we to the gods;
> They kill us for their sport.

There are moments when it might seem so—to those at least for whom mankind is imprisoned in a closed, self-contained system. But there is another explanation. Not only the problem of apparently pointless suffering, but the radical instability in nature itself, demand the acceptance of our relative helplessness. Humility, faith, prayer are not devices of self-deception; they are expressions of the deepest insight into the human predicament. We have the assurance that "the burthen of the mystery" is not insupportable, that behind and above this at times unintelligible world there is both a promise and its fulfillment. The ineradicable optimism which underlies all sane thinking, the conviction that "God writes straight with crooked lines," are born of the knowledge that our gaze is fixed on the hither side of a vast tapestry each thread of which has its place, being woven into a pattern of "dexterous and starlight order."

Does there exist a creator God whose providence extends "from end unto end mightily and orders all things graciously"? This is the question of questions. Compared with it all others are of trifling importance. From the answer we give the consequences deduce themselves, as the Marxists have perceived more clear-sightedly than we of the West. "If there is no God," said Dostoevski, "then everything is permissible." We should not forget that Communism has its own morality; it can inspire a greater degree of self-dedication and concern for man's temporal well-being than that evoked by an emasculated Christianity. Its sins are not notably those of the flesh; it knows all about the virtues of asceticism. But in denying the existence of an absolute standard of right and wrong—which is what practical atheism amounts to—its code of conduct is based on mere expediency, the line of action demanded by the interests of the Party. Marxism dispenses with any concept of God because this implies a dualism between Creator and creature, it sanctions an opposition between the ideal and the real inconsistent with an uncompromising materialism. The error of the Christian religion—the "opium" with which it dopes the people—lies precisely in its preoccupation with a transcendent ideal. Whereas this "ideal," according to Marxism, is in fact embedded in the material process itself; it will be unearthed as the class struggle develops and finally realized in the establishment of the classless society. This last is the "god" which Communism worships with its "religion" of dialectical materialism. Thus the Marxian philosophy is not a form of nihilism; it draws its strength from its positive content. Marxism eliminates Christianity's vertical dimension but transposes on to a horizontal plane the Christian's forward-looking vision and sense of expectancy.

The complexity of Communist atheism, however, leaves unaltered its essential character. All flows from the postulate—there is no God, no wisely ordered providence. Against this denial Catholicism sets its face in irreconcilable opposition. Not to acquiesce in the reality of a supreme Being is the sign of a weakened or perverted intelligence. Common sense, which is the foundation of any sound philosophy, accepts the notion as demanded by all the evidence. True, there are sceptics who

affect to be unimpressed by arguments from manifest effects to
an ultimate unifying cause, or by Aristotle's inference of an
unmoved mover from the fact of ubiquitous flux and change,
but such agnosticism conceals a lie in the soul. To refuse to
commit oneself here, to allow the mind to become "sicklied o'er
with the pale cast of thought," is to exchange dreams for a
vision of the world as it is. No people, confronted by the witness of their senses, as St. Paul pointed out in his own day, has
any rational excuse for atheism. "The knowledge of God is
clear to their minds; God himself has made it clear to them;
from the foundations of the world men have caught sight of
his invisible nature, his eternal power and his divineness, as
they are known through his creatures" (Rom. 1:19-20).

That man and nature are the creation of God, that they are
wholly dependent on Him both in their existence and their
activities, is Christianity's first premise. It is this, and this alone,
that makes sense of civilized man's respect for absolute values,
his conviction that there exist intellectual and moral standards
which no amount of wishful thinking can alter. His nostalgic
pursuit of the true, the good, the beautiful has its term precisely here.

> Yet all experience is an arch wherethro'
> Gleams that untravell'd world, whose margin fades
> For ever and for ever when I move.

What we are perpetually in need of being reminded of is not
so much this presence, attested by conscience, of an order of
reality higher and better than we fully apprehend, as the fact that
it is grounded on a righteous God. For such an admission brings
with it obligations that we are not always ready to welcome.
These obligations are what Catholicism regards as its chief
concern. The Church does not leave them, as it were, in an
embryonic state, to be made more or less explicit according to
the moral perceptiveness of this or that individual; it focuses

our attention upon them and all that they involve. The result of this is not, as might be supposed, to add to life's burdens; rather it is to impart that sense of poise and basic security which must necessarily follow from an elucidation of the laws of man's being and the whole delicate structure of relationships between creature and Creator.

To reduce the matter to its simplest terms, it may be said that the Catholic Church exists on earth for the sole purpose of insisting, in season and out of season, that God be recognized for what He is, and as so recognized, worshipped. The Church is society's permanent rampart against idolatry. This is the ultimate, in a sense it is the only, sin, the root of all disorder. Significantly its prohibition takes first place in the Decalogue; it dominates and pervades the whole as the condition *sine qua non* of religion. Not only are the various manifestations of self-centeredness and excessive human affection so many species of idolatry, but the same is true on a larger, if less obvious, scale of every attempt to treat man's temporal well-being as the primary object of human endeavor. This is to substitute the lower for the higher and, by thus introducing a radical fault into the hierarchic constitution of the universe, prevents the achievement even of what is aimed at. The State, the race, the Party are our modern baals and golden calves, whose true character has yet to be unmasked before their worshippers.

When Christ Our Lord declared that God was to be loved above all things and that a man was to love his neighbor as himself—"On these two commandments, all the law and the prophets depend" (Matt. 22:40)—He was consciously enunciating the gravitational principle which keeps the human community in its orbit. If we set it aside, as we are free to do, what follows is disaster; not as a penalty arbitrarily imposed from without, but as arising from the situation itself—the personal and social disintegration which are the direct consequences of lawlessness. This principle, then, or to be more exact, its living embodiment in Christ, is the keystone in the arch of the whole political and social structure. To maintain it in its place, despite all attempts to dislodge it, is the *raison d'être* of Catholicism.

3

Individual or Community?

WHICH is the more important, the individual man or the community to which he belongs? There is no simple answer to this question. To make choice of either alternative is to find ourselves in difficulties. If, with the Fascists and Communists, we take sides for the community, we appear to give our vote to the dictator and our support to the totalitarian State. We countenance the exploitation of the human person in the supposed interests of "the people"—for, the world being what it is, that is what community government amounts to. If, with the liberals, we assign first place to the individual, we have apparently forgotten the lessons of *laissez faire,* the social injustice and economic anarchy that result from uncontrolled private enterprise. Evidently we are not here concerned with one of those *either/or* decisions such as occupied us in the last chapter. To continue Kierkegaard's antithesis, we are amid the perplexing contingencies of *both/and.* From one point of view the individual comes first, from another the community. To hold the correct balance, to discover and maintain the right priorities, between the one and the other is the chief task of civilized governments. They have not always been conspicuously successful.

In an attempt to elucidate the problem we may first recall some of the familiar facts about man himself. Modern psychology, though it has thrown much light on various aspects of human behavior, has not yet evolved a more satisfactory description of man than that which the traditional Catholic philosophy inherited from Greece. Man is a rational animal. Compounded of matter and spirit, each acting and reacting on the other, he shares much in common with the animal creation, yet has powers that are obviously denied to the animals. They have senses, often more highly developed than ours, which answer to appropriate stimuli; they possess memory and can even associate images; but there is no evidence that they think as we understand thinking. They attain to no abstract ideas, produce no intelligible speech, engage in no purposeful activity not accountable for as a response to their immediate environment. These are the characteristics which distinguish man, revealing him as a being not bounded by what is seen and heard and touched. When, for example, Marxists claim to be working for "social justice"—as universal an idea, involving the abstract notions both of "society" and "justice," as was ever conceived by the mind—they unconsciously saw off the philosophical branch on which they are seated. No materialist view of man's nature can explain why it is that he finds justice so compelling a motive for action, "fairer than either morning or evening star." An animal is aware of its needs; it has no conception of *rights,* whether of itself or others. The idea of "right" has a universal application; it is not the less complex for being an accepted commonplace. The apparently self-evident principle that each man should be given his due—which gives rise to a host of problems as soon as we start to apply it—was only arrived at after long reflection by the human spirit.

But it is not only the materialists who have erred. There is an excessive intellectualism which fails to give an adequate account of the body-spirit relationship. In emphasizing the reality and functions of the mind it understresses the part played by the physical organism. Man is looked upon, if not merely as a soul imprisoned in a body or, more extravagantly, as "a ghost in a machine," at least in such a way that his bodily elements come to be regarded as so many more or less obedient instruments of the spirit. This not only overlooks the fundamental oneness of the human personality, it gives rise to a jejune psychology. Its underlying assumption is that man's rational consciousness is capable of embracing the whole self and that the seemingly irrational constituents in his make-up have only to be examined and controlled by reason to be completely explained. One does not need to be a disciple of Freud to be aware that this is a gross oversimplification. The bewilderment of so many intellectuals in face of the forces that operate most powerfully in modern society is proof that their highly rationalized account of man and his motives hardly corresponds with the facts. It should in fairness be added that when this underestimate of the bodily factors is allied, as it sometimes is, with a religious other-worldliness, neither religion nor the world it aims at interpreting is likely to benefit.

To stress the validity of instincts and emotions, of feelings and unconscious impulses, is not to deny the paramount importance of mind and will. If it is perilous to treat the sub-rational elements in our nature as if they were other than they are, it is no less so to make no attempt to co-ordinate them with reference to their respective functions in the human psyche. This unquestionably demands the highest attainable degree of conscious awareness and a corresponding control by the will. Otherwise we are left in fatal ignorance of ourselves, victims of our own temperaments and helpless before every emotional storm that blows our way. The goal to be achieved is the integration of our whole personality. An inner disharmony, the pull of the lower against the higher, the fact that so often we approve the better yet choose the worse, conspire to warn us that so it is. But this inward conflict does not point to any essential disunity within man's nature, as if body and spirit stood radically opposed. The tension arises from the predicament in which the human race now finds itself. This we must briefly consider.

We shall not here discuss the historical background to the Catholic doctrine of original sin. Rather let us ask ourselves whether the implications of that doctrine do not throw a flood of light upon our present theme. It has been said that even orthodox Christians tend to give too much attention to sins, to cataloguing their vices and faults, too little to the nature of sin itself. This is to be like a doctor who is so preoccupied with the symptoms of ill-health that he fails to diagnose the disease. St. Augustine, than whom no one has meditated the matter more deeply, traces the origin of sin to an initial flight from reality within the mind. More exactly, it lies in man's refusal to accept his dependence on a law higher than himself, conformity to which is in turn a law of his own being. This lawlessness, whether or not it be so recognized, is in fact nothing less than an act of rebellion against the lawgiver, God. *"Non serviam"*: "I will not serve." Following upon this radical insubordination —which is another name for "original sin"—there arises a disturbance of right order, a disintegration, within man's whole nature. His mind and will, no longer held at their proper tension in the grip of those realities whose ground is God, become slack and lose their power to control his bodily impulses. These in their turn are now insubordinate—instincts, emotions, feelings and the sub-rational elements in human nature generally seek their gratification without regard to the well-being of the whole. The result is man as we know him—a creature who, having disavowed the master-servant relationship in which he has the subordinate role, is unable to reproduce that same relationship where it no less rightfully belongs, that is to say, within himself. "So free we seem, so fettered fast we are!"

The chief consequence of this state of things is the all-pervading phenomenon of self-centeredness. The self has its rights, but how seldom are they kept within bounds. Sin having entered the individual, it proliferates on a vast scale throughout the community. The immense aberration of a man-centered world is but the inevitable consequence of the self-centeredness within each of its component parts. In passing it may be noticed that the moral theologians, in their study of sin, have perhaps given their attention too narrowly to one of its departments, that of sexual irregularity. There are good grounds for such preoccupation with the abuses of this most imperious of human instincts, but it is surely regrettable that the effects of original sin, summed up in the heavily charged word "concupiscence," should have become almost exclusively colored by this association. We tend to lose sight of the symptoms of the same disease revealing themselves throughout the whole range of man's activities. The root of the matter is a wish for independence, for security on our own terms. When this ineradicable desire is unrelated to a living trust in God and His providence, its excesses know no limits. We compensate for our unacknowledged fear and sense of inadequacy by all manner of self-assertion. Egoism first betrays itself in the child's anxiety to be noticed, develops through the various manifestations of our concern to exercise influence, to culminate, if unchecked, in exorbitant ambition and an uninhibited lust for power. The wish for recognition, to perform a function proportionate to our capacities, are not in themselves signs of disorder; they are bound up with our status as persons; but the amount of human misery to which these impulses give rise is the measure of our inability to keep them under control.

What adds to the pathos of this whole situation is that we have not at our command the resources necessary for its cure. We cannot, as the phrase goes, hoist ourselves aloft by our own shoelaces. This elementary truth is apt to be overlooked both by the empirical psychologists and the progressive secularists of our day. The teaching of Catholicism that personal integrity comes to us as a gift from on high is strongly reinforced by the evidence which emerges from reflecting upon the facts. Man's reason may convince him that God exists, his will reach out to that Goodness which is beyond his grasp; he may assent to the truth expressed by Browning, "On earth the broken arcs; in the heaven, a perfect round"; yet still be unable to give such reality to this vision as will make it the motive force of his actions. The mind remains clouded, the will inevitably falters, unequal to the demands made upon it. What we need and, if ready to accept, receive is a creative gesture from God Himself. As a result, the reason is enlightened by faith, the will strengthened and uplifted by divine love, and the vital substance of the soul endowed with a gracious quality making it fit to become its true and better self. This regenerative process is the condition of finding our rightful place in the cosmic scheme of things. Only so are we on the way to repairing the havoc caused by man's egocentricity. We have to be saved from ourselves. But this need for redemption cannot be satisfied until it is first acknowledged.

We may now return to a closer scrutiny of the relations between the individual and the community. Human nature has been damaged by self-will, but its essence remains intact. At a deeper level than the psychological "personality" which calls for integration is the unalterable substance of the person itself. What are the characteristics of personality in this basic ontological sense? It is here that we may find the solution to our problem whether the rights of the individual harmonize or conflict with the claims of the community. The person is commonly defined by Catholic philosophy as "an individual substance of a rational nature." This apparently meager description contains more than we might at first sight suppose. It not only points to the obvious fact of individuality but qualifies this with the attribute of reason. Man is an individual with a difference. He is aware of a uniqueness that cannot be ascribed to material, or even animal, bodies. How shall we measure the gap that lies between the realities signified by the colorless word "it" and that singular pronoun, charged with undefinable significance, "I"? If we may coin the term, it is precisely this "I-ness" that makes us persons. For practical purposes we may sometimes speak of each of our organs and limbs, of the body and even the mind itself, in terms of the impersonal "it." But that is not how they lie within our consciousness. They are all comprised and enveloped in the uniqueness of the "I." In reality it is I, not my body, that feels warm or cold, I, not my eyes and ears, that see and hear, I, not simply my mind, that thinks.

St. Thomas Aquinas held that the person is higher in the scale of values than anything else in nature. Fortunately this is still the view of the Western liberal tradition. But there is a further qualification to be noticed of which modern liberalism often fails to take account. Within the indestructible unity of the *ego* we may distinguish between man considered as a person and man as an individual of the human species. This distinction can best be illustrated in the light of experience. We are aware that, despite what marks us off from other men, in fact we share the universe with them. "One touch of nature makes the whole world kin." We are caught up in a system whose lifeblood is community of interest. We acknowledge the fact of mutual interdependence, the need for give-and-take in every sphere and at all levels of man's activity. The accepted aim is the *bonum commune,* the common good of all. Compared to the common good the maintenance of any given social structure—a hierarchy of "classes," for example—is unimportant.

From this point of view we are parts of a greater whole. Hence we are prepared to admit that our rights and desires, in some respects at least, must be subordinated to the well-being of society. To further this end we submit to restrictions, being ordered about, deprived of a measure of property. We will even tolerate arrangements which touch closely our private lives, such as legislation concerning health and education, so long as we are persuaded that the general interest is genuinely being served. All this has to do with our character as individuals. However uncongenial we may find it, justice compels us to acknowledge that to be wholly unco-operative here is to indulge the individual to excess. We may even discover that, so considered, there is something about individuality itself that tends to be irrational and exorbitant.

But the case is very different when we come to view ourselves strictly as *persons*. Here we will permit no liberties to be taken, no infringement of inalienable rights. We must be allowed to call our souls our own. In circumstances where the supposed requirements of the common good conflict with our personal conscience we have to stand true to ourselves even at the price of being reckoned antisocial. The mind may submit to no law but truth itself, the will be enforced by no inducements but what it sees to be good. There are moments when we must be ready to say with the Apostles, "We ought to obey God rather than men" (Acts 5:29). What underlies and explains the inviolability of the person is its inherent relation to realities which cannot be manipulated for our own purposes. They control us, not we them. Of these, again, the source and ground is God Himself. None but He can take charge of our personality and do it no violence. Where any creature attempts to do so, as in the familiar instance of a misguided and possessive affection, there results a sense of invasion of what is proper to ourselves. However close the intimacy of friendship—and this is true even of the marriage relationship—there remains an inner citadel in both parties which each must respect. Love at its best, so far from feeling constraint on recognizing this, rejoices in finding itself ennobled by a reverence for what is sacred. No small proportion of the breakdowns in our mutual relations are due to a failure precisely at this point. We forget that, because the personality is God's most evident handiwork, it is so constituted that it may enter free and full communion only with its author.

Each of us, then, is both an individual and a person. Here it may be suggested that these two aspects of the one *self* have not received enough attention from contemporary psychologists and political thinkers. The same can perhaps be said of certain Catholic publicists. Their writing often betrays an incapacity to distinguish the basis of political liberalism, which gives rise to an exaggerated stress upon individual rights, from the much deeper foundations of the Church's doctrine of personal freedom. We need not quarrel about words, with the usage that treats individuality and personality as synonymous terms. But to equate the realities they signify is another matter. In the light of the foregoing paragraphs, let the student of psychology ask himself what he means by the development or integration of the "personality," and similarly, the student of politics what he means by the liberty of the "individual." At least both the one and the other should make sure that he has carried his analysis to sufficient depth. Individuality and personality are, of course, inseparable; each in its own way is identical with the self; but, as we have seen, they are distinguishable and respectively denote diverse attitudes and tendencies in human nature.

It will have been noticed that what preoccupies man as an individual is whatever makes for his security as a member of the species. Such things, for example, as food, drink, clothing, shelter and all that ministers to his physical well-being, including bodily sensations and desires. To which may be added wealth, honors, influence, prestige and the various intangibles that add to his stature in the eyes of his fellows. These, within limits, are human nature's legitimate concern. But they give grounds for caution, a caution that is increased when we reflect that individuality derives from the material, as distinct from the spiritual, element in our make-up. We notice further that the objects here being pursued are not inexhaustible; they are attainable only on a competitive basis where one man's gain is another man's loss. Thus they all too easily become a source of strife and division in society, a scramble in which the prizes go to the strong, or the lucky, while the rest go to the wall. Hence to foster our individualism without regard to wider considerations is, at best, to become an eccentric egoist, at worst, to make common cause with the careerists and go-getters so aptly described in Wordsworth's well-known lines:

> The good old rule
> Sufficeth them, the simple plan,
> That they should take, who have the power,
> And they should keep who can.

If we wish to promote political unity and social co-operation, it is to man as a person rather than as an individual that we must turn. Personality is rooted in spirit. While material things divide us from one another, the things that are spiritual bring unity and cohesion. The truth that is in my mind, for example, deprives no one else of the same truth. On the contrary, it is enlarged by being more generally known. Love, beauty, justice, moral goodness have no confines. Their nature demands that they be shared. The paradox of personality is that it is something alone and unique without being either solitary or isolated. The growth and development of the person takes place at no cost to others. It proceeds by a movement that is both upwards and outwards. Upwards to its regulative principle: the region of transcendent truth and goodness reflected in the light of conscience, which is nothing other than the created impress of God's own personality. Outwards to embrace and unify, while permeating to their depths, all the elements of self, so that we may come to full stature not merely as individuals but as a *person.*

We are now in a position to restate in its proper terms our problem of the relationship between the individual and the community. The business of government is to curtail the excesses, both actual and potential, of individualism without encroaching upon the prerogatives of the person. Or, put in another form, to foster the growth of personality while discouraging self-centered egoism. But, as soon as this has been said, we are again presented with the crucial dilemma which confronts the modern world—the choice between totalitarianism, by whatever name described, and representative democracy. Totalitarianism is to be ruled out since it extinguishes personality; its ends bear no relation to the worth and inexhaustible aspirations of man considered as a person. The claims of Western secularist democracy, however, are hardly less questionable. The so-called "open society" of liberalism is almost as great a myth as the classless society of the Marxists. It is based upon that negative conception of freedom whose deficiencies we have already examined. Having no agreed philosophy of the person, it can neither protect man from a state of chronic insecurity, which is the by-product of individualism, nor safeguard him from ruthless exploitation by the totalitarians.

When we come to consider the claims and counterclaims arising from each man's assertion of his right to a share in the good things of life, we observe that the elements of conflict can be resolved in one of two ways. Either an agreed solution is reached by reference to a law acknowledged by all parties or the dispute is settled by *force majeure*. Human nature being what it is, those who have superior power tend to exceed their rights. To seek agreement by an appeal to law is the method dictated by reason; it indicates submission to the idea of justice. In other words, it resolves the conflict by an essentially *personal* act. When, however, an element of power is thrown into the scales, these are at once weighted in favor of individual self-assertion. This is not to say that power can be dispensed with, or that its employment need be unjust. A law without sanctions is for practical purposes no law at all. But power not harnessed to the aims of the person, that is to say, impersonal and therefore irresponsible power, is no more than an instrument in the service of egoism and self-assertion. "The love of liberty is the love of others; the love of power is the love of ourselves." The modern tragedy is that we have vast resources of power but are without the secret of their effective control.

This conflict between the use of force and the claims of justice, between might and right, can be moderated wherever the public conscience is instructed and alert. But, again, the achievement of such social stability as is here implied depends upon the fullest possible recognition being given to man's status as a person. Yet this duty is hardly more effectively discharged by treating him deferentially as an autonomous individual, knowing no law but enlightened self-interest, than it is by exploiting him ruthlessly in the interests of the State machine. The real point of the contemporary protest that we are too closely governed, too much legislated for, is, or should be, that we are governed at an insufficiently high level, constricted by regulations that force us into an impersonal mold. In the last analysis, Western man suffers from a lack of government, a want of that external pressure upon his conscience and motives for action which is the condition of personal well-being. This cannot be supplied by

political leadership, however inspired, or by constitution-making
on the widest and most democratic principles; though these may
have their place. The need can only be met by reviving a general awareness of the significance of the human person, its
dignity and limiting conditions, above all, its subjection to a law
which is both native to man's own being and so transcendent as
to assign him his true place in the hierarchy of creation. We need
not have an uncritical admiration for Burke to acquiesce in the
abiding relevance of his famous words: "There is but one law
for all, namely, that law which governs all law, the law of our
Creator, the law of humanity, justice, equity—the law of nature,
and of nations."

When we review the world scene as it is today, we find the
deficiencies just considered startlingly revealed. The human
community has so far proved incapable of evolving for itself a
coherent political and social structure. Even the desire for it
has yet to be effectively stimulated. Ideally it may be agreed that
the resources of the earth should be made available to all men,
but a concrete program to this end remains outside the sphere
of practical politics. The West is still reluctant to accept the
Marxian thesis—one to which a Christian need take no
exception—that political without economic unity is a mirage.
The chief fear is that world unity, whose advent is sooner or
later inevitable, will be imposed from above by a process of
revolutionary conquest. This, of course, is the Communist
totalitarian solution. Westerners have so far striven to defend
themselves by engaging in the struggle for political and economic power, that is to say, by meeting Marxian materialism on
its own ground. Necessary as are these countermeasures for
confronting Communism with the one form of opposition it
respects, they are conditions for survival and not a positive policy. The American gesture of Marshall aid set a precedent at the
economic level for what needs to be done on a world-wide

scale. Until the native populations of Africa and India, of both Near and Far East, are assured that we are as much concerned for their well-being as the Marxists profess to be, we fight a losing battle. Whether, too, the demands of social justice are being adequately met nearer home, in Italy, France and Spain, possibly in America and England themselves, remains for many an open question. Men's souls are not to be saved without due regard for their bodies. Where the standard of living falls below a certain minimum, where glaring inequalities pass unheeded, the worth of our much vaunted liberty will be judged by our readiness to make men free of the material possessions we affect to regard as secondary. The advance of Communism will not be arrested by rhetorical denunciation, but by those able and willing to deliver the same goods on different terms. What is indicated is a selfless creative effort of unparalleled generosity, as sustained and all-pervasive as the Marxian dynamic itself. But from what quarter, for us of the Western world, is this to draw its inspiration?

We lack neither the potential resources nor the political and economic instruments by which they can be distributed. There exists, too, a widespread recognition of some such need. What is wanting is a sense of corporate responsibility, an awareness that, after all, we are our brothers' keeper, that we have duties to human society as a whole and not merely a call to maintain in being the Western way of life. Unfortunately we will the end without willing the means, we strive for unity while refusing the sacrifices that are necessary for its achievement. When we look realistically at the proceedings of the United Nations Organization, for example, we can detect a basic inconsistency fatal to the attainment of any lasting objective. Where there is no universal law by which all concerned acknowledged themselves bound, one that cannot be vetoed when its application becomes inconvenient, the only motive powerful enough to enforce action is the same as that which actuates men as individuals—calculated self-interest. When, further, the business of power politics is carried on under a semblance of law, in alleged conformity to high moral principles, real unity is weakened because the law which forms its basis is discredited. A short-term objective may be achieved, but in the long run it is always better to be quite honest and call things by their right names. As a provisional measure, pending the much-to-be-desired re-emergence of the idea of "natural law" [1]— which is repudiated by Marxists and, generally speaking, given short shrift by Western liberals—there is surely much to be said for conducting affairs between nations on the contractual basis of direct negotiations in the interests of each. Dubious as are the devices of diplomacy, they at least have the negative advantage of eliminating the necessity for mass propaganda and the erection of a façade of unity which bears no relation to the less picturesque realities. This is not to decry the value of the United Nations as a venue for discussion and the settlement of minor disputes. As a focus for world opinion, its benefits have already been demonstrated. [2] But of its nature it is "human, all too human." It brings us no resources but our own.

Thus we are left with twentieth-century Western man clinging to his ideal of individual freedom while it is rapidly being emptied of all content under the pressure of forces which he is powerless to control. These arise partly from himself, in his desperate attempts to build up a protective rampart of personal independence, partly from outside, in the seemingly irresistible onslaught of totalitarian society. He can associate with others on given conditions and for limited objectives, but is unable to enter the disinterested communion and larger fellowship which

[1] For a discussion on Natural Law, see pp. 179-98.
[2] See John Foster Dulles, *War or Peace* (New York: The Macmillan Co., 1950), chap. 6, "The United Nations in Operation."

his situation demands. He shuns such self-commital with the greater abhorrence lest, in surrendering to one or other of the "isms" that clamor for his allegiance, he should forgo the last shreds of personal liberty that remain to him. Among these "isms," let it be admitted, he often includes the Catholic Church. For what in the last analysis is there to choose between the authoritarianism of the Vatican and that of the Kremlin? At least he owes it to himself to consider the difference. Catholicism claims both to unite him with his kind in a unity as flexible and comprehensive as life itself and to bring him the perfection of freedom, "the glorious liberty of the children of God" (Rom. 8:21).

The legitimacy of this claim we have now to consider. Should it prove groundless, the prospect is truly forbidding. If there exists no world-wide social organism in which the rights of the individual and the demands of the community can be effectively harmonized, then man's future on this earth may fairly be depicted as a return to the conditions described by Thomas Hobbes: "No art; no letters; no society; and which is worst of all, continual fear and danger of violent death; and the life of man, solitary, poor, nasty, brutish, and short." Could it be that the alternative between Communism and Catholicism is finally to prove an *either/or* no more to be escaped than those presented in the preceding chapter? We may bring these inconclusive reflections to a close on a less insistent question mark—with Bishop Butler's celebrated, though always pertinent, platitude: "Things and actions are what they are, and the consequences of them will be what they will be: why then should we desire to be deceived?"

4

Towards a Solution

IF the argument so far has led to any conclusion, it can be
summarized as follows: Man's supreme need is to discover
a way of life which allows him to be fully a person and at
the same time to function as a member of a community whose
interests he shares and for whose welfare, so far as in him lies,
he is corporately responsible. If he cannot be himself, or is
denied a sense of fellowship with others, he becomes perforce
something less than human. Can Catholicism make good its claim
to meet just this situation? That is the question with which we
shall be engaged throughout the following pages.

THE LARGER BACKGROUND

Historically, it might be said, the Church has had its chance
to supply the mass of men with the conditions for the good life
and has failed in the task. Possibly there is some truth in this.
At any rate, we may let it pass. Certainly the theocratic ideals
which had their vogue in medieval Christendom are inapplicable
today. Inapplicable, because the spirit of free inquiry and the
rise of democratic institutions, whatever their attendant shortcomings, are acquisitions which no civilized man can be per-

suaded to relinquish. When the secularist looks from without at
the external structure of Catholicism, he may be impressed by
its magnificence, puzzled and even resentful at its strange
undeniable power, but its charms, such as they appear, have no
allurements for him. The Catholic Church provides an obvious
refuge for the ignorant and superstitious; it offers much common ground to religious and political traditionalists; it has
resources that meet the needs of conscientious aesthetes and
defeated intellectuals. All this may be admitted. It can also be
explained; at least by anyone with sufficient history and psychological insight, provided he has the mental balance and
courage to face the facts. Was it not Hobbes himself who
summed up the whole matter in a sentence? "The Papacy is not
other than the Ghost of the deceased Roman Empire, sitting
crowned upon the grave thereof."

On this it is fair to comment that if Catholicism contains a
hidden source of light, strength, and inexhaustible vitality, there
is no reason to suppose that such creative energy will reveal
itself to the eye of the secular historian, fruitful as are the lessons
of the Church's history. Nor can the inner secret be laid bare
from an inspection of the outward pomp and circumstance, the
splendors of ecclesiastical ceremonial. The onlooker is still free
to question whether this ancient pageantry is not, like Prospero's
cloud-capped towers and gorgeous palaces, a baseless fabric. It
is not for him to know that, "like stories from the land of spirits," it is pregnant with unguessed meaning. Only from the
highest vantage point, at the meeting place between the human
mind and Truth itself, can Catholicism be seen for what it is.
Political and social systems contain no essential mysteries.
Given the facts and the necessary intellectual equipment, they
can be fully understood. Catholicism, by definition, cannot be
so comprehended. What is required is that we should take our

stand at its highest and most central point and contemplate the Church's externals precisely from this level.

The detached spectator is likely to be daunted at the suggestion that he should take so precarious a leap in the dark. He is being invited to consider evidence whose real significance cannot be apprehended from his accustomed standpoint. But the difficulty is not insurmountable. Let him, as in any scientific investigation, begin with an unproved hypothesis: in this case, the postulate that the viewpoint of the Christian faith—for it is of that we are now speaking—is a valid one. Let him then ask himself whether what follows on this basis tallies with the ascertainable facts; whether it makes sense of a series of otherwise inexplicable phenomena; whether it in any way answers to his own need for fulfillment and self-realization. Beyond doubt wishful thinking is an uncertain guide in the quest for truth. We must check its steps by critical reflection at every stage of the journey. Things are not different from what they are by our desiring to have them so. But there are no dreams that do not mirror, however grotesquely, the everyday world. Vast as are the possibilities of self-deception, they have their limits. The mind and heart are so constituted that their innate unsatisfied longing for a solution to life's mystery, for secure and abiding happiness, for "the blessed vision of peace," cannot but be evoked by the ultimate Reality on which all such aspirations are grounded.

> Not where the wheeling systems darken,
> And our benumbed conceiving soars!—
> The drift of pinions, would we harken,
> Beats at our own clay-shuttered doors. . . .
>
> Yea, in the night, my Soul, my daughter,
> Cry,—clinging Heaven by the hems;
> And lo, Christ walking on the water
> Not of Gennesareth, but Thames! [1]

[1] Francis Thompson, "The Kingdom of God" ("In No Strange Land").

"God was in Christ, reconciling the world to himself" (II Cor. 5:19). If there is a single text in the New Testament that sums up the meaning of Christianity, it is this one. In and through Christ the purpose of human life is once and for all made known. God meets man's need by a creative act of self-giving, so solving the problem which lies at the root of all his troubles— his own self-centeredness. Here it must at once be said that any conception of Jesus of Nazareth which falls short of the Catholic doctrine of the Incarnation is irrelevant to these requirements. All attempts to attenuate Christ's equality as God with His Father are fundamentally unrealistic. That this is so has been overlooked by not a few professing Christians. Thus to say that Jesus is the uniquely perfect example to man of what he should be, and to add that He was endowed with incomparable insight and moral force, is to say what is true. But to stop at this is not to take either Him or His message with sufficient seriousness. If He is thought of as differing only in degree from a Confucius, a Buddha, or a Socrates, then He is not understood. What it is essential to grasp is that not only did Christ represent and embody "the power of God and the wisdom of God" (I Cor. 1:24) but that, as their author and norm, He exercised these divine attributes in His own right. Herein lies the cosmic and unrepeatable character of the Incarnation—that the same God who created and controls the universe chose to perfect His work by entering into intimate personal communion with our human nature in one man, Jesus Christ, and through Him to bring to its climax His providential plan. "In Christ the whole plenitude of Deity is embodied, and dwells in him, and it is in him that you find your completion; he is the fountain head from which all dominion and power proceed" (Col. 2:9-10).

Having stressed the crucial importance of Our Lord's divinity, we must insist with no less emphasis on the reality of His manhood. It may be that some among orthodox theologians, preoccupied with working out the theoretical implications of His Godhead, have not always avoided an unduly *a priori* treatment of the New Testament witness to that undiminished human nature which, as "the first born among many brethren" (Rom. 8:29), He shares with us. The only element of our created nature that was absent from His was precisely that man-centered self-concern, the origin of all sin, from which He brings us deliverance. Christ, by His very being, is the one absolutely God-centered man the world has seen. For the rest, He experienced to the full our constitutional weaknesses. Hunger, thirst, fatigue, mental depression, fear, temptation to wrong-doing—He knew them all. Nothing more clearly shows the extent to which Jesus of Nazareth embraced our common lot than the memorable words, as consoling as they are full of pathos, of the Epistle to the Hebrews. "Christ, during his earthly life, offered prayer and entreaty to the God who could save him from death, not without a piercing cry, not without tears; yet with such piety as won him a hearing. Son of God though he was, he learned obedience in the school of suffering, and now, his full achievement reached, he wins eternal salvation for all those who render obedience to him" (Heb. 5:7-9).

The sum and substance of Christ's message is the truth embodied in His own person. The transcendent God, who holds the universe in the hollow of His hands, must be acknowledged by His creatures for what He is. Fundamentally it is as simple as that. Christianity contains a revelation of God's mysterious nature; it offers the final explanation of life's purpose; it presents us with a symbolic ritual whereby divine favors are mediated to man; but there is nothing either mysterious or symbolic about its ultimate basis. This is none other than the Creator-creature relationship in which God and man, by the absolute necessity of their respective beings, confront one another. Non-reality thinking, our capacity to take refuge within the fortress of the ego in pride and willfulness, may lead us to refuse to accept what this position implies, but nothing that we may do can alter it. What Christ did was to bring this situation to the forefront of the world's stage and compel men to fix their gaze upon it. From the ultimate point of view it may be said that He did not come to inform men's minds with a new and unheard of doctrine but to remind them of what they were. Not to urge them to practise some superhuman idcal but to invite them to accept their own condition and its consequences. His mission was not to institute a better form of religion than had hitherto existed, not even to impose upon His disciples *His* religion, but to disclose in the clearest possible manner religion itself. He came, that is to say, in order to demonstrate that the true frame of reference for each of man's activities is the encircling bond which binds the creature to his Creator. Compared to the understanding of this, all other human interests are of no account.

Thus we find that when Jesus was asked by one of the scribes to expound the secret of eternal life (Luke 10:25 ff.), He answers with a corroboration of the great text in Deuteronomy: "Hear, O Israel: the Lord our God is one Lord. Thou shalt love the Lord thy God with thy whole heart, and with thy whole soul, and with thy whole strength" (6:4-5). This, in its most positive and persuasive form, is the age-long fulmination against idolatry in whatever guise. It is the focusing of man's mind and heart where they belong. What is prohibited is not only idolatry but any yielding to self-concern. The "whole" of our energies are to be directed to God, the self being considered simply in its relation to Him. To obey this commandment, on the word of Christ Himself, is to live. To disobey, that is, to give less than our all, is by so much to be subject to self. So failing, we remain compassed by sin and thus prove unequal to mastering life's secret. This is the message, in universal terms, which fills the

Synoptic Gospels. Men must submit themselves utterly to the Kingdom (i.e., the *Rule*) of God. The Kingdom was now uniquely realized in Christ's own person. How this was so He declared to Pilate, who had questioned Him on His claim to kingship. "What I was born for, what I came into the world for, is to bear witness of the truth" (John 18:37).

This is the clearest single statement in the Gospels of the meaning of Our Lord's mission and the nature of God's kingdom. All sovereign States, since they "belong to this world," lack the basis of ultimate truth. They are far from representing the ideal of what human society should be. Their claim to be a real community of peoples is largely a legal fiction. Each State is no doubt upheld by sentiments of kinship and good will among its members. This sense of solidarity may reach as far as the well-being of the national group; but that it does not extend further, that its limits are just what give rise to many political and social units, indicates how far they fall short of the *truth*. What Christ came to bear witness to was quite otherwise —"my kingdom does not take its origin here." His rulership was based on the real constitution of the universe in its relation to God. This was the *"Truth"* to which He would testify. A truth to be realized progressively as mankind, listening to Christ's voice, joined with Him in common brotherhood under the Father. "There can be neither Jew nor Greek, there can be neither slave nor freeman, there can be no male and female, for you all are one in Christ Jesus" (Gal. 3:28).

When the New Testament affirms that it was God's "loving design, centered in Christ, to give history its fulfilment by resuming everything in him, all that is in heaven, all that it is on earth, summed up in him" (Eph. 1:9-10), we are being told something of unparalleled significance. This is what it most of all concerns man to know. Jesus Christ in His very person is religion incarnate. Religion, considered not in any restricted conventional sense of ritual devotion and personal piety, but as the ultimate constitutive element, fundamental and all-pervasive, of created human nature as related to its first cause and last end—God. To demonstrate this truth at the highest possible level of intelligibility, and to impress it upon men's minds with the most compelling urgency, was the purpose of the divine-human *crisis* we call the Incarnation. This is what explains the piercing intensity of Our Lord's words, the almost terrifying single-mindedness of His actions. Not a saying but reveals His absorbed preoccupation with man's relation to God. Not a deed but serves to strengthen it and remove all impediments to our awareness of its paramount importance. For Him religion is not one interest among many; it is the only interest, including within itself all others. Of conscious design He set it in isolation from every other human concern, so that there might be no mistaking the absoluteness of its claims. He resisted every attempt to involve Him in the current political controversy, between the aspirations of Jewish nationalism and loyalty to Rome (Mark 12:17), and refused to act as arbiter in any secular dispute (Luke 12:14). His mission was to put an end to unrealistic dreams, to show the worthlessness of every project but the supreme one, in short, to awaken man to his position face to face with God. Compared to this no other task merited a moment's consideration.

But then, as now, men were being invited to a change of heart of which, from their own resources, they were incapable. The most they could do was to recognize their need, accept the situation, and dispose themselves for its relief by an attitude of self-distrust. "Lord, to whom shall we go? Thou hast the words of eternal life" (John 6:69). The lifework of Jesus Christ was to make possible for the world in general the God-centeredness which He embodied. This achievement, however, was conditioned by His power to bring order out of universal chaos. His vocation was that of restoring the harmony between man and God broken as the result of human selfishness. He must perform an act of cosmic significance, by which the whole process of disintegration should be arrested and set in reverse. As the veritable Son of Man, He bore within himself all the elements of man's nature. These He would consecrate afresh to the God from whose dominion they had fallen away. As God's suffering servant, Christ's destiny was to do this by freely accepting, as directed against Himself, the frightful consequences of the world's self-centeredness, absorbing their full force. Having thus allowed malice to expend its energy, He could, by a divinely human act, master the resultant situation and turn back man's perverted will into its right course. On Calvary Our Lord suffered and acted as the representative figure of all mankind, to whose salvation He was dedicated. "So it is that the Son of Man did not come to have service done him; he came to serve others, and to give his life as a ransom for the lives of many" (Mark 10:45).

About all this there was nothing fortuitous. Jesus of Nazareth was fulfilling His appointed task. No conviction was more firmly rooted in His mind than that He was doing what God required of Him. "The Son of Man goes on his way, for so it has been ordained" (Luke 22:22). Self-centeredness brings with it the penalty of suffering, not as an arbitrary infliction from without, but by the law of its nature. By standing proxy for self-centered man, Our Lord removed the cause of egoism's necessary frustration and final undoing by first sustaining its effects. What should not be overlooked, however, is that in the concrete historical situation in which He found Himself, the tragic outcome of His ministry was, humanly speaking, no less inevitable. Jesus' attempt to broaden and deepen the existing conceptions of religion, to reinterpret the Jewish Law, as it was commonly understood, in terms as comprehensive as the divine

Law itself failed. The old wineskins could not contain the new wine. The Messiah was brought to a head-on collision with the upholders of the ecclesiastical *status quo*. The challenge He threw down to the Israelite leaders touched them at their weakest and tenderest spot, and they could not abide it. They were exploiting religion itself in the interests of their personal prestige and self-esteem, seeking man's approval rather than God's. When to this was added the claim that their predicament could only be resolved by making common cause with Him, the cup of their indignation was full. The dilemma was resolved on Calvary, those responsible assisting at the sublimest act of tragic irony in history. Their seeming triumph was in fact their own downfall, the vindication both of the Critic and His criticism. The Crucifixion would give the world its supreme assurance that in the conflict between might and right, right will always win in the end.

But this was not the conclusion of the story. So far as it concerned the peoples outside Palestine, it was only the beginning. Jesus of Nazareth, who died on the Cross, rose from the tomb alive again on Easter morning. Christianity stands or falls by this truth. The central importance of the Resurrection must here be emphasized. There are admirers of Jesus and the Christian ideal who affect to regard this preternatural event as unhistorical, a myth evolved from the legend-creating faith of the first disciples. It has even been argued, following the Marcan account, that Our Lord died in dereliction and despair. This was the tragedy whose lesson we must somehow make our own. To append a resurrection epilogue, so these critics tell us, is to be guilty of sentimental bathos. In reality it is those who take this view, in defiance of our written records, who are the sentimentalists. They remove the truly tragic element from Calvary and reduce it to a drama which satisfies, not a sense of justice, but their own somewhat dubious aesthetic taste. Christ's "failure" was analogous to that of the poet Keats. (The comparison has actually been made;—surely the most pathetically absurd mis-interpretation that has appeared in print!) Jesus was a "hero" who learned by suffering. The message of His life and death, though of deeper significance, is not essentially different in quality—a catharsis, through terror and pity—from what can be gathered from Shakespeare's *Lear*.

To romanticism of this kind it must be pointed out that the Christian doctrine of the Resurrection is concerned with nothing so trivial as dramatic suitability. There was no spectacular triumph about the appearances of the risen Lord, such as might well have been devised by anyone sufficiently interested to in-vent, or add color, to the story. In fact He showed Himself to a mere handful of chosen witnesses (Acts 10:41); though in a manner so unmistakable as to enable them to carry their con-viction of its truth to the confines of the Roman Empire. The Resurrection was truly fitting in that it demonstrated that a manhood whose life it had been to adhere to God, Himself the Author of life, could not be separated from Him by death. From the world's point of view the Resurrection was necessary as the indispensable condition of man's conquest of self-centeredness. Here, again, a romantic humanitarian Christianity falls sadly short of the mark. What it overlooks is that the Christian life is not constituted by man's independent efforts to follow Christ's ideals and put His teaching into practice. The disciples during their Master's lifetime were not notably successful in this respect. Then, as now, a radical change of heart was called for, a re-orientation of men's whole outlook. But how could this be effected? Only by a work of divine power bestowing upon them a share in Christ's own life, an infusion of the same motive force into their minds and hearts as actuated His. Hence they were to be as dependent on Him for their status as Christians as are the branches on the parent vine (John 15:5).

If man is to live the God-centered life—and it was the whole purpose of Christ's mission that he should do so—then he must be raised from his natural state of egoism and furnished with the needful strength. It was for this reason that Our Lord had first to offer the supremely selfless sacrifice of His death and then, with the executive authority of the risen Saviour, complete His work. Of this need and its fulfillment the disciples, in the newly born faith of the Resurrection, were conscious to the depths of their being. During His lifetime they hardly understood Him, much less were they able to follow His example. But with the Pentecostal outpouring of the Spirit all was changed. They knew that He was their living Lord in heaven, knew that it was through a communication of vital energy from Him that they too lived and worked and bore Him witness. "And yet I am alive; or rather, not I; it is Christ that lives in me. True, I am living, here and now, this mortal life; but my real life is the faith I have in the Son of God, who loved me, and gave himself for me" (Gal. 2:20). This is the kind of language —found in what is probably the earliest Christian document known to us, St. Paul's Epistle to the Galatians—that demands explanation by those who would deny the reality of the Resurrection.

Let us suppose, for argument's sake, that the sceptics' contention be admitted, that the appearances of the risen Lord were no more than an unconscious hallucination on the part of a small group of devoted followers, that they spread the story in all good faith, and that thus it found its way into our present Gospels. The theory that the first Christians deliberately concocted a resurrection legend may be dismissed as a psychological absurdity. But individual and even mass hallucination is not unknown and men—and, so it is said, especially women!— have a remarkable capacity for seeing what they want to see. The "unconscious" can play strange tricks with the visual faculty. With those who hold antecedently that a bodily resurrection cannot happen and accordingly that all evidence in its favor is to be rejected *a priori* it is, of course, useless to argue. We must leave them in their dogmatic slumber. But even those with an unprejudiced interest in objective truth and a disposition to accept facts, however remarkable, have a case for regarding the visions seen after the discovery of the empty tomb as due to self-deception. After all, an optical illusion is a more frequent phenomenon than that a man who was crucified should rise from the dead. What puts this explanation out of court, quite apart from the Gospel narratives, is the known teaching given to the primitive Christian communities as this emerges from the Acts and the Pauline Epistles.

The aspect of Christianity which dominated the mind of the early Church was neither the life story of Jesus nor the doctrine contained in the Sermon on the Mount but, precisely, the Resurrection. The disciples were engaged in a continuous proclamation of the fact that the Master they had known, Jesus of Nazareth, the acknowledged Messiah and Son of God, had been crucified and was now risen from the dead. The Apostles, as witnesses to the Resurrection, were concerned to get it accepted it they died in the attempt. They knew as well as any man in the twentieth century that the thing was wonderful and unparalleled. They had good reason to guard against illusion, being fully aware that if the Resurrection were not true, then they were impostors (I Cor. 15:13). Being contemporaries of the event, they had every opportunity for examining and comparing the evidence. The sequel shows them to have been so convinced of its authenticity that they place it in the forefront of their preaching and demand belief in it as an indispensable condition of any fellowship with them. Large sections of the Gentile world might have accepted a Christianized form of Judaism—itself a loftier religion than anything they had yet discovered—had it not been for the stumbling block of the Resurrection. St. Paul's experience with the Athenian intelligentsia was typical; they were interested—up to a point; but "When resurrection from the dead was mentioned, some mocked, while others said, We must hear more from thee about this. So Paul went away from among them" (Acts 17:32). It was to other hearers that he could more profitably expound the final issue of the life and death of Jesus. "That is why God has raised him to such a height, given him that name which is greater than any other name; so that everything in heaven and on earth and under the earth must bend the knee before the name of Jesus, and every tongue must confess Jesus Christ as the Lord, to the glory of God the Father" (Phil. 2:9-11). The genesis of these ideas, rooted as they were in a primitive tradition (I Cor. 15:1 ff.) quite independent of St. Paul's experience on the Damascus road, is what the advocates of a de-supernaturalized Christianity have never been able to explain.

The Christian Church, as we find it in the Acts, had been prepared for during Our Lord's public ministry. He gathered about Him a group of disciples, the faithful remnant among the chosen people. They would form the nucleus of what St. Paul describes as the newly constituted Israel of God (Gal. 6:16). The ancient Israel had rejected its Messiah; its inheritance was now to be the lot of the nations (Matt. 8:11-12). There was to be a holy community of believers, bound with indissoluble links to Christ Himself, His representatives before the world. Through a living faith they would strive to adhere to God in the manner He had shown them, selflessly and with singleness of mind. The two great commandments—a wholehearted surrender to God and a fraternal love of one's neighbor—which had been overlaid by the minutiae of Jewish legalism were now revealed as the sum total of religion. Displayed in their essential clarity in Christ Himself—now and forever the ideal embodiment of what man's relations with God and his fellow creatures should be—their implications in terms of everyday life would be worked out by His followers.

It is not only as instruments for attaining eternal salvation that these requirements were to be observed. Their frame of reference was applicable everywhere and always. The stability of human society, whatever touches man's temporal welfare, would be conditional upon his conformity to what had once for all been disclosed as the twin laws of his being. That is to say, an acknowledged dependence upon a supreme Lawgiver and the recognized obligation to concede to all men the rights inherent in each. So stated, these might be described as the secular counterparts of the twofold Gospel precept, were it not that secularism is now an anomaly, being a perversion in nature whose only source is the secular heart of man. Given this fundamental adjustment to reality, nothing need be subtracted from the whole realm of created values, since these now fall into their rightful place. The Christian may attach a richer meaning than their pagan author's to the famous words, *"Homo sum; humani nil a me alienum puto."* He has a positive invitation to give his thoughts to whatsoever is lovely or of good report (Phil. 4:8). It was a Catholic instinct in Thomas Traherne that inspired him to the classical expression of the only legitimate humanism, a philosophy and aestheticism centered upon God.

You never enjoy the world aright, till the sea itself floweth in your veins, till you are clothed with the heavens and crowned with the stars: and perceive yourself to be the sole heir of the whole world, and more than so, because men are in it who are every one sole heirs as well as you. Till you can sing and rejoice and delight in God, as misers do in gold, and kings in sceptres, you never enjoy the world (*Centuries of Meditations,* Cent. i, § 29).

The Christain community was not to live simply on the memory of its crucified and ascended Lord. What was demanded of them depended for its fulfillment upon the abiding presence of His promised Spirit. Failing that, they had no lawful claim to be His followers (Rom. 8:9). Christ Himself would always remain the Head of His Church, controlling and guiding it from His exalted place at the Father's right hand; but He was also immanent within it by His Spirit. This was its vital principle, its "soul," informing the Church with divine-human energy. The Holy Spirit constituted the Church the one God-centered community on earth. For this reason St. Paul describes the Church's fundamental character as that of the "Body" of Christ. Not, as is obvious, His unique physical body, but a social, "mystical" body; so called because it is a mysterious, sacramental manifestation of Christ's person still present in the world. The Church is thus an extension in space and time of the original Incarnation; its *raison d'être* is to be precisely this. Our Lord concentrated His uniquely personal work within a short lifetime on a narrow stage; but what He was and did would be embodied throughout history in His mystical Body. The Church is thus an absolute necessity to Christ's saving purpose. Without it His representative office as the type of God-centered humanity has no significance. He could no more be Messiah without the Israel of God, a Redeemer without the redeemed, than He could be Head without the members of His Body. Christ and the Church together form an organism whose parts reciprocally contribute to the life of the whole. This mutual interdependence marks the Christian community at its deepest and most vital level, the living union of the Saviour and those being saved, the *Christus totus*.

Hence it is only "in Christ" that we can follow Christ. The Church has one all-embracing task, that of testifying to and portraying Christ to the world. It has inherited His mission of transforming man's natural self-centeredness into God-centeredness. The Church's members are not volunteers for a cause; they are a chosen community. But their election concedes nothing to their self-esteem. This was the mistake made by the Israel that failed. They assumed that they were not as other men, thought of themselves as a chosen people after their own fashion, enjoying privileges and a prestige denied to "lesser breeds without the Law." So they would continue to cultivate their divinely given preserve. Having the Law and the Prophets in their possession, they had nothing more to learn. Let others come and join them if they would. After due submission, they would be welcome. But those who could boast that they had Abraham for their father need make no move. As for any sense of obligation to the nations at large, they went on their way regardless. In the issue they were engulfed by the nemesis which follows all corporate self-preoccupation. Not knowing how to share their treasure with others, they could not keep it for themselves. They were to learn that God could raise up children to Abraham from whatever material He chose (Matt. 3:9). The Gospel was to show that the condition of retaining God's favors is our willingness to share them with others (Luke 6:38). This tragedy is not perhaps without its lessons for Christians today. The only basis left them for exclusiveness is the cause of divine truth. On this they can perforce yield nothing. But the New Israel, like the Old, has its vested interests; its members were not granted immunity from the spirit of faction. Not only could they fall into heresy and schism; they could retain the truth while proving unequal to its demands. By a kind of Christian Pharisaism they would be able to promote sectarianism at the expense of religion.

The universalism of Christianity is compatible with, though it is certainly obscured by, a lack of insight on the part of its adherents. The Church has been well served by men with their full share of those, after all, typically human failings, an excessive mental rigidity and shortsightedness. Psychologists will no doubt account for such limitations by pointing to an unconscious fear and sense of insecurity. Ignorance and stupidity, too, to put it bluntly, have perhaps had their part to play. Preoccupation with a cause has had its natural result, that of subjecting the mental vision to the requirements of the will. Yet these defects can go together with the highly Christian virtues of courage and singleness of purpose. What they do not easily combine with, however, is a responsiveness to every aspect of God's truth; they may foster "a zeal for God, but not according to knowledge" (Rom. 10:2). In the last analysis we are committed to nothing except the revelation that is in Christ Jesus. The Christian's privileges, therefore, are to be measured not by any personal prerogatives but in terms of a unique responsibility. He is called, like Christ Himself, to a life of witness to God and unending service of his fellow men.

The Church, then, is the mystical Body of Christ. It is a holy community, the living temple of God's spirit, bearer of the Christ-life to all the world. That life each of the Church's members derives from Christ their Head; they sustain it by reciprocal communion with one another. But living as they do by faith and not by sight, their response to the God-centered ideal tends to be fitful and uncertain. The Church is still in process of realizing itself, of conforming ever more faithfully to the pattern given it by Christ. If its members are finally to attain the fruits of His achievement, they must first share His sufferings (Rom. 8:17). To be purified from the disordered sensuality which is lust, to have pride removed from the mind and willfulness from the heart, are the prerequisites of the ultimate self-giving. The Church is thus building itself up through love (Eph. 4:16). This enterprise is what constitutes the only genuine progress of mankind. We are concerned to "build up the frame of Christ's body, until we all realize our common unity through faith in the Son of God, and fuller knowledge of Him. So we shall reach perfect manhood, that maturity which is proportioned to the completed growth of Christ" (Eph. 4:12-13).

Not otherwise than in the context of what St. Paul here calls the "fulness of Christ" can the problem of the relationship between the individual and the community be resolved. We have seen that the impediments to its solution lie, on the one hand, in man's ignorance and uncertainty as to the purpose of his existence, and on the other, in the absence of a corporate will effective enough to reconcile the apparently conflicting claims of the person and the community to which he belongs. "God made me to know Him, love Him and serve Him in this world, and to be happy with Him for ever in the next." These simple words of the catechism, which the Catholic child learns by heart in infancy, contain life's philosophy in a sentence. They provide the one satisfying answer to the supremely urgent question. All that we ever learn afterwards is but a filling in the details of this great scheme of things. The saving knowledge of faith is what gives the mind its needful center of gravity. The love of divinely infused charity supplies the dynamic without which knowledge remains ineffective. With these are blended the Christian's unconquerable hope. Not a blind, instinctive optimism or an uncritical acceptance of the view that "whatever is is right," but an unshakeable conviction, based on God's power and mercy, that those who trust in Him will not be left helpless victims before His enemies. Like Christ, they may know no lasting triumph till the resurrection, but there will be no mistaking it then. "For now we see in a mirror, dimly; but then face to face. Now I know partially; but then I shall know completely, even as I am completely known. And now there remain faith, hope, love, these three; but the greatest of these is love" (I Cor. 13:12-13).

The knowledge which comes by faith supplies the key both to our understanding of society as a whole and an appreciation of each of its members. We see mankind, not as a vast conglomeration of autonomous individuals sharing only a common nature, a *genus homo,* but as an interrelated organism each of whose parts is in vital dependence on each. A vague sense of brotherhood and community of interest, which reason itself discerns, are motives insufficiently powerful to unify and give effective cohesion to the human race. What we need and, given the will, receive is a supra-rational insight into the truth that together we are the children of our Heavenly Father, and Christ is our Brother. We are bound together not merely by ties of blood but through a spiritual rebirth enabling us to live with an immortal, God-centered life. What brings unity to society as so conceived is the veritable Spirit of unity (Eph. 4:3), the only power in existence that can unite men in a common cause with no possibility of violence to their personal integrity. For God's law—though more exacting than any other, since it is the law of love—knows nothing of despotic controls and arbitrary restraints. It sacrifices no individual to the common welfare, because this is the level at which the interests of both coincide. It even modifies the law of nature itself and eliminates its element of ruthlessness, since God now treats with humanity not as a Creator with His creatures but as a Father with His children. "The Spirit himself thus assures our spirit, that we are children of God; and if we are his children, then we are his heirs too; heirs of God, sharing the inheritance of Christ" (Rom. 8:16-17).

PERSONAL RELATIONSHIPS

The respect due to each individual person, combined with the fact that we share a common destiny, is what gives point and purpose to the Gospel precept of mutual charity. The observance of this, according to the mind of Christ, is to be the chief characteristic by which the members of His mystical Body will be known for what they are. "The mark by which all men will know you for my disciples will be the love you bear one another" (John 13:35). Here indeed is the heart of the matter. The well-being of society clearly depends less on the soundness of its underlying philosophy than on the quality of its individual members, particularly the quality of its leaders. Accordingly it may now be in place to review our present theme in less general terms. What follows is an attempt to translate into a more personal idiom much of what has so far been considered.[2]

When Our Lord told His disciples that they were to deny themselves in order to follow Him, their attention was being drawn, not so much to themselves who were to be denied, as to Him who was to be followed. Christian renunciation is best thought about from the positive rather than the negative point of view, as being a detachment from self only in so far as it is an attachment to God. This process, the change over from self-centeredness to God-centeredness, is one way of describing the whole business of living. To speak of the stages of such a transformation in terms of "love" is no mere flight of fancy, a romanticizing of a theme at once too serious and too engaging for sentimentality. Let not the abuse of the noblest of words, or perhaps our odd, self-conscious reluctance to employ it accurately, debar us in this context from calling things by their right names. A man in the last resort is to be judged only by what he loves. It may be helpful, sometimes, to state the issue thus plainly to ourselves.

The disturbing thing is that love begins with and, if we are not careful, ends with self. There is, of course, a lawful kind of self-love; the kind which is to be the model for the love of our

[2] The following, revised and adapted to its present context, originally appeared in the *Tablet* as a series of articles entitled "The Dialectic of Love." Acknowledgement is due to the Editor of that journal for his kind consent.

neighbor. The trouble arises when the main drive of the will and of our affections is centered upon the ego. Moreover the human situation is such that, unless something intervenes to save us, this becomes our all but inevitable plight, even though we may remain only faintly conscious of it. By original sin man lost the God-centeredness given him by grace. There followed the darkening of the mind and enfeeblement of the will which lie at the root of most of our ills. All sin is a betrayal, a failure to live up to the light; or else it is a breakdown in love. In our self-absorption we see the scene out of focus; misguided self-will leads us astray and our actions mar and spoil. A man's mind and heart, instead of reaching outwards and upwards to make contact with things as they are, turn back upon themselves. He now begins to live, not among the realities God has made, but in a world of his own of which he is the center. His vision is clouded by self-consciousness, his power to love frustrated by self-concern. Unloving, and therefore unloved, he may console himself with the song of the Jolly Miller: "I care for nobody, no, not I, and nobody cares for me."

Egoism, happily, seldom reaches its logical outcome, which is self-worship. But we know how many and various are its forms, from the God-denying megalomania of the political despot down to the pitiful self-preoccupation of the sensualist. In this latter connection we may note in passing that the abuse of the sex function is wrong, not because it is pleasant, but because it is selfish. On the wider stage, the irreligion and secularism of our day are a form of cosmic selfishness—a refusal to give God His due lest something of our own thereby be lost. The outward forms of sin may change, but its chief motive remains what it has always been: man's desire for self-sufficiency, to be a law unto himself.

Yet apart from the easily tabulated sins, how pervasive is the influence of self-love gone astray! We see it in our own un-

generosity, in the craving for praise, in our failure to take
account of other people's feelings, in the at times damaging
thoughtlessness and forgetfulness, which we excuse as absence
of mind, but whose real source is lack of interest and of something more. Small wonder that we find Our Lord to have been
immeasurably more concerned with the wellsprings of human
conduct than with the casuistical discussions of the scribes and
Pharisees. "Many sins are forgiven her, because she hath loved
much" (Luke 7:47).

We know how possible it is for virtue itself—austerity of life,
for example—to be made the instrument of self-love. This was
the fault of the Stoics of the ancient world—"Through the rent
in your garment, Cleanthes, vanity peeps out!"—and is perhaps
not unknown among Christians. The resuscitated Stoicism of
Pelagius was officially condemned, but his heresy is by no means
extinct. How much easier do we perhaps find it, because more
rewarding in terms of a personal achievement, to mortify the
flesh than to be affable and kindly to those about us! The Gospel
warns us that it is the respectable folk, not the flagrant sinners,
who are most likely to be blind to their own self-complacency;
none the less so for being acutely aware of it in others. At any
rate, we may profitably reflect on how much of self obtrudes
itself upon the best, as well as the worst, of what we do.

There is a time for asceticism, as also for reminding ourselves
that holiness does not consist in austerity of life but in the love
which is the fulfilling of the Law. Thus, in contrasting the poverty
of our own motives with the selflessness of Christ, so strikingly
exhibited in the Gospel narrative of the Temptations, we may
well experience the bitter sweets of what Kierkegaard called
"creative despair," that distrust of self which is our one sure
ground for confidence. In the wilderness Our Lord was prompted
to self-display. What emerged from that most significant incident
is the condemnation of all self-interest, which not even the

highest objective motives can redeem, and the absolute primacy of the divine will over every human desire. Any giving to creatures (ourselves included) of what belongs to God is a form of idolatry. So Christ reminded the tempter, "Thou shalt worship the Lord thy God, and serve none but him" (Matt. 4:10).

Self-love, unlike self-knowledge, has few rewards. For one thing, it incurs the penalty of loneliness; the complete egoist is without that precious sense that he "belongs," whether to another person or to some wider fellowship. To know ourselves, what are our gifts and our shortcomings, is a part of wisdom. Thereby we may be led to humility before God and a right attitude towards those around us. But to love oneself, except as included in something bigger and more significant than self, is to go against nature. We were not meant to stand alone. Hence we must contrive to get away from, without forgetting, ourselves. This, of course, is widely recognized. No one courts isolation for its own sake. Even the most self-reliant feel the need for companionship and diversion. The ways in which men attempt to throw off the burden of being alone are broadly reducible to three. By the adventures of the mind, through some kind of bodily experience, and by love. Clearly these are not rigidly exclusive divisions; in the concrete they fuse and overlap. But they depict types distinctive enough to be worth glancing at separately.

What hopes of emancipation from self lie before us in the fascinating world of intellect and imagination? The student or the creative artist, in following his chosen bent, may have made a promising start, but he must become something more if he is to reach the great objective. Without in any way belittling the work of the philosophers and scientists, or being insensitive to that of the poets, painters, and musicians, we may risk a generalization and say that their personal lives are not rich in salutary lessons for the rest of us. The *amour propre,* the touchiness and vanity, to say nothing of the less reputable vices, that afflict the less gifted of their fellows are shared by them in full measure. Nor is there any reason why it should be otherwise. Knowledge of itself, as Aristotle observed, moves nothing. We can know and appreciate the truth while our hearts remain untouched. The same, alas, may be said of the sense of the beautiful; its charms provide no stimulus to purposeful action. To no one more tragically than the poet Keats did experience lay bare the age-old aesthetic fallacy, that the relation between truth and beauty comprises all that is worth knowing on earth. Truth and beauty must come linked with goodness—"three sisters that doat upon each other . . . and never can be sunder'd without tears"—before they have power to win us release.[3]

If not in the mind, then certainly not through the body, shall we escape from self-centeredness. Travel and a change of scene may refresh the brain and reinvigorate the nerves, but they cannot remedy a disease of the spirit. To take part in games and sport, a healthy tribute to the child that is in all of us, seemingly has a neutral effect upon character. Its palpable physical benefits and value in fostering the team spirit can be more than offset by a dulling of awareness at deeper levels and the not always happy results of setting a premium upon skill in itself of little consequence. Not along that path, at all events, shall we catch sight of the "many-splendoured thing." Least of all can the mere gratification of the bodily senses bring us nearer the goal. Here the moment of ecstasy is quickly followed by "the journey homeward to habitual self." The most delusive of all pleasures, when taken out of its proper moral context, leads on to the discovery that "in the very temple of delight veil'd melancholy has her sovran shrine." We are so made that we can reach fulfillment only in a happiness that is, like bloom on a flower, an

[3] For some further remarks on the relation between the true, the good, and the beautiful, see pp. 109 ff.

afterglow, the by-product of right functioning. Not to know this is to be always seeking and never finding, the fate of the hedonist unable to account for his own disillusionment.

There remains the way of love. Not, save in rare moments, the melting mood of keen emotions and tender feelings, but the fixing of our desires and energies upon objects able to satisfy them. In practical and prosaic language, this means getting on with the job, keeping our eye on the ball. Thus mind and body, leading us astray when left to follow their separate courses, find their true scope in the service of a rightly ordered will. To put the best we have into our work, however apparently insignificant, to see it, not simply as a profession or livelihood, but as the carrying out of God's will and our obligations to society, is to be well on the way out of the prison of self.

On the longer view, what is implied is knowing why the world was made and the worth of the people in it. This, too, is only possible when mind and heart are focused ultimately on God. For here is contained both the answer to life's secret and the ideal of our own best selves. God's own idea of us is just what we are meant to become. All this is no more than commentary on Our Lord's soul-searching paradox: "The man who tries to save his life will lose it; it is the man who loses his life for my sake and the gospel's sake that will save it" (Mark 8:35). There is no evading the call to abandon ourselves, in one form or another, to the cause. In so doing we are given back, renewed and marvelously enriched, what we imagined we had sacrificed.

> All which thy child's mistake
> Fancies as lost, I have stored for thee at home:
> Rise, clasp My hand, and come! [4]

Our Lord has taught us that there is no path to God which by-passes our neighbor. "Believe me, when you did it to one of

[4] Francis Thompson, *The Hound of Heaven*.

the least of my brethren here, you did it to me. . . . When you refused it to one of the least of my brethren here, you refused it to me" (Matt. 25:40, 45). We are faced, then, with the problem of personal relationships. "Blessed is the man that loves Thee, O God, and his friend in Thee, and his enemy for Thee. For he alone loses no one that is dear to him, if all are dear in God, who is never lost." So, unmistakably and inimitably, St. Augustine. The peace of the City of God is the fellowship of perfect order and harmony in the enjoyment of God and one another in God. And, more explicitly: "the love (*caritas*) of man towards man is the surest stepping-stone to the love of God." Whatever Christian detachment may imply—and it implies a great deal— it demands a consecration, and not an uprooting, of natural affection.

Human love is normally made up of desire and the impulse to self-giving. Where the former element predominates, there is passion, merging all too easily into possessiveness and egoism; where the latter, there is friendship, disinterested well-wishing. We shall presently enlarge on the qualities of this last, the noblest of human emotions. For the moment we are thinking in more general terms, not to exclude that aspect of the matter—the delights of loving and being loved—to which St. Augustine again has given characteristic expression. *"Nondum amabam et amare amabam . . . Amare et amari dulce mihi erat."* All love worthy of the name is fecundating and creative. Of this the marriage union, the divinely appointed means for perpetuating the race, is the prototype. A man and a woman, happy together with their children, are a surer witness to the sublimity of love than any, be they the brightest "pair of star-cross'd lovers" in romantic fiction, whose amours are so often tragic largely because they are too intense and self-consuming to be fruitful.

It is a mistake, fostered by the Freudian psychology, to regard human affection as based wholly on sex. If we are to oversimplify, we shall be nearer the truth in discussing love in terms of spirit rather than matter, as rooted in the soul far more deeply than in the body. When the saints discourse upon friendship—and a number of them do so at length—it is open to psychoanalysts to say that their language betrays (in the appropriate jargon) a "sublimated," or it may be, a "suppressed" eroticism. The fact remains, however, that they could achieve in their lives a fusion of self-control with emotional responsiveness, of virginal detachment with warmhearted affection, which shows that they had solved the problem of how "to care and not to care." There are elements, not least in the marital relationship itself, that sexuality cannot account for: the unconditional well-wishing, the non-possessiveness, the respect hardly distinguishable from reverence, the reticence, on occasion, of the mutually understood *noli me tangere,* which have their place in even the most intimate union of person with person. Indeed, we know that this union can sometimes be closest where there is no opposition of sex to add enchantment; as when, in the story of King Saul, "the soul of Jonathan was knit with the soul of David." "Very pleasant hast thou been unto me," David was later to lament over his friend, then dead. "Thy love to me was wonderful, passing the love of women."

Personal relationships, if they are not to defeat themselves by becoming hopelessly absorbing and exclusive, need a background of social obligation and wider fellowship. The sentimentalist's delusion, that a devoted attachment is an excuse for disregarding the claims of society, that "the world is well lost for love," is a product of the very self-centeredness from which it is man's aim to be delivered. We may recall that when Our Lord spoke explicitly on our present theme, bestowing on His disciples the title of "friends," it was within the framework of His exposition of their living union with Himself, and with one another, in terms of Vine and branches—a metaphor which contains a hidden reference to the Old Testament imagery of Israel as God's "noble vine," planted for the salvation of men, but doomed to destruction if proved faithless. The privileges of the ancient Israel have now passed to the Catholic Church, the new Israel of God, reconstituted by Christ the Redeemer. Whence it follows that there can be no effective approach to God, and no ultimate harmony among men, in dissociation from the Church. Those secularists who profess humanitarian sentiments, while behaving for all practical purposes as if the Church did not exist, stand convicted of either ignorance or bad faith. With their laboriously thought-out schemes for promoting good will, they are like men lighting torches to look for the sun. Or is it that they prefer darkness to light? The Church alone has inherited the saving mission of her Lord, for which no merely human polity can avail—"to bring together into one all God's children scattered far and wide" (John 11:52).

A truth about the social animal called man, which has been confirmed to the point of demonstration by Henri Bergson in his great work *Les Deux Sources de la Morale et de la Religion* (Paris: Librairie Alcan, 1932), is still overlooked by the leaders of popular opinion. To the well-intentioned but over sanguine "world-betterer" it seems that there is a relatively simple solution to our problems. What we have to do is to extend outwards in ever widening circles the benign sentiments we naturally cherish towards our friends and neighbors. Thus we shall embrace progressively, first the members of our own social group, next the larger unit of village or town, then our country, and finally, to realize the internationalist's dream, the whole world. Now the relevant truth here is not merely the obvious one that this is not what happens, but the far more significant one that it *cannot* happen. Man is not made like that.

We must face the humiliating fact that the effective range of spontaneous well-wishing is limited to small groups. Under the influence of conscious reason we may learn to control the cruder expressions of clannishness and insularity, but the herd impulses are seldom far below the surface. That strangers and foreigners excite not amiability but distrust is not to be accounted for simply by irrational prejudice and bad will. It is the instinct of self-preservation asserting itself before the unknown, which it senses as a possible menace, an instinct rising quickly to irascibility and combativeness. The same which leads men, even modern "civilized" men, with a part of their personality, to exult in bloodshed and war. By these means self-assertiveness is given its fullest scope, an enemy is destroyed, a threat removed, and the well-being of the group kept intact. So much for the instinctual basis for world fellowship and co-operation.

If then, as Christians, we are to strive to realize the ideal of good will towards all men, it cannot be along the part of instinctive natural affection, even when rationally controlled, as suggested by our simple-minded internationalists. Whoever may be right, they at any rate are wrong. What is needed, and what is possible, is not a broadening outwards but—to continue the spatial metaphor—a rising upwards to attain a new vision and a fresh fountainhead for our endeavors. There are many who perceive the necessity for this; the point that eludes them is that we cannot achieve it by our own efforts. That the people who like to be thought progressive are, for the most part, unaware of this incapacity is because, being intellectuals cut off from their Christian roots, they are bemused by philosophical abstractions. Forgetting the origin and history of their own ideas, they misapply them in practice and thus bring an essentially noble ideal into discredit. The abstract notion of "humanity" we owe to Greek philosophy, but the attempt to give concrete expression to the brotherhood of man is due, not to philosophy, but to the Christian religion. Moreover this project, from the necessities of the case, could only take effect from above downwards, not from below upwards. Initiated by God, who would have us look upon Him as Father, it was to be brought to perfection by Jesus Christ His Son.

Any approach to the ideal of the social life is thus contingent upon a recognition of God as our Father and Christ as our Brother. The refusal of the modern world to accept this condition inevitably brings with it the frustration of its hopes. For a precedent in wrongheadedness to mankind's attempt to evolve from within itself the pattern of the perfect society we must go back in history to the construction of the Tower of Babel. Divine revelation apart, a New Jerusalem descending from on high, with all its apocalyptic imagery, embodies an idea far more creditable to human intelligence than schemes for world unification devised at the political level, to be so quickly stultified by events and whose unreality robs them of all conviction. "Pitiable creature that I am, who is to set me free from a nature thus doomed to death?" Twentieth-century man, undeceived by the shallow optimism of his would-be guides, can make his own this cry of St. Paul. To be given new heart on learning the all-sufficient answer, "Nothing else than the grace of God, through Jesus Christ our Lord" (Rom. 7:24-25).

To think of Jesus Christ Our Lord, for authentic Christianity, is to think of His Church. In the Church the Incarnation is continued down the ages; it is the complement, the "fulness" of Christ. The Church has no mandate to absorb within the ecclesiastical system the administration of temporal affairs; but she is a living demonstration of the fact that an intellectual and moral union among men is not a will-o'-the-wisp, that there are forces making for cohesion stronger than the disintegrating influences of unregenerate human nature. Despite the numberless infidelities of the Church's members, on the ultimate questions concerning God and man they are at one. Of no society on earth, except the Catholic Church, can this be said. As touching the love for one another demanded by Our Lord of His disciples, which is itself bound up with community of belief, the faithful have all the means and every incentive to its achievement. They may stumble on the journey, but at least they know where they are going.

"I have a new commandment to give you, that you are to love one another; that your love for one another is to be like the love I have borne you" (John 13:34). St. John records these words as spoken by Our Lord to His disciples less than twenty-four hours before He died. He had chosen the moment they were least likely to forget to make His most exacting claim— not for Himself, not even for the Father, but for themselves, and for those later to be of their company, whom also He would call His "friends." This was not simply to repeat in another way His words on the love of one's neighbor. He points now to what is to be the *quality* of that love; it is to be "like the love I have borne you." Here, precisely, is what makes it a "new" commandment.

Christ's was a sacrificial and redemptive love; it entailed a willing surrender to death and a winning back to life of the unlovable. In this lies the difference between God's love and man's: natural human love is something evoked from us, an emotion stirred into being by the attractiveness of its object, its goodness or beauty or what you please. But God's love requires no stimulus; it is not a reaction, in its essence passive; it is active, "creating and pouring out," as St. Thomas says, "the goodness that exists in things." Thus God does not, as we, find men lovable and so love them; He loves them first, creatively, so that they become focal points of His love, held out of nothingness by it. In this manner of loving, Our Lord, as man, shared to an unique degree.

The human mind and heart of Christ were centered upon God the Father. It is as they are in God's sight that He looks on men, as lost children needing to be brought back to their Father's house. Yet He is concerned with us, not as disembodied spirits but as complete personalities, individually and not merely as members of the human race. "He calls by name the sheep which belong to him." From Christ's redeeming love the Church was born; by handing over His physical body to death He brought His mystical Body to life. The grain of wheat, so He had taught, "must fall into the ground and die" before it can yield "rich fruit."

Perhaps the easiest point of passage from the pure light of Christ's love to our own sullied imaging of it is the ground He gives for calling us His "friends"—"I have made known to you all that my Father has told me" (John 15:15). This is the unmistakable mark of friendship, the sharing of inmost thoughts, the not holding back of confidences. To have a friend is to give him our trust; that he will keep it we take for granted, not spoiling things by asking him for any assurance. So it is with Jesus; having found His own, He kept nothing from them except what they could not bear. We must know how to be reserved, decorous, discreet, as charity and good sense demand; not, however, with a view to walling ourselves up within the would-be invulnerability of self. For Christian love to flourish it must grow under the sun of truth breathing the air of freedom. Hence, since "we receive but what we give," nothing mars personal relationships more effectively than any artificiality or constraint, whose purpose, whether conscious or not, is almost always concealment. We too must learn, like Christ, to come before others just as we are.

We are able, too, to share in the creativeness of Christ's love: by seeing those around us as He sees them and acting as He would act. This implies a highly positive attitude of selfless generosity; not being blind to, but making allowances for, faults, having an eye for good qualities, ready to uphold, encourage,

inspire, build up from promising, or even unpromising, beginnings towards some fruitful achievement. And all this with
no undue possessiveness or wish to dominate. We are concerned
to help others to become their own best selves, not to fit them
into our scheme of things. Even parents with their children must
know how to "have 'em and love 'em and let 'em be." How
much self-effacing charity lies in the graceful art of letting people
be! There is point, as well as cynical humor, in the jest at the
expense of the overzealous lady bountiful. "She devoted her
life to others; you can tell the 'others' by their hunted look."
Where we have responsibility for others, especially the young,
we must of course guide and direct; yet so skillfully as not to
confine the spirit's freedom or crush self-reliance. Just as the
aim of the good teacher is to render his own presence superfluous, so the highest form of love is wholly concentrated on
the well-being of its object. "And yet I can say truly that it is
better for you that I should go away . . ."; so Our Lord spoke
to His disciples at the very hour when for the first time He
called them His "friends."

Inevitably all this is linked with sacrifice, that is, with self-
giving, however unspectacular. As of Christ, so of each, should
it be said, he "did not come to have service done him; he came
to serve others. . ." And He served them gladly, enduring the
Cross "for the joy that was set before him." We note, too, that
at the washing of the disciples' feet, there is no suggestion that
it cost Him anything, that He is lowering His dignity. It was
Simon Peter who saw it that way. Here, then, is the solvent of
fear and pride. No pain is too great to be borne, no service too
lowly to perform, when prompted by love. We know this to be
true with those naturally near and dear to us. It is meant to
become so with Christ Himself and all the members of His
mystical Body.

We have already outlined the Christian conception of world

unity: a community of peoples, not without their local and national differences, but where "all are one in Christ Jesus." This achievement, as is painfully evident, lies still in the future. But we go astray and mislead others if we lose sight of what is the goal. Patriotism, in Edith Cavell's famous phrase, is not enough. The same may be said of all sectional and party loyalties; they pale into insignificance before the claims of Christ and His Church. The perfection of love, coming from the mind's being centered on God, has an all-embracing quality; it takes on something of the divine non-exclusiveness. We have to learn, not only to see God in creatures, but, what is better and rather different, to see creatures in God. To see them, that is to say, as eternally cared for by Him and bathed in His redemptive love. If they are heedless of their own condition and we have to try to win them over, let it be clear that we are concerned, not to capture them for a cause, but to mediate God's truth and goodness to them. Which can only be when those qualities are to be seen in us.

After Christ's witness to Truth on Calvary there followed, in the Resurrection, the triumph of Love. For the first time in history the human spirit, by virtue of its dedication to God, had overcome death. We ourselves, body as well as soul, are to rise again as Christ did and enjoy God's presence. As yet our bodies tend to preoccupy us with self. Good in themselves, in their every aspect and function, they still need to be transfigured by the power of God's Spirit, so that they may become like that of the risen Lord. It is thus that the body is fashioned a fitting partner for the soul, for their mutual joy in the whole personality's final surrender to God, wherein is total fulfillment. Even now, under the touch of grace, the body can take on "the festal air, the radiant look," as of one making ready for a marriage; it is the first breath of the resurrection-life later to be its native element.

Meanwhile, unseen, that life is vivifying the Church, Christ's mystical Body. The whole Body, the *Christus totus,* as a compact structure, is growing up unto God, to share in the triumph of its Head. The individual member does not live by his own life but by the life of the Body. Hence he must be united, not only to the Head, from whom the living influx comes, but also to the other members, each of whom, in his own sphere, transmits that life to him. Such, then, is the climax of the life-long journey away from self-centeredness. When we are at one with the mind and heart of Christ's Church we are leading the God-centered life. "May Christ find a dwelling-place, through faith, in your hearts; may your lives be rooted in love, founded on love" (Eph. 3:17). This, St. Paul's benediction, has for its answering thought his further words, "With us, Christ's love is a compelling motive . . . Christ died for us all, so that being alive should no longer mean living with our own life, but with his life who died for us and has risen again. . . " (II Cor. 5:14, 15). Along what other path but this can we achieve the harmonious balance between the rights of the individual and the claims of the community to which he belongs?

5

Response to Reality

SELF-KNOWLEDGE, according to an ancient philosophy, is the key to wisdom. Modern psychologists, while interpreting this principle in less intellectualist terms, substantially agree; their aim is to persuade their patients to accept themselves for what they are. But the theologian would go further: it is not enough to have self-awareness, to acquiesce in our limitations and take comfort from our possibilities, if we understand neither our relative place in the world nor the purpose of human life. Man lives, develops, and grows to maturity by doing things. He cannot act successfully without being adjusted to those universal laws which, being changeless and beyond his control, he must master, paradoxically, by a willing acceptance. It is with this adjustment, at its deepest level, that we are now concerned—that response to reality which can never be complete until it issues in the conscious worship of God.

WORSHIP IN SPIRIT

"God is a spirit, and those who worship him must worship him in spirit and in truth" (John 4:24). Worship has the same derivation as the word "worth." Man's primary duty is to

91

acknowledge God's worth; to pay Him, that is, the tribute due from the creature to the Creator. Unless a man's mind and heart are in the first place directed to this objective, he cannot successfully discharge his obligations to society. He will fall into the blunders which always arise from confusing means with ends. The culminating point of worship is an intimate personal communion between man and his God, an encounter in which each individual soul experiences the influence of God's Spirit—"like light caught from a leaping flame," as Plato puts it in his Seventh Letter. But even at its beginnings our approach to God must always be by an impulse of the spirit—*gressibus amoris,* in St. Augustine's words, "by the steps of love." In stirring the energies of the soul to acts of faith, hope, and charity, we are in fact performing the highest functions of religion. Without this interior activity, the execution of an outward ritual, whatever its intrinsic significance, avails us little.

These principles are important and practical enough to be worth dwelling on. There is much consolation in knowing that in no circumstances is God inaccessible to the soul, provided it be willing to seek Him. To be alone and bedridden, for example, cut off from a priest and unable to enter a church, would still leave us living members of Christ's Body, able through grace to grow in faith and love. A group of Catholic Christians, wrecked on the proverbial desert island, can apply to themselves with full assurance Christ's words, "Where two or three are gathered together in my name, I am there in the midst of them" (Matt. 18:20). Though deprived of Mass and the sacraments, they need lose nothing essential to full communion with the Church, since the God who willed these ordinances controls by His providence all such seeming accidents. Whatever his situation, no one is debarred from giving expression to the thoughts embodied in the great collect for the thirteenth Sunday after Pentecost—a compendium of all things necessary for salvation.

"Almighty and everlasting God, grant us an increase of faith, hope and charity; and that we may deserve to obtain what Thou dost promise, make us to love what Thou commandest. Through Jesus Christ our Lord."

All such irregular cases being allowed for, we may now consider the normal consequences that flow from the religion of the Incarnation. When the Son of God embraced our human nature He committed himself to the gracious purpose of taking men as He found them. Now one of the more obvious things about man is that he is not a pure spirit. He is bound up with matter, dealing most naturally with what he can see and hear and touch. Only by means of his senses and with difficulty can he ascend to what is immaterial. A merely spiritual religion may suffice for angels but it will not do for man. Our Lord, needless to say, took full account of this fact. True, in line with the greatest of the Hebrew Prophets, He was keenly aware of the dangers inherent in an organized ritual. It could become a substitute for, instead of an expression of, the worship of the heart (Mark 7:6). But He sanctioned by His presence the Temple liturgy and the public prayer of the Synagogue. Whatever the apparent defects of ceremonial routine and set forms of prayer, however they may seem to curb the spontaneous outpourings of the spirit, they are activities so essential to man's religion that it becomes meaningless without them. Christ may have given a new and undreamt of significance to liturgical worship, but the thing itself enters into His whole plan of reconciling men with God and with each other. The relations between the corporate Christian community and its individual members come most clearly to light in this context. Accordingly it provides the appropriate setting for an attempt to elucidate further our central theme.

We have seen that Christianity is much more than a philosophy of virtuous living. As a revelation, it embodies the truth that God has established, through Christ, a unity for mankind, a plan to resolve the elements of conflict. He would draw men out of their misguided independence, resolving their isolation and mutual enmity, and gather them into a world-wide family, a fellowship whose expression is none other than His Church. Christianity denies that men can make their approach to God simply as individuals, each for himself. The only way is for them to come to Him "in Christ," that is, as members of Christ's mystical Body. This is the culminating point of the entire Biblical revelation, the "mystery, kept hidden from the beginning of time in the all-creating mind of God" (Eph. 3:9). The purpose of Christ's coming was "to bring together into one all God's children, scattered far and wide" (John 11:52). His message was something much deeper than a demand for the individual's moral and spiritual reformation. It was a call to men to enter a pre-established order which their Heavenly Father had prepared for them, a community in which collectively they could lead the God-centered life. The Kingdom of God is portrayed in the Gospels as existing prior to the individuals who are invited to enter it: it is a wedding feast to which they are summoned as guests, a sheepfold to which as lost sheep they are brought back, their Father's house to which as prodigals they return. Jesus Christ came into the world as the Heavenly Messiah bringing to men, as incarnate in His person, the Kingdom of God.

How all this is related to liturgical worship and to its supreme expression, sacrifice, we have now to examine. If we turn to the New Testament document, the Epistle to the Hebrews, we shall find the necessary clue. This essay—for it is cast in that form rather than as a letter—may well have been written for the benefit of a particular group of Hebrew Christians. They were under pressure from their Jewish fellow countrymen, at the outbreak of the Jewish War which led to Jerusalem's destruction by Titus in A.D. 70, to take their stand with them in defense of the national cause against the common enemy. There was no need for them to deny that Jesus is the Christ; He was indeed a great prophet and moral reformer. But this admission is quite compatible with their continued observance of the Old Testament sacrifices. Were not these left unaltered by Jesus Himself? What, then, was there to hinder His Hebrew followers from being Jews and Christians at once? The writer of the Epistle will have none of this. To take such a course would be to compromise what is essential to Christianity. The choice is between going into the wilderness with the Christian Church, so abandoning Judaism, or apostatizing irrevocably from Christ (Heb. 13:13).

The recipients of this message, impressed by the age-long splendors of the Jewish sacrificial system, were evidently tempted to regard it as destined to endure for ever. The writer's whole effort aims at convincing them that the Temple ritual was no more than a temporary dispensation. This has now been superseded by the coming of Christ (Heb. 8:1-2). Jesus by the very fact that He is the Messiah is also High Priest after the manner of Melchisedech. It is true that Jesus was not a Jewish priest; He offered no Levitical sacrifice. But as Messiah, in opening God's Kingdom to all believers, He has realized at a higher level all that lay implicit in the Old Testament sacrifices. These indeed underlined the truth that sacrifice is natural to man, that somehow, through the offering to God of what was held precious, could be found a way to reconciliation and the removal of human guilt. But how could the blood of bulls and goats conceivably remove from men's hearts the self-centeredness which is sin? What was needed was the self-offering to God of man himself.

All that the Old Testament sacrifices had been striving to achieve has been brought into effect by the life, death, and resurrection of Jesus Christ. Being the Messiah, He is also priest; in this capacity He offered not the shadow-sacrifice of a dumb animal but the one real sacrifice of which all others were symbols—the whole giving of human life to God. "I am coming to fulfil what is written of me, where the book lies unrolled; to do thy will, O my God" (Heb. 10:7). In Christ the archetype, the exemplary pattern of sacrifice has descended to earth. The old Levitical sacrifices are no longer needed. The message that they were attempting so inadequately to express has been once for all delivered by Him (Heb. 1:1). The old sacrificial system falls into its true place as the preparation for what He was to do. Its validity was only for a time: now it is fulfilled.

To His Palestinian contemporaries Jesus appeared as a prophet, a preacher of repentance and righteousness, apparently little concerned with the accepted notions of sacrifice. But now that His lifework is over, He is seen to have brought to completion the Old Testament sacrifices by raising the principle that underlay them from the merely ritualistic level to that of the spiritual oblation of man to God. Sacrifice is no longer to be understood as an atonement for ceremonial uncleanness; it is a means whereby radically to "purify our consciences, and set them free from lifeless observances, to serve the living God" (Heb. 9:14).

The sacrifice of the Cross has thus a unique significance. It perfects, not only the Old Testament ritual, but even the sacrificial worship of the heathens. Students of comparative religion have discovered many lines of continuity between Calvary and the ancient pagan rituals.

A wonderful continuity, this. We are accustomed to read the Old Testament with the New: the Epistle to the Hebrews applies to Christ the sacrificial conception of Israel, in all its fulness and depth of meaning. But a day is coming when the science of religions will have learnt to interpret the much wider continuity of our Saviour's death and resurrection with the ancient pagan rituals.

There also it will see a prophecy and a fulfilment: it will see types created by the longing of the human soul and its dim perception of reality, till the time came for them to take flesh and blood. Then it will be seen how strangely Christ fulfils even the idolatrous rites of weeping for Tammuz, which the women in the eighth chapter of Ezekiel are seen carrying on in the Temple of Jerusalem; and how the Roman soldiers had a dim sense of an inner meaning, when they arrayed Pilate's prisoner as a king of May revels, with purple robe and crown.

For very many years I have had to busy myself with these subjects in thought and study; and still my wonder never loses its freshness. I can never cease marvelling, how since primeval times our race has connected suffering with its deepest idea of the Divine —till in the end an instrument of execution became the greatest of all religious symbols: the Cross.[1]

Much the same thought—so congenial to the Catholic, who holds that grace perfects and does not destroy nature—has been expressed with regard to the sacramental representation of what took place on Calvary. "If, in speaking of the Mass, one may speak, without offence, with the tongues of the historian and anthropologist, then, using this language, one may describe the Sacrifice of the Mass as the mature form of a most ancient religious rite of which the rudiments can be traced back to the worship of the fertility of the Earth and her fruits by the earliest tillers of the soil." [2]

It is not, however, from this level that the true meaning of the Mass can be understood. If Jesus by His own death was to abrogate the ancient rites, He nevertheless met man's need to proclaim his worship through signs and symbols by instituting a new rite, one that would embody the highest expression of religion. On the night before He died He took bread and, fol-

[1] Archbishop Söderblom, *The Mystery of the Cross* (London: Student Christian Movement Press, 1933). Quoted from A. G. Hebert, *Liturgy and Society* (London: Faber & Faber, 1935), pp. 56-7.

[2] Arnold Toynbee: *Civilization on Trial* (Oxford University Press, 1948), p. 242.

lowing the sacred custom, blessed it, broke it, and gave it to His disciples with the words, "Take ye; this is my body" (Mark 14:22). The breaking of the bread may have been a kind of acted parable, in the manner of the prophets (e.g. Jer. 27)—a foreshadowing of what Christ was to undergo on the morrow. But it was immeasurably more, as we should expect from Him who had come to fulfill the prophets and what they foretold. The days of a merely symbolic ritual were over. Thus Christ could not consistently institute a rite whose substance was to be no more than a commemoration—a *"nuda commemoratio"*— of the Last Supper. This would have been simply a refinement, backward rather than forward looking, of the ritual which He had superseded. Instead He created a unique rite, in which His sacrifice on Calvary could be re-enacted; He, as both priest and victim of that sacrifice, would be sacramentally present in what was ritually being offered in worship. His Eucharistic presence would be in the order of signs but also in the order of reality, a *real* presence; though not in any sense that involved a new experience for the ascended Lord now in heaven, much less a physical re-enactment of His sufferings. His body and blood would literally be *re*-presented on the Christian altar, yet in a manner so transcendentally mysterious as not to bring them into any new relation with space and time. [3]

We recall that ever memorable night. Sacramentally Our Lord makes present His body and blood under the appearances of bread and wine. We can gather from St. Luke (22:19-20) how this act looks forward to, is in some sense one thing with, what is to take place on the Cross the next day. Christ's body is here and now "given for you," his blood "poured out for you"; St.

---

[3] St. Thomas raises the question whether the body of Christ is locally present in this sacrament (*Summa Theologica*, III, 76, 5). He concludes his discussion with the words: *"unde nullo modo corpus Christi est in hoc sacramento localiter."*

Matthew adds, "for the remission of sins" (Matt. 26:28). Thus the first Eucharistic sacrifice—the "Mass," as it was later to be called—was celebrated by Christ Himself. In a symbolism which made real what it signified He anticipated His sacrificial death, destined to be a historic fact but a few hours afterwards. On the Cross alone could man's redemption be achieved; only thus could he be "sanctified through the offering of the body of Jesus Christ once for all" (Heb. 10:10). But here, on this solemn night, was its sacramental counterpart. The separate consecration, first of the bread and then of the wine, was the ritual foreshadowing of that act whereby the Victim's body and blood would in truth be separated by death. In this immolation Christ, the true Passover Lamb (I Cor. 5:7), was sacrificed and all man's sacrifice save this forever made void.

The unique offering on Calvary was to endure, a living memory, throughout the ages. So the commission had been given to the Apostles: "Do this in remembrance of me" (Luke 22:19; I Cor. 11:24). With these words Our Lord made them priests, giving them a share in His own priesthood. The eleven and those they would appoint were to be the guardians of the New Convenant, which, now being anticipated in sacramental form, was to be consummated on Calvary. So the Christian Church has understood the matter from the beginning. "It is the Lord's death that you are heralding, whenever you eat this bread and drink this cup, until he comes" (I Cor. 11:26). *Until He comes* —this is why the Mass has always been, and will remain, the vital center of the Church's worship. It is her most sacred trust: to be faithfully discharged, as a pledge of the remission of sins, of propitiation, thanksgiving and worship, until "the end," when Christ "hands over the kingdom to God and the Father, when he abolishes all other sovereignty, authority and power" (I Cor. 15:24).

This rite was later to be elaborated by the Church and its

symbolism enriched, but its essential character as the unique sacrifice of Christ, as Head of His mystical Body, remains unchanged. It is He who, through the ministry of an ordained priest, is the true celebrant of every Mass, as the link between the Consecration and Our Lord's words of institution in the Roman missal makes abundantly clear. The close association between the Church's present sacrifice and the Last Supper is again illustrated, for example, in the touching commemorative prayer in the Mozarabic rite:

Be present, be present, O Jesus, thou good priest, in our midst, as thou wast in the midst of thy disciples: sanctify this oblation, that we may receive the hallowed gifts by thy holy angel's hand, O Holy Lord, eternal redeemer.

The offering of gifts by the faithful people—which took the form, in early times, of the actual bread and wine to be consecrated—is a concrete symbol of their desire to offer themselves to God. It is here that the act of self-giving by the Church, the mystical *Corpus Christi,* provides as it were the material for the sacramental *Corpus Christi.* Thus, as in St. Paul, the two senses of the "Body of Christ" intermingle: the offering up of the body of Jesus Christ in the Sacrament becomes one with the offering up of His mystical Body which is the Church. This process begins with the Offertory and is consummated in the Communion.

The Offertory and Communion have a particular bearing upon the lives of the faithful; for it is just at these two points that symbolism is merged with reality. "In the activities of a great church," writes John Macmurray in his *Conditions of Freedom* (London: Faber & Faber, 1950), "the communion of its members can only be *symbolised* in its service and rituals. It can be *realised* only in the direct fellowship of the persons who constitute its membership." It was precisely for the purpose of removing the dichotomy between symbolism and reality that the Mass was instituted. "By its very nature the external rite of sacrifice must necessarily make manifest a worship of the heart (*cultum internum*). The supreme Sacrifice of the New Law signifies that worship by which the chief offerer, Christ, and with Him and through Him all the members of His mystical Body, give due honour and veneration to God." [4]

If, however, the oblation by which the faithful offer the divine Victim to the Heavenly Father in this Sacrifice is to have its full effect, something further is required. They must offer themselves in the manner of a victim. Nor is this latter immolation to be considered merely in terms of the liturgical Sacrifice. Since we are built upon Christ like living stones, the Prince of the Apostles would have us be a "holy priesthood, to offer up that spiritual sacrifice which God accepts through Jesus Christ" (I Pet. 2:5). Again, St. Paul is speaking without regard to any particular time when he exhorts Christians as follows: "I appeal to you ... to offer up your bodies as a living sacrifice, consecrated to God and worthy of his acceptance; this is the worship due from you as rational creatures" (Rom. 12:1). [5]

Without this essential element of interior self-dedication "religion becomes an empty ritual and mere formalism." [6] The symbolism of the Offertory is thus the outward expression of man's striving away from self to attain the region of God-centeredness. This self-renunciation reaches its climax at the moment of the Consecration, when man's gifts—which, if they are to have value in God's sight, must stand for man the giver—are transformed into the very body of Christ, so being enhanced with the value of His unique act of self-giving. Here the Godward movement is complete; it has reached its term. What follows is God's response to man, an answering gift whereby

[4] Pope Pius XII, encyclical *Mediator Dei* (*Acta Apostolicae Sedis*, Vol. XXXIX, No. 14, p. 556).
[5] *Ibid.*, pp. 557-8.
[6] *Ibid.*, p. 531.

we are enabled to commune with Him and with each other. The Offertory, though having a social character, since it is an oblation by the Church, may be considered as the personal act of each individual. Each brings himself, as embodied in his gifts, and surrenders it to God. But the Communion is by definition an act of the Christian community. The grace of the sacrament, making real what is outwardly symbolized, tends to remove the barriers of individual selfhood and unite person to person in the bonds of divine charity. The Eucharist is not only the symbol of Christ's sacramental presence; it is par excellence the sacrament of His mystical Body. "We have a cup that we bless; is not this cup we bless a participation in Christ's blood? Is not the bread we break a participation in Christ's body? The one bread makes us one body, though we are many in number; the same bread is shared by all" (I Cor. 10:16-17).

The Eucharistic liturgy, in its ordered progress through the seasons, is a continuous drama which presents the various aspects of Christ's saving work. The liturgical year, with its two series centering respectively on Christmas and on Passiontide and Easter, recalls in detail the mysteries of the Incarnation and Redemption. A new series begins at Pentecost, which commemorates the coming of the Holy Spirit; and, since the Church lives with the life of the Spirit, every Christian Sunday can truly be thought of as a "Sunday after Pentecost." The central rite is placed within the appropriate scriptural setting, so that those who take part may grow ever more familiar with the historic origins of their faith. On All Saints' Day, for example, they hear the opening words of the Sermon on the Mount, the Beatitudes, spoken no less directly to them than to their first hearers on a Galilean hillside. Let no one say, then, that the Catholic liturgy is concerned with anything but the essence of Christianity.

The ever-recurring double principle—that of stressing man's

complete dependence on God and showing that salvation can be found only in Christ—underlies the whole sacramental system of Catholicism. The sacraments operate by God's power, not by man's; they have their sole efficacy from Our Lord's life, death and resurrection. If material elements surround our initiation into the Church through Baptism, this is because Christ willed that sense-bound human nature should be led to what is spiritual precisely by these means. In the same way He would consecrate the progressive stages of our earthly existence: the attainment of adolescence, the purification from post-baptismal sin, the call to the high responsibilities of marriage, the special vocation to share in His own priesthood, and finally, the decline into mortal sickness. Each of these rites exemplifies what may be described as the spirit-through-matter principle that accords with man's nature, having its prototype in the Incarnation itself. Each of them has both its direct relation to the living person of Christ and its wider reference to His mystical Body. Each of them, that is to say, is an invitation to break out from the constricting bonds of individual egoism and consciously to take our place in the fellowship of God's universal family.

When we come to consider the Church's liturgy from a less objective and more psychological standpoint, we notice its extraordinary restraint. The implications of this fact are worth considering. Are we after all to find no outlet for that intensely personal relationship with God which is the heart of religion? There are no grounds for such misgivings. In the first place it should be remembered that the liturgy is by its nature a *corporate* act. It is the Church's "official" prayer; hence the almost invariable use of "we" rather than "I." The liturgy has rich emotional overtones—as, for instance, in the *Gloria in excelsis,* or for that matter, in many of the collects—but it is emotion kept in restraint. A little thought will show the necessity for this discipline. Prayer intended for the everyday use of a large body of people must be controlled in its expression. Otherwise, if the language employed is highly charged with personal sentiment, those who make use of it will either feel obliged to force themselves into the appropriate emotional attitude, or they will give no real assent to the words they say. It is in order to avoid these unwelcome alternatives, and for a further reason to be mentioned presently, that the Church exercises such strict control over the liturgical formulas.

The Psalter, which is the Church's prayer book, comprises a wider range of experience than that of any individual. The "I" of the Psalms does not stand for each separate worshipper; it represents the person of Christ, speaking for Himself or in the members of His mystical Body. Their varied and alternating moods are what now find corporate expression; whether of courage or despondency, joy or sorrow, triumph or defeat, zeal for all that is best or a falling away into apathy and faintheartedness. The Psalms are not intended to be used, in the manner of a modern hymn, as personal religious poems. Taken over from the ancient Israel, they have become the common prayer of the reconstituted Israel of God, so illustrating how the new fulfills the promise of the old. While reciting the Psalms the faithful are called upon to realize their solidarity with the whole human race as redeemed by Jesus Christ.

Thus the liturgy invites us to that wider charity which is the greatest need of our time. It is a challenge to rise above the level of limited individual concerns to share more fully the mind of the universal Church. It is a reproach, not merely to the inadequacy of humanitarian "good nature" but to those narrower "charities" which reflect so little of what is essential to Christian good will. It reminds us that Catholicism is not attained simply by a profession of the orthodox faith. Just in so far as our thoughts are dominated by the parochial outlook, unreasoned prejudice, insularity, bigotry, party spirit, or any local or domestic interest to the detriment of the whole truth as it is in Christ, by so much do we fail as Catholic Christians. The lawyer in the Gospel (Luke 10:25-37) was quite ready to be charitable to his neighbor—that is, to the people next door, to his friends and acquaintances, even to any one of his countrymen. He had to learn from the parable of the Good Samaritan the limitless implications of neighborliness.

The same lesson, in another medium, is embodied in the liturgy. It is brought into striking relief by the greatest of all liturgical prayers, the Our Father. We are not to say *my* "Father" but only, as members of a world-wide family, *"our* Father." When Jesus taught His disciples to pray, He did not compose for them any such affective aspiration as "O my God, I love Thee." About this there might have been too much of the ego—*"my* God," *"I* love." Instead we find that the consecrated formula, giving liturgical expression to man's wish to fulfill the first commandment of the Law, is *"Thy* kingdom come, *Thy* will be done." Again there reappears the motif of God-centeredness. We ask that we may be surrendered unreservedly to the Father, submitted to His dominion over our world, acquiescent in His kingship and mastery of it.

But when all this has been said, it must be added that liturgical devotion is not the only way of approach to God. Through taking part in the liturgy the individual acquires the "grand manner" in the spiritual life. The grand manner, however, is for special occasions. The strictly official character of the liturgy and the splendors of outward ceremonial are not without their dangers. "This people does me honour with its lips, but its heart is far from me" (Mark 7:6). Without the worship of the heart liturgical prayer becomes a matter of formal routine; its technically finished performance may give aesthetic pleasure, but the spirit has gone out from it. That is why the

Church has been at pains to curb the ardor of its own liturgical enthusiasts. [7]

Whatever may have been the deviations of individuals in drawing a sharp contrast between public worship and private devotion, Catholicism admits of no opposition between the "institutional" and "mystical" elements in religion, between the "religion of authority" and the "religion of the spirit." Nothing must be allowed to interfere with the free and direct access to God which is the personal right of each of His children. "There is one Spirit," writes Pius XII, "but 'it breathes where it will' (John 3:8). The Holy Spirit leads to holiness the souls which He enlightens by means of various gifts and in different ways. The liberty of these souls and the Holy Spirit's activity within them are sacrosanct. They are therefore not to be interfered with or violated on any pretext." [8]

If the Church's public worship is embodied in the liturgy, this is entirely without prejudice to whatever is of value in the individual's religious experience. The witness of the Christian mystics is part of the heritage of Catholicism. Such saints as Augustine and Bernard, Teresa and John of the Cross, found no incompatibility between a full participation in liturgical prayer and an intimate personal union with God. No doubt "mysticism," like "liturgy," has its pitfalls. The refinements of mystical experience may turn out to be the individualist's escape from his social obligations and a source of antinomian illusions. Just as the liturgy may give scope to an aestheticism which, falling short of the moral content of religion, is essentially frivolous. But the Catholic conception of mysticism—a truth that is still widely unrecognized—takes Christianity at its deep-

---

[7] For a fuller discussion on how liturgical worship and private prayer are related I may perhaps be allowed to refer to the chapter on "Prayer" in my book *The Love of God* (London and New York: Longmans, Green & Co., 1939).

[8] *Loc. cit.,* p. 585.

est and most serious level. Substantially it has nothing to do
with visions and ecstasies, with neurotic states and preternatural
marvels; [9] much less is it to be identified with that partly sen-
sual, partly intellectual, apprehension of the unity underlying
nature whose charms have been sung by Wordsworth:

> ... a sense sublime
> Of something far more deeply interfused,
> Whose dwelling is the light of setting suns,
> And the round ocean and the living air,
> And the blue sky, and in the mind of man.

Provided this be not taken as the climax of man's search for
ultimate reality, it may not be unrelated to religion. It may even
point the way; but it is not the thing itself. The content of
Christian mystical experience is the conscious clinging to a
personal God. Personal, not in any sense directly known to us
—a projection upon the Holy Trinity of human limitations—
but as the uncreated source of what constitutes personality,
namely, a transcendent intelligence and will existing in self-
subsistent Unity. He is a God who cares for His creatures, who
answers their prayers, with whom they can hold communion
in the knowledge which is faith and the love that is charity.
Knowing and loving, raised to the highest pitch of awareness,
are what make the stuff of Christian religious experience. Here
there is no merging of our personalities in a supposedly
impersonal "Absolute"; but an "I-and-Thou" relationship, the
same in kind for the Catholic mystic as for the Israelite Psalmist.

> For what have I in heaven?
> And besides Thee what do I desire upon earth?
> For Thee my flesh and my heart hath fainted away.
> Thou are the God of my heart, and the God
> that is my portion for ever...
> But it is good for me to adhere to my God,
> To put my hope in the Lord God:
> That I may declare all Thy praises (Ps. 72:25,26,28).

[9] Again I may refer to my *The Love of God,* pp. 225 ff.

The secret of Catholicism's capacity to harmonize liturgical worship with the demands of personal devotion lies in the fact that both the one and the other are a response to the same reality. Each is focused on the God who reveals Himself in faith, who attracts the mind by being unalloyed truth and the heart in virtue of His infinite goodness. In religion, as in all rational activity, the mind must direct and control the desires of the heart. The life of love can only be led under the light of truth. This is the fundamental principle of Catholicism, the *articulus stantis vel cadentis ecclesiae.* It explains why the Church insists that the liturgical formularies shall conform to revealed truth; it is the touchstone by which the legitimacy of any supposed religious experience may be judged. "The law of faith prescribes the law of prayer." No act of corporate worship, however impressive its ceremonial, is of value if it fails to give sensible expression to the Christian creed. No mystical transports need be taken seriously if they do not embody a response through faith to God's unchanging truth.

WORSHIP IN TRUTH

The primacy of truth, the precedence to be given to the *logos* over the *ethos,* has its bearing not only on divine worship but on every department of life. This principle is so important, and in practice so commonly disregarded, that it demands separate consideration. Even a theoretical justification of the reversal of right order, so ranking the will before the intelligence, has been attempted. It made a notable appearance in the science of ethics, thanks to the philosopher Kant; it was given dramatic embodiment by Goethe. He represents Faust as taking it upon himself to substitute for the Johannine, "In the beginning was the Word" the un-Biblical and basically irrational "In the beginning was the Deed." By this piece of legerdemain he released man from any obligation to conform to an objective order not of his own creating. Man was thus left free to make his own laws according to an arbitrary *fiat,* unembarrassed by any restraint upon self-indulgence and the lust for power. *"Hoc volo, sic iubeo, sit pro ratione voluntas."* It is an old barbaric philosophy, as old as the primeval declaration of self-sufficiency, "I will not serve." Let us attempt, then, briefly and not too laboriously, to elucidate in general terms the relation between knowing and willing.

It would not be difficult to show that whatever is of value in human activity is in some way an expression of man's instinctive worship of that celebrated triad, "the true, the good and the beautiful." The philosophers and savants, the saints and moral reformers, the artists and poets proclaim their homage by their respective functions. They walk within the sanctuary of this trinity and offer their gifts as its chosen votaries. As surely, if less evidently, the more familiar ways of life, the commonplace actions of every day, bring their own witness. To read a newspaper is to admit a need for knowledge, which is another name for truth—however precarious may be this particular means of obtaining it. To smoke a cigarette is to satisfy a craving, assuage desire, that is, to acquire goodness within a limited field. To gaze upon an object, or to pause and listen, for no other reason than that it is delightful is to pay tribute to beauty. Even the merely useful occupations: washing, dressing, eating, journeying, making, machine-minding (assuming for argument's sake that these various activities are no more than "useful"), if they are informed by reason at all, are directed to something beyond themselves, to the acquirement of a state of well-being which answers to the potentialities of mind and heart and senses. At every level of thought and action the claims of truth, goodness and beauty are inescapable. In the final analysis we may discover that they coalesce, three in one.

But if truth, goodness and beauty are but three aspects of ultimate reality, they differ in our manner of apprehending them in a way that it is of the highest importance to appreciate. In the language of the schoolmen, they present us with three quite distinct "formal objects," and consequently dictate three equally distinct methods of approach. This is borne out by the existence of the respective sciences of metaphysics, ethics and aesthetics. For all *practical* purposes truth is not to be identified with goodness or beauty.[10] Truth holds an ontological primacy from which every effort to supplant it involves ruinous cost. Truth is the life of the mind, the very stuff of which rational existence is made up. Attempting the define something so elemental that it defies definition, the philosophers have called it the "equating of the mind with the thing" (*adaequatio intellectus cum re*). Truth is the grip of the rational creature upon reality; it is as vital to mental health as air to the body. So necessary is truth to the intelligence that, in default of it, the mind will fashion for itself a substitute, whether it be some intellectual caprice or an object arbitrarily imposed by the will.

Nor is truth—and here, surely, is a common illusion—identical with sincerity. The sincere mind has only the duty of being self-consistent; it is its own judge and can withdraw from the scrutiny of the world at large to seek contentment in the consciousness of its own good will. The true mind cannot but be sincere, yet experience shows that the sincere mind is not always true. Sincerity of itself does not render us immune from the

[10] The philosophical insufficiency underlying the often quoted lines of Keats:

> 'Beauty is truth, truth beauty,'—that is all
> Ye know on earth, and all ye need to know—

could not be better illustrated than by the life of that poet. A. C. Bradley's essay "Keats and 'Philosophy,' " published in his *A Miscellany* (London: Macmillan & Co., 1929) throws valuable light on Keats in particular and the relation between truth and beauty in general.

defects of subjectivism, particularity and even fanaticism. Where
emotion and prejudice take the place of intelligence, sincerity
can be the worst enemy of what it counterfeits, the love of truth.
Truth is on a different plane; it has a higher impersonality
rooted in the universal order of things. Its interest is rather in
facts and principles than in points of view and personal opinions.
It is critical in the proper sense of that word—it judges—and
invites criticism in return. It seeks always for evidence and will
submit only to an authority that can show worthy credentials,
examining all testimony in the light of first principles. It concedes no peculiar privileges to priority in time and allows of no
proprietorship of person. And yet, paradoxically, the seeming
arrogance of truth is but the obverse of its humility. Considered
in itself, the mind is destitute; its first task is to submit to reality,
to conform to what *is*. The nature of the intelligence is not to
create but to discover. The condition of its functioning is that it
should be docile before the objects it desires to know. "In the
search for truth," says St. Augustine, "the first step is humility,
the second, humility, the third, humility, and as often as you ask
I will make the same reply." Without this attitude of submission
to what is presented to it, the mind becomes incapable of passing judgment upon the objects with which it deals and truth is
inevitably excluded. As soon as the mind turns inwards upon itself, being discontent with its proper function of recording in
intelligible terms the evidence before it, preferring rather to
form its own object of thought, to work out a personal "theory,"
we have no longer truth but, at best, sincerity.

The moral life—for the Christian, the life of active charity—
if it is to achieve the poise and self-realization which are its
due, must recognize that the pursuit of goodness presupposes an
insight into truth. The mind, of its nature, cannot contravene the
universal law that "nothing is loved unless it is first known" but
it can act without conscious advertence to that law, that is,

without paying due tribute to truth. We must know what we are about before we begin to act at all. To fail in this, even though "good will" remains, is to countenance the capricious and irrational. The tactlessness which sometimes goes together with the best intentions arises from attempting to put goodness before truth; the mistake is simply a lack of perception. Wrongdoing in general is as much due to ignorance as ill will, though an ignorance for which ill will may be responsible. Sin itself is a misguided striving after goodness, the pathetic *bonum apparens;* its malice lies in a willful infidelity to truth. Conversely, good action, virtue, alive to every demand made upon it—the needful thing gracefully done—is no more than the response of the will to what is true. The virtuous man is the follower of truth in action.

The will is not only the faculty which controls our rational activities; it is the seat both of desire and joy. In these matters, too, it functions soundly only when following the light given to it by the intelligence. Its desires must be directed towards objects which the mind perceives to be worth while; its joy can only rightly be the *gaudium de veritate.* "It is not in our power," as St. Augustine remarks, "to determine a thing to please us." True pleasure arises from the delightful qualities of what the mind and senses contemplate. Hence the need to know in what genuine pleasure and happiness consist. A reversal of the due subordination of will to intelligence, by which activity and desire (in themselves unenlightened) usurp or anticipate the guidance of the mind, lies at the root of the pitiless and despotic dealings with men and things of which the modern world affords so many examples. On a smaller scale it is non-reality thinking, the "lie in the soul," which produces those uncertain efforts we make to achieve the appropriate attitude, rather than react to the situation as it is. In the same way duty can become a phlegmatic response to a blind "categorical imperative" and morality an unenlightened conformity to an external code, instead of the natural and balanced expression of what are in fact the soul's true laws. It is frequently forgotten, sometimes by masters in Israel, that the life of virtue is but the development of the life which is natural to man. As St. Thomas has pointed out, "An aptitude for virtue is in us by nature, even though this needs to be brought into effect by practice or through some other cause. Hence it is clear that virtues perfect us so that we follow in a due manner those natural inclinations which are ours by right." [11] St. Thomas's conviction of man's absolute dependence upon God for all the good that is in him did not obscure from his mind, as it did with the sixteenth-century Reformers, the truth that "to detract from the perfection of creatures is to detract from the perfection of God's power." [12] Catholicism will allow of no disparagement of human nature to the supposed exaltation of grace.

If the pursuit of goodness without due reference to truth can have unhappy consequences, this is perhaps even more strikingly evident in the case of the third member of the great triad, beauty.[13] Beauty in its subject is the perfection arising from the harmony of its parts precisely as apprehended, whether by the senses (not necessarily only by that of sight) or by the mind. To be struck with beauty is not (I submit), strictly considered, to receive an accession of truth. The impression of the beautiful is independent of, and does not in fact require, an intellectual

---

[11] *Summa Theologica,* II-II, 108, 2.

[12] *Contra Gentiles,* III, 69.

[13] I take beauty to mean the splendor of form, the integrity and perfection of a thing such that the very contemplation of it gives pleasure: *id quod visum placet.* So considered it has a different *ratio,* or constitutive principle, from truth; though, of course, the term can be quite justifiably employed with a more extended meaning than its strict connotation. St. Augustine, for example, who so often uses the word "beauty," *thought* of it as truth; or so it seems to me. It is significant that St. Thomas, who subordinated every other interest to that of truth, has little beyond the all-important essentials to say of beauty.

judgment about the existence of the object which conveys the impression; and yet it is only by such a judgment that we arrive at truth! To rejoice in Bach's *B Minor Mass* or Beethoven's *Fifth Symphony* requires no assessment of their truth content. The aesthetic pleasure induced by reading *The Tempest* or the "Ode to a Nightingale" is unaccompanied by any preoccupation with the historical likelihood of the characters of the one or the real existence of a bird that could evoke the emotions described in the other.[14] Beauty, to an immeasurably greater extent than truth and goodness, depends upon sensibility, upon the responsiveness of the senses and the mind. The measure of a creative artist's greatness is his capacity so to work upon our powers of receptivity, both mental and sensuous, that their very operation causes delight. The lover of beauty is concerned above all else with the experience of what is pleasing; he seeks logically an ecstatic existence of perpetual intoxication, through eye and ear and mind, with beautiful objects—to find inevitably

> . . . Beauty—Beauty that must die;
> And Joy, whose hand is ever at his lips
> Bidding adieu; and aching Pleasure nigh,
> Turning to Poison while the bee-mouth sips.

Not that aesthetic experience, even at its most intense, is in any way immoral. Such sensibility can and should, when controlled by the virtue of prudence, and still more, by the theological virtues, lend grace and attractiveness to the moral life. But so strong are the allurements of beauty to those who can respond to their call, that the appreciation of them tends all too often to degenerate into mere aesthetic indulgence. Beauty, for

---

[14] This is not intended to suggest that such works of art are not manifestations of ontological truth. Truth is of their essence; it is in proportion to their truth that they are beautiful. The point here being made is that the personal realization of their beauty is something distinct from the recognition of their truth; and further, that aesthetic sensibility, as such, is not concerned with truth, still less with moral goodness.

us, is not the equivalent of truth and goodness. It does not compel us to an existential judgment and hence the mind is not carried into the real world, which is the condition of our acquiring truth. It makes no demands upon the will, which is the function of goodness. This last is of capital importance and often unfortunately overlooked. The moral life aims at possessing what is good and achieving for itself a permanent state of well-being. To this end the will goes out in desire and gives effective direction towards its realization; *amor meus pondus meum.* But the appreciation of beauty postulates no such striving; the worshipper at this shrine does not wish to possess, he is content merely to "stand and stare." The

> ... daffodils
> That come before the swallow dares, and take
> The winds of March with beauty...

have not to be plucked at. All their charm lies in being seen, and, it may be, seen more alluringly under the magic of Shakespeare's imagination than as they exist in nature. So it is with all beautiful things; they give a repose that borders closely upon enervation. It has been said that "hereafter we shall all be aesthetes"; yet this does not touch the root of the matter. In heaven we shall be contemplators of Truth—*visio est tota merces,* possessors of all Goodness, spectators of eternal Beauty; three in One; but in order—Truth, Goodness, Beauty.

For the moment, however, we are still upon earth. Human nature, despite the Fall, is essentially sound and can never embrace evil for its own sake; but it may hanker after the phantoms and creatures of wrong desire. It surely would not be an error to diagnose the peculiar evil of our time as an infidelity to truth, as this is manifested in an implicit denial of any absolute standards of morality binding upon all men. But sanity will not be restored by the simple advocacy of a return to truth. To discern the evil is not to cure it. Men in the mass have little love for abstractions; the philosopher cuts a poor figure beside our contemporary demagogues. Still, the mind and heart have their exigencies which will not be denied. *"Naturam expelles furca, tamen usque recurret."* There is a sense in which it will always be true to say that "We needs must love the highest when we see it." The average man, despite himself, cannot resist truth in the concrete. If he is impatient of argument, he will be convinced in the long run by what he can see and feel and touch—a fact which those who are concerned for the spread of God's kingdom must recognize and act upon. Perhaps the most efficacious means for proclaiming truth to our contemporaries is by what might be called the dynamic apologetic of sanctity. Holiness, it has been well said, is the only unanswerable argument. The world, we have been told, is crying out for saints. When they come they will testify to truth not to the philosophers only—perhaps least of all to them; but to the simple and unlearned and those outside the pale. They will *do* the truth (I John 1:6).

Thus we are brought back to the dominating theme in man's relation to God, namely, the creature's self-dedication to the Creator in worship. Material agencies, man being what he is, are necessary to initiate and maintain this ideal, but its vital power comes wholly from the spirit. The energy generated by the exercise of the three theological virtues is what constitutes the life force of Catholicism. "With unceasing desire we pray always in faith, hope and charity." [15] Not only does this energy inform both the Church's liturgy and the individual's private devotion; it imbues the members of Christ's mystical Body with something of His own spirit—the spirit which the Church would have "pervade private and domestic life, man's social activities, and

[15] Pius XII, *loc. cit.*, p. 541, quoting St. Augustine (*Epist.* 130, *ad Probam.* 18).

even the sphere of politics and economics." [16] Again we are shown the level at which the conflict of interests between the individual and society is transcended. Faith, hope and charity link each person directly to God, so raising the individual above the constraints which might hamper his true development. But the three theological virtues also join him in fellowship, not with a collective mass of human beings, but with a community of persons sharing the same privileges. To bring this project into effect is the enterprise to which the total effort of Catholicism is directed—"until we all realize our common unity through faith in the Son of God, and fuller knowledge of him. So we shall reach perfect manhood, that maturity which is proportioned to the completed growth of Christ" (Eph. 4:13).

[16] *Ibid.,* p. 536.

6

The Setting

WE must now give our attention, not so much to the essentials, as to the external conditions indispensable to man's success in leading the God-centered life. It has often been argued that the saying in the Fourth Gospel, that God is to be worshipped "in spirit and in truth," amounted to an implied attack, if not upon religious ceremonial, at least upon organized ecclesiasticism. What have the officialdom of a priestly caste and an elaborate administrative system to do with the unfettered intercourse of man's spirit with God's? Was it not precisely this attempt to canalize the divine elixir of faith and love along the approved channels of some social institution that Jesus was concerned to frustrate? Or was it? To speak without prejudice and in all reverence it may be said that, if it was the substance and not the shadow of religious organization that He would have done away with, He showed a strange and elsewhere undiscoverable failure to come to grips with the human situation.

Never has religion been purely and entirely individual; always has it been, as truly and necessarily, social and institutional, traditional and historical. And this traditional element, not all the religious genius in the world can ever escape or replace: it was there, surrounding and moulding the very prenatal existence of each of us;

it will be there, long after we have left the scene. We live and die its wise servants and stewards, or its blind slaves, or in futile, impoverishing revolt against it: we never, for good or for evil, really get beyond its reach.[1]

When we consult our earliest records we find, as we should expect, that Jesus lived and acted in perfect conformity with these principles. He was born into a community whose religion, besides being corporate and institutional, was actually embodied in sacred books and a traditional doctrine. He shared His peoples' veneration for the Jerusalem Temple, insisting on its being regarded as the House of prayer. He asserted that what He taught was written in the Law, which He had come to fulfill and not to destroy. He illuminated with an unprecedented insight the significance of the doctrine, but exempted neither Himself nor His followers from its basic requirements. He recognized in the "chair of Moses" (Matt. 23:2) the existence of an official magisterium (Matt. 23:13). He taught obedience to the rule of the Israelite hierarchy, while pointing out the insufficiency of their example. He thus drew a distinction that was to be valid for all time, namely, that between an ecclesiastical office and the personal qualities of its occupant. But He incited none to disaffection from lawful authority, even while those who exercised it were blind to the implications of the religion they professed and the tradition they upheld.

The central theme of Our Lord's preaching was the "Kingdom of God." [2] It is to oversimplify to say, with Bousset, that "there was no need for Jesus to enter into a detailed explanation of what He meant by the phrase, for every child in the country could have told Him." What is certain, however, is that the idea

---

[1] Friedrich von Hügel, *The Mystical Element of Religion* (London: Dent & Sons, 1909), Vol. I, p. 59.

[2] For a fuller discussion of this, see the present writer's *The Christ of Catholicism* (New York and London: Longmans, Green & Co., 1947), pp. 294-309.

of the Kingdom dominated the minds of His contemporaries. Had not John the Baptist revived their expectations with regard to it? The prevailing notion was that of a divinely created institution located in Palestine. It was not man-made but God-given; a heavenly Personage was to make His appearance in order to establish it. If it was in some sense a spiritual Kingdom, it was also essentially corporate. Our Lord's disciples are to be found, even after the Resurrection, inquiring about the Kingdom as so conceived (Acts 1:6), just as they had earlier contended for official precedence within it (Mark 10:37). He characteristically broadened and deepened the traditional teaching on the Kingdom, as we have seen Him do with reference to the two great commandments of the Law, but that He thought of it as a corporate structure existing here in this world there can be no manner of doubt.

That this is so clearly emerges from the variety of ways in which Our Lord illustrated the nature of the Kingdom. Its concrete visibility may only have been hinted at when, in the great Sermon, he compares the Christian community, now slowly taking shape, to "a city set on a hill" (Matt. 5:14), but there can be no mistaking the implication of the Parables. The comparisons of mingled wheat and tares, of good and worthless servants subject to the same king, wise and foolish virgins associated together, a vineyard entrusted to a group of men, all point to something that is corporate rather than personal. The parable of the net cast into the sea (Matt. 13:47-50) can only be understood to refer to an organized structure whose function it is both to include all kinds and to differentiate those within from those without. Even the much debated saying—"the kingdom of God is within you" (Luke 17:21)—suggests only an apparent inconsistency. The Synoptic Gospels show "the Kingdom" to have a double meaning: that of God's *rule,* in which sense it is personal, bearing directly upon each individual soul;

and that of God's *dominion,* where it connotes God's world-wide *imperium* as embodied in a corporate society. The second of these meanings is clearly an extension of the first: to be under God's rule is to be within His Kingdom. Thus while a man may rightly think of the Kingdom being within him, in as much as in his personal conscience he is faithful to God's law, by this very fact he is in his turn within the Kingdom considered as a corporate community. The context of Our Lord's words just now quoted shows that He was addressing the Pharisees. He could not have meant that the Kingdom was "within" them, since He had earlier excluded them from it (Matt. 5:20). But He could truly say to hearers of good will that the Kingdom was in their midst; for where Christ and His disciples were, there was the Kingdom already present.

We notice further that, although the Kingdom already exists, its manifestation to the world will be gradual. This is the lesson, for example, of the parable of the mustard seed. Again, the Kingdom is like leaven; it slowly makes its influence felt in the individual or society that receives it. The Kingdom, which includes both good and bad, will be perfected hereafter; nevertheless it is present and not merely future. This is strikingly illustrated by Our Lord's words, "But if I by the Spirit of God cast out devils, then is the kingdom of God come upon you" (Matt. 12:28). The Kingdom would be powerfully manifested within the lifetime of Christ's hearers (Mark 9:1). In fact it is the long-promised Messianic Kingdom over which the Messiah himself will preside.

How is the Kingdom as so understood related to the Church? The Synoptists suggest that Jesus habitually used the word "kingdom," whereas there are only two recorded occasions where he employs "church" (Matt. 16:18; 18:17). On the first of these—the promise made to Simon Peter—Our Lord combines in the same sentence the words "I will build my church" with "the keys of the kingdom." Before touching on the significance of this passage, which is well known to be a basic text for the Catholic position, it is only fair to state that many modern critics have striven to undermine it at its source. Guignebert, for instance, asserts that the phrase "my Church" was quite alien to the thought of Jesus. The idea, it is suggested, was read back into the earliest period by the later Christian community to which Matthew belongs. The "Church" as a corporate institution is a Pauline development, and even St. Paul thought of it as the Church of God and not as the Church of Christ. Thus there are no solid grounds for supposing that Jesus Himself actually employed the words *"my* Church."

On this it may be remarked, whatever is to be thought about the word actually employed, that the *idea* of the Church was evolved from the mind of St. Paul is a view no longer taken seriously by modern Biblical scholars.[3] The word occurs in the Greek Old Testament, the Septuagint, as the equivalent for "synagogue" (cf. Acts 7:38). Moreover, since Our Lord refers

[3] On the Matthew texts see Karl Ludwig Schmidt, *The Church* (Bible Key Words from Gerhard Kittel's *Theologisches Wörterbuch zum Neuen Testament*) translated and edited by J. R. Coates (London: A. and C. Black), pp. 35-50. Before alluding to the " 'Protestant,' and above all 'Modernist,' efforts to get rid of the *locus classicus* for Papal primacy," Schmidt points out (p. 36) that "The text of Matt. 18:17, and still more that of 16:18, are above suspicion. We have no Greek MSS. or ancient translations which do not contain Matt. 16:17-19 or at least 16:18; and it can safely be asserted today that no objection to the verses under discussion can be based on their occurrence or nonoccurrence in patristic writings from the time of Justin Martyr onwards." And further (pp. 40-41) "Thus we not only become more and more certain that, so far as facts are concerned, Matt. 16:18 does not stand alone, but also realise— an important point—that this conception of the complex of ideas (Jesus, Messiah, Son of Man, Disciples, Community, Lord's Supper) leads directly to the Pauline and sub-Pauline doctrine of the *ekklesia,* which on the one hand is 'from above' and on the other is 'the Body of Christ,' just as Christ is at the same time highly exalted and present in the midst of the community. The question whether Jesus himself founded the Church is really the question concerning his Messiah-ship."

to the Kingdom as "His" (Matt. 13:41), there is no inconsistency in a similar claim with regard to the Church. It has been
fairly conjectured that He must have used an Aramaic phrase
or word (now rendered as "church") to designate the community
of His disciples, knit together by their belief in His divine son-
ship, and commissioned to propagate His teaching. What has
given rise to critical doubts at this point is not the Biblical texts
but the assumptions on which they are to be interpreted. A
repudiation of Christ's divinity has for its corollary the denial
that He constituted a Church as the New Testament reveals it to
have been. If Our Lord had no power to send the Holy Spirit
upon the primitive Christian community and imbue it with
divine-human life, then the Catholic conception of the Church
is an elaborate imposture. But the same must be said of the
ideas and alleged facts embodied in the Acts and Pauline
Epistles. Thus the query raised earlier in these pages with regard
to the Resurrection again presents itself. Who is in the better
position to know and understand the true nature of primitive
Christianity? St. Paul or the dogmatic rationalist of today,
whose real character remains unaltered under the guise of a
"Modern Churchman"?

The decision we give here will also determine our view on how
Christ's words, which suggest that the end of the present world
order is imminent, are to be reconciled with His constituting a
Church destined to exist throughout the ages. Do they imply
that He thought the end to be actually at hand? Or do they
combine an apocalyptic prediction of the coming destruction
of Jerusalem and its Temple—which was certainly the end of
organized Judaism and the greatest of the many calamities in
Israel's history—with an urgent, dramatically illustrated, warning of the Christian need to be ever on the watch? That the latter
is the true explanation can be gathered, for example, from such
explicit assertions as that "the end is not yet" (Matt. 24:6),

and that before it comes "this gospel of the kingdom shall be preached in the whole world, for a testimony to all nations" (Matt. 24:14). This is confirmed by those parables of the Kingdom which indicate that its extension is not to be instantaneous but a slow development (e.g. Mark 4:26-28; Matt. 13:24-30).

It must be acknowledged, however, that even at the moment when Our Lord promises to Simon Peter the "keys of the kingdom"—a point to which we shall return—He does not explicitly identify the Kingdom with the Church. There is no text in the New Testament which does this. But the fact that Peter is both the Church's rock foundation and the Kingdom's key bearer shows that Church and Kingdom are intimately connected. The evidence as a whole points to the Church being the temporal embodiment of the Kingdom, and so justifies the traditional Catholic description of Christ's Church as the Kingdom of God *on earth,* but the two ideas are not quite synonymous. There are grounds for a distinction of which it is important to take note. The Church exists as an historic actuality; its members do not await its establishment at some future date; but they are required to pray that the Kingdom may "come." The Church, it seems, is still on the way to self-realization as God's Kingdom.

But we may not draw from this conclusion the further inference, as has been done, that the Church is in some way subordinate to the Kingdom. It is an error to equate the two ideas *sans phrase,* but it is no less so to draw a sharp distinction between them. If Our Lord habitually spoke of the newly constituted Israel of God in terms of the Kingdom rather than the Church, the explanation is not far to seek. The word He would have been obliged to use for "church" was open to interpretation by His hearers as a variant of "synagogue." This, with its national and local associations, would have precluded their understanding that the community in which they were invited to become members was to be world-wide. Even so, they found its larger implications hard enough to accept. St. Paul, on the other hand, was preaching the Gospel to the Gentiles, in a milieu where the Roman authorities looked with no favor on a potentially hostile "kingdom," with its correlative of a rival "kingship." It is not therefore surprising that the Apostle preferred to speak of the Church rather than the Kingdom; though the latter term does in fact appear a dozen or more times in his Epistles. When, for instance, he speaks of the Father having "transferred us into the kingdom of the Son of his love" (Col. 1:13), this is hardly to be distinguished from admission into the Church.

We notice further that it is through Baptism that the believer enters into God's kingdom, while this cleansing is what initiates him into the Church. His relation to the Kingdom is strengthened and made more intimate by the sacrament of the Eucharist, which is a sacrificial gift belonging exclusively to the Church. The parallelism between Kingdom and Church is complete: the Kingdom is on earth, likewise the Church; the Kingdom includes both worthy and worthless, so does the Church; the Kingdom is both present and future; it is the same with the Church. Here, at any rate, Loisy's judgment may be accepted: the Gospel of Jesus had already the rudiments of a social organization, and the Kingdom took the form of a Society. Jesus proclaimed the Kingdom; what resulted was the Church.

The case—argued, for example, by Harnack—that Jesus did not shape the original company of disciples into a visible institution, that He left it only with the spiritual cohesion supplied by a common belief in the fatherhood of God and the brotherhood of man will not survive an examination of the evidence. In fact, as the perfect realist, He organized it in the most workmanlike manner. This was the principal occupation of His ministry. From the multitude of His followers He selected the Twelve Apostles (Mark 3:13-19; Luke 6:13). The number represented the twelve tribes (Deut. 1:23) and this company constituted the chiefs of the New Israel. They were to be their Master's companions and to go out preaching in His name (Mark 3:14). To them He explained the meaning of the parables; to them He gradually made known the mystery of His personality; to them He gave the benefits of a spiritual retreat under His own guidance (Mark 6:31). He bound them in loyalty to Himself and companionship with one another in a union, save for one defection, never afterwards to be broken.

Of the Twelve Simon had been appointed chief. "Thou art Petros (stone) and upon this Petra (rock) I will build my Church" (Matt. 16:18). In the Aramaic spoken by Our Lord the two words would be indistinguishable, the difference only appearing in the Greek because the feminine Petra could not be applied to a man. The symbol of the rock had been employed earlier by Jesus (Matt. 7:24-25); it was an Old Testament usage familiar to His hearers and much commented on by rabbinical writers. One instance (Isa. 51:1-2) is especially significant: Abraham, the father of the faithful, is here designated rock. We can appreciate the role now being assigned to Simon Peter in the light of a passage from the Jewish Midrash.

God is like unto a king who wished to build himself a house. He digged and digged, but in each place water sprang up and destroyed the foundation he had dug. At last he chanced to dig where deep down he came upon a rock (petra); then said he: "Here will I build." In like manner God, wishing to create the world, looked out upon the generations of Enoch that would be, and that of the flood, and said: "How can I make a world out of such sinners, who will people it with those who will annoy me?" But when he saw Abraham he said: "Ah, here is a rock upon whom I can found a world" (*Yalkut Shimoni*, i, 766 on *Nu.* 23:9).

Peter similarly, as the man of faith, is the rock upon which the Son of God will build the community of the faithful. Peter alone is the foundation on which the Church is to arise. St. Paul speaks of Jesus Christ being the "foundation" (I Cor. 3:10-11), but the context shows that the allusion is to the truth that Jesus is the Messiah—precisely that truth for the professing of which Peter is here being rewarded. Israel lay in ruins; through the debris Our Lord had dug down until He had struck rock. Now He could perform the great Messianic act foretold by the Prophets: "I will come back, and build up again David's tabernacle that has fallen; I will build up its ruins, and raise it afresh; so that all the rest of mankind may find the Lord, all those Gentiles among whom my name is named, says the Lord, who is the doer of all this" (Acts 15:16-17). Peter and the Apostles are thus not so much the first stones of an entirely new building as the leaders of Israel's "faithful remnant," through which the divine purpose was destined to be fulfilled. In the deepest sense there is only one Ecclesia of God and His Messiah—Our Lord's use of "*my* Church" suggests, needless to say, no contrast with what is God's (John 17:10)—and that is the continuous life of the "Israel of God" (Gal. 6:16) from the call of Abraham until the end of time. Our Lord is the Church's "Founder," not as bringing into being what did not exist before, but by a creative act of building up, as opposed to breaking down (cf. Jer. 1:10). He reconstituted and reorganized the remnant of Israel, "edified" it, so that through it God's plan of salvation could be made manifest.

Peter's office—later confirmed (Luke 22:31-32) and formally bestowed (John 21:15-17)—was not simply that of doorkeeper. His function is parallel to that of Eliakim ben Hilkiah who was appointed as minister and key bearer of the house of David (Isa. 22:15-22; cf. Apoc. 1:18). In other words, Peter was to act as administrator or steward of God's kingdom on earth. Like a faithful and wise steward, he is to provide the household with food at the appointed time (Luke 12:42). His office is the reverse of that of the scribes, who were taking away the key of knowledge (Luke 11:52) and so shutting the Kingdom of Heaven against men (Matt. 23:13). What is being emphasized is Peter's authority to teach (cf. Matt. 13:52) and, as is shown by the words that follow (Matt. 16:19), to enforce discipline. "To bind" and "to loose," in the technical language of the Rabbis, refer to the powers of a doctor of the Law to adjudicate definitively on disputed questions and, where necessary, to pronounce excommunication. Such decisions were held to be acknowledged in heaven in the sense that God would sanction and endorse what had been decided on earth. Thus Peter is here endowed by Christ with a divinely recognized authority to preside over, teach and discipline the future Christian community— an authority which we find him exercising without dispute after the Pentecostal outpouring of the Spirit (cf. Acts 5:1-11; 15:6-12 etc.).

There can be few impartial New Testament scholars who would today query the substantial accuracy of the exposition outlined in the foregoing paragraphs. As K. L. Schmidt observes, "Just as the Good Shepherd is the same as the Lord so his flock is the same as his Church. This group or company is, to begin with, the college of the twelve disciples appointed by Jesus. He separated a small band from the rest of the Jews, sharply opposed to the Pharisaic scribes and ultimately to the whole impenitent nation, to constitute the true *ekklesia* or people of God. Thus Matthew 16:18 gives us more than an item in the life of Jesus: this is an event in the history of the Christ." [4] Where, however, there is less agreement is on the question whether Peter's prerogatives were personal to him, so terminating at his death, or whether they could rightly be claimed by his successors, on the assumption that he was intended to have any. It has been pertinently asked, with a firm negative as the implied answer: Was

[4] *Op. cit.,* pp. 38-9.

Our Lord creating an office which could be held alike by Peter and Pope Alexander VI?

We may pause for a moment at this point before returning to our original sources. The general position of the Catholic Church with regard to the successors of St. Peter is well known, though its implications are still widely misunderstood. The basis of that position, by which it stands or falls, is that Our Lord, in virtue of His divine authority as Messiah and Son of God, gave to the Church a permanent constitution, valid not for the Apostolic age only but for as long as the Church on earth would last (cf. Matt. 28:18-20). This necessitated both that Peter should have successors and that these should be endowed with Peter's office. They would profess and uphold Peter's unfailing faith; they would declare its meaning with the same authority as he did; they would rule, "bind" and "loose," teach, and exercise discipline because Peter's status in the Christian community had now passed to them.

But Peter's successors were to be no more immune from human limitations than he was. Moreover Peter personally enjoyed divine favors which were no part of the office handed on to his successors. He had lived and worked and grown in holiness under the direct guidance of his Lord; he was the recipient of immediate revelation from God, enjoyed the plenary inspiration of the Holy Spirit. None of these privileges could be claimed by those who came after him; only the divine assistance necessary to preserve wholly intact the Church's faith. It is historically significant that no Pope has ever assumed the title Peter II. Peter might be regarded as speaking "through" his successor, as is shown by the acclamations given to Pope Leo's message at the Council of Chalcedon, but there has been only one Peter. He could be God's instrument in extending the actual content of the revelation that was in Christ Jesus. Peter's successors might elucidate, but essentially they could add nothing to, what had been committed to their trust (cf. I Tim. 6:20). Their status was thus official, not personal; it was compatible, though to the grave scandal of the Church, with moral unworthiness. Our Lord attached no assurance of either holiness or wisdom to Peter's office: there could be wicked and foolish Popes. He guaranteed that by means of it the faith would not be perverted into error or the powers of evil prevail against His Church. No image could suggest permanent duration more strikingly than that of "rock." If the Church as an organized structure was intended to endure, then so was its rock foundation.

Once more, from the purely Biblical standpoint, the question whether Peter's role was official or only personal turns on the answer we give to the antecedent question: Who was Jesus of Nazareth? A strict exegesis of Matthew 16:18-19 could conceivably point to an office being conferred upon Peter alone, but, as has been well remarked, "A deeper and broader foundation is reached when the discussion is extended so as to include the question whether, and in what sense, Jesus regarded himself as the Son of Man, and whether, and in what manner, he instituted the Lord's Supper. If Jesus understood his Messiah-ship in the sense of Daniel 7, this will open up new vistas when we are considering the nature and importance of his founding of the Church. For the Son of Man in Daniel is not a mere individual: he is the representative of 'the people of the saints of the Most High' and has set himself the task of making this people of God, the *ekklesia,* a reality." [5] The intimate connection between the founding of the Church and the Last Supper is of great significance; for, as we have already seen, it was on the night before He died that Jesus instituted the New Covenant in His blood, which abrogated the Jewish sacrificial system and gave to the reconstituted Israel its own form of worship. Our Lord ordained this rite in the full consciousness of His dual role as the Heavenly

[5] K. L. Schmidt, *Op. cit.,* pp. 39-40.

Messiah, as suggested by Daniel 7, and God's Suffering Servant, as portrayed in Isaiah 53. Kattenbusch is surely correct in his profound observation that "When he founds the *ekklesia,* a community in his name, through the Last Supper, he does not forget the title [Son of Man] he chose for himself out of Daniel, but puts it in the foreground (Mark 14:21), indicating the nature of the Son of Man by means of a reference to Isaiah 53."

It is noteworthy that modern Biblical scholarship, after a long period of individual aberrations, has been forced as a result of its own researches to return to an acceptance of the central position held by the Church in the lifework of Jesus of Nazareth. If Jesus is the Messiah, then He is unintelligible without His Church. The following are four typical conclusions: "The title, Christ, demanded of him that he should bring the perfect community into being" (A. Schlatter). "Christ has an independent existence, just as much as each of those who are his, but is only himself in the *soma* [i.e. Christ's mystical Body]; without this he would not be what his name indicates; . . . he must so shape his personal life that he really is, and can claim to be, the type of a people of the saints of the Most High; and he must create and build up this people among men" (Kattenbusch). "The saviour is only saviour as the creator of a new, redeemed and justified people; . . . the *Christos* can no more be Christ without the *ekklesia* than the *poimēn* can be shepherd without the *poimnion*" (Gloege). "The Messiah is not a private person; a community belongs to him; to the shepherd belongs the flock" (Linton). When these findings are read in the light of the Fourth Evangelist and St. Paul, we are left with the full Incarnation doctrine of Catholicism and the Church as Christ's mystical Body—as essential a part of authentic Christianity as the person of Jesus Himself.

We may therefore conclude that the Christian message cannot be understood merely as a doctrine, an ethical code and a way of life, though it includes these three elements. It embodies in a corporate society both a sacramental religion and the highest form of worship. It was so designed by Our Lord Himself; He laid its foundations during His ministry, sealed it with His own Covenant—in a representative symbolism at the Last Supper, in historic actuality on the Cross—and impregnated it with His Spirit at Pentecost. Whitsuntide, according to the Acts, signifies nothing other than the birth hour of the Catholic Church. The gift of tongues represents by anticipation the universalism of the centuries to follow. The regenerative effect of Christ's life, death and resurrection are becoming intelligible to all nations.

What followed may be briefly outlined. At its first head-quarters in the primitive Jerusalem community the Church contained in germ all the essentials of Catholic institutionalism: dogma, hierarchy, and sacraments. Dogma, with its corollary, an agreed and accepted faith, controls the situation. The Creed, as we should expect, is rudimentary but its character is unmis-takable. No one could be admitted into the Christian fold—an initiation perfected through Baptism—unless He believed that Jesus was the Messiah and Son of God, that He was Head and Lord over all, having died and risen again for men's salvation. This is in substance the content of the early chapters of Acts. The ecclesiastical hierarchy is evident in the respect paid to the Twelve, with Peter as their acknowledged chief. The fifteenth chapter of Acts, drawing a clear distinction between "apostles," "presbyters," and "brethren," indicates the basis for the hier-archical organization of the later Church and the subordination of the laity to the clergy. The original leaders of the Christian community, as we have seen, did not receive their authority from their fellow disciples but from Christ. Accordingly, they at first retained it as a prerogative of their office and later imparted it, by a principal of transmission consisting in the laying on of hands, to chosen co-operators and successors.

Appointment to the ministry was no doubt preceded by a scrutiny of the candidate's qualifications, moral, spiritual, and intellectual (cf. Acts 6:3). Whatever may have been the functions of the "deacons," the ministry in general was *priestly*. The stewards and ministers of God's household would have to feed and rule, but also to represent both Master to household and fellow servants to Master. As B. J. Kidd remarks, "priest and steward alike mediate or intervene, and priesthood is simply stewardship *in sacris*." [6] If the New Testament speaks only of the priesthood of the laity (I Pet. 2:5,9)—a reality always recognized by Catholicism [7]—this is because the traditional term *hiereus* (never used in the New Testament for the ministerial priesthood) would have been misleading. Christian ministers are correctly called *leitourgoi* (Acts 13:2; Rom. 15:16)—a term used for the Old Testament priesthood (Isa. 61:6) and applied to Our Lord as High Priest (Heb. 8:6)—since this implies, by contrast with *hiereus,* a ministry manward, and by contrast with *latreuein,* priesthood in an office. No more precise term could have been found for the Christian ministry. [8]

The office of "presbyter-bishop," as well as that of "deacon," appears always to have been closely connected with the need for a celebrant and an assistant at the Eucharist. Duties of supervision and instruction would *ex officio* fall to them, but the *raison d'être* of their ministry was to attend upon the Eucharist. As Harnack is obliged to admit, "The root of the specific ecclesiastical priesthood is rather the specific sacrifice, as it developed in the conception of the Lord's Supper." [9] It was the

---

[6] B. J. Kidd, *A History of the Church to A.D. 461* (Oxford: Clarendon Press, 1922), Vol. I, p. 40.

[7] Pius XII, encyclical *Mediator Dei* (*Acta Apostolicae Sedis,* Vol. XXXIX, No. 14, p. 557).

[8] See R. C. Trench, *Synonyms of the New Testament* (New York: Redfield, 1854), § xxxv.

[9] A. Harnack, *Constitution and Law,* p. 118.

permanent need for the celebration of the Eucharist which led to the formation of a local rather than a general and itinerant ministry. The Apostles and Prophets and their immediate associates exercised their ministry over a wide field and journeyed from place to place. In this way "they kept the life-blood of the Church in circulation and preserved its unity, for it is to them we owe the fact that there is one Bible everywhere received in the Church, one Creed, one weekly Holy Day, one Baptism, and one Eucharist." [10]

But the ministry of Apostle and Prophet was temporary. It was for laying the foundations (Eph. 2:20); when these rose above ground the need was for permanent officials. St. John was the last Apostle; and the Prophets, of whom we hear much in the Apocalypse, have disappeared twenty years later in the Epistles of St. Ignatius. Just as the gift of tongues and the power to work miracles had their part to play in the early days, as a spectacular demonstration of the Holy Spirit's presence in the Church, but were to give place to the real business of the Christian (cf. I Cor. 13), so the sacramental ministry succeeded to the miraculously endowed. In the same way, with the subsidence of the apocalyptic expectations of the Lord's second coming, the Church's organization took permanent shape. The ordinary gifts of the Spirit succeeded to the extraordinary and, in matters of discipline, preternatural sanctions no longer appear. But the principle of ecclesiastical discipline, as part of the Church's original constitution, was always operative. Excommunication was held as a weapon in reserve; it was used to extirpate moral disorders (II Thess. 3:14) and—a fact that has sometimes been overlooked—for heresy (I Tim. 1:19-20) and schism (Rom. 16:17; Titus 3:10). It was thus that the Church's unity in doctrine and worship, as the indispensable conditions of a deeper unity in faith and love, could be protected and

[10] J. Wordsworth, *The Ministry of Grace*, p. 148.

preserved. Failing that unity, it would no longer be the Church of Christ's foundation, no longer God's instrument for unifying mankind.

Such, in brief and imperfect outline, is what we learn from our earliest records of the outward structure of primitive Christianity. There are local Churches, but no sects or "Christian denominations"; the "churches of God" (I Cor. 11:16) are so many local embodiments of the Church Universal. "For in one Spirit we were all baptized into one body, whether Jews or Greeks, whether slaves or free men" (I Cor. 12:13). St. Paul could no more conceive of a "divided" Church than he could of a divided Christ (I Cor. 1:13). He had his difference on a point of discipline with Peter—the manner in which he records it (Gal. 2:11; *see* verse 7) is an inverted tribute to the preeminence of that Apostle—and, of the two, he had doubtless the deeper insight. But not to have shared Peter's faith, or to have countenanced a fundamental disagreement with him, was unthinkable (cf. I Cor. 1:12). It would have been to withdraw from Christ's mystical Body.

Thus it is not merely in terms of the interior worship of the spirit, but at the level of institutional Christianity, that we find an underlying harmony between the aspirations of the individual and the demands of corporate society. That this must necessarily be the case is implicit in the message of St. Paul who, after Our Lord himself, is the dominating figure in Christian history. He insists that the Church is a single organism made up of Head and members: the personal union of the individual convert with Christ is attained only by incorporation into the Body of Christ. Apostolic Christianity therefore knows nothing of attempts to lead the Christian life apart from membership of the institutional Church and holds that the distinction between those within and those without is fundamental. Each individual Christian has his separate functions, each has his special gifts, but these come from one and the same Spirit and so unite each to all in a single community. What more appropriate title could be devised for this corporate fellowship than that which it was later to receive —the one Holy, Catholic, and Apostolic Church?

Catholicism has been imbued by St. Paul with the conviction that there can be no opposition between the individual and social aspects of religion. Christ had spent Himself for the benefit of the unique personality of each, concentrated His love upon it as if nothing else need be considered. The Son of God "loved *me* and gave himself up for *me*" (Gal. 2:20). But equally, He was concerned for the corporate welfare of His Church. It had existed as an ideal in Our Lord's mind before it took shape in the world of space and time. That ideal He loved; He lived and died and rose again so that it might be realized as an accomplished fact; it was as a community, a social body, that the Israel of God was redeemed. "Christ loved the *Church* and gave himself up for *it*" (Eph. 5:25). St. Paul, as has often been remarked, had all the characteristics of a born individual-ist, a man not easy to manage. We know more about him than of any other personality in early Christian history. The evidence points to a conspicuous independence and sense of leadership, a powerful intelligence combined with immense moral strength, qualities which raised him head and shoulders above his asso-ciates; to which was added the consciousness of a personal religious experience vouchsafed to no other. And yet he insisted that the way of salvation was only to be found in the subordina-tion of self to the corporate interests of the community. He had learned on the Damascus road that to persecute the Christian Church was to persecute Christ, and he drew from that stagger-ing revelation the only possible conclusion: A life which has God as its center must be led in fellowship, or not at all.

Christianity, supremely a religion of the spirit, was not only embodied in an institution. Unlike the legends of pagan mythology, it was set firmly within the framework of world history. The Church's awareness of the importance of this fact emerges from the primitive Creed. Along with the great doctrinal truths, the faithful are reminded that Jesus Christ was crucified at a known date and place: under the Roman procurator of Judaea, Pontius Pilate. The Christian community had visibly grown and expanded under the aegis of the Empire. The extension of the Church, from Jerusalem through Antioch to Rome, is the underlying theme of the Acts of the Apostles and the Pauline Epistles. From St. Paul, as soon as the conflict with his Judaizing opponents begins to subside, we hear no more of the Second Coming. A wider vision is opening out. There is a repeated anticipation of seeing Rome (Acts 19:21; 23:11; cf. Rom. 1:13; 15:24, 28), of the conquest of the capital for Christ, and so of the world. With the presence of both Peter and Paul in that city, the recognized center of the Christian community had shifted from Jerusalem to Rome. On the destruction of the Jewish state in A.D. 70 that position was finally stabilized; the metropolis of the Empire and the headquarters of the Church coincided.

The tradition with regard to the origin of the Roman Church is stated in its fullest form by St. Jerome. "Simon Peter . . . prince of the Apostles, in the second year of the Emperor Claudius . . . came to Rome and there for twenty-five years occupied the episcopal throne till the last year of Nero." [11] The joint ministry and martyrdom within the capital of Peter, designated the "rock" foundation by Our Lord Himself, and Paul, the no less divinely chosen Apostle of the Gentiles, make Rome the "Apostolic Church" *par excellence*. The functions of the Papacy, and of the hierarchy in subordination to it, were later to be multiplied, as the declining Empire proved unequal to its

[11] Jerome, *De viribus illustris,* § 1 (Op. ii. 827; P.L. 23, col. 607). For a discussion on the authenticity of this tradition, as stated by Jerome, see B. J. Kidd, *op. cit.,* Vol. I, pp. 51-3.

responsibilities. The episcopal dioceses largely conformed to the existing administrative units and the procedure of the Papal curia was modeled on that of the Imperial civil service. But this necessary adaptation to circumstances—the "secularization" of Christianity, as some have unfairly described it—wrought no essential change. The Church's faith was centered upon the person of its Lord and God's saving revelation as once for all disclosed in Him. Christian worship was expressed in the original Eucharistic Sacrifice, the Mass, as it had now come to be called.

Towards the end of the second century of our era, St. Irenaeus, perhaps the best qualified witness of his day, is to be found referring to the Roman Church as "the embodiment of tradition in miniature." It is interesting to note that the contemporary verdict, as expressed by one of the most distinguished living historians, is not substantially different. "The Church in its traditional form thus stands forth armed with the spear of the Mass, the shield of the Hierarchy, and the helmet of the Papacy; and perhaps the subconscious purpose—or the divine intention, if you prefer that language—of this heavy panoply of institutions in which the Church has clad herself is the very practical one of outlasting the toughest of the secular institutions of this world, including all the civilizations." [12] It is well to be reminded of the necessity for "toughness" in the Church's external structure; for it is a quality in which her enemies are by no means deficient. But there are those who will see a juster statement of Catholicism's *raison d'être* in a passage written by the successor of Simon Peter.

The Church, therefore, has one and the same purpose, office and function as the Incarnate Word: that is, to teach the truth to all men, to rule and guide them aright, to offer to God a pleasing and acceptable sacrifice, and thus to re-establish between creatures and their sovereign Creator the close relation of harmony which the

[12] A. J. Toynbee, *Civilization on Trial,* p. 242.

Apostle of the nations thus describes: "You are no longer exiles, then, or aliens; the saints are your fellow-citizens, you belong to God's household. Apostles and prophets are the foundations on which you were built, and the chief corner-stone is Christ Jesus himself. In him the whole fabric is bound together, as it grows into a temple, dedicated to the Lord; in him you too are being built in with the rest, so that God may find in you a dwelling-place for his Spirit" (Eph. 2:19-22). [13]

[13] Pius XII, *loc. cit.*, pp. 527-8.

7

The Problem Reconsidered

MANY of the difficulties put forward in the opening chapter of this essay should appear in a different light in view of what has followed. But a number of loose ends remain to be gathered and, if possible, woven into a coherent pattern. It was no less a celebrity than Lenin who, on being faced with some awkward queries, blandly remarked that a fool can ask more questions in two minutes than a wise man can answer in an hour. When, as in this case, the questioners are themselves among the wise, the task of providing a brief and effective reply is the more delicate. Since, however, we are not concerned to score debating points or to prove that the right has always been on one side, we should be able to retrace our steps without undue embarrassment. First, then, the various forms of secularism, ranging from the typical representatives of scientific positivism, through the sociologists and political thinkers, to those near-Christians, the liberal humanists.

VARIETIES OF SECULARISM

The controversy between religion and science has not always redounded to the credit of the respective disputants. No Catholic can look back with satisfaction upon the classical example of how not to do it—the case of Galileo. The two-way principle laid down by St. Thomas—that what is essentially a revealed truth of faith is of necessity undiscoverable by reason, and contrariwise, that whatever human reason can attain to does not in itself come within the sphere of faith—has sometimes been overlooked by those who should have known better. The Bible has been ransacked for information which it was not designed to provide and the supposed findings used as a stick with which to beat the back of the honest scientist. But the central Catholic tradition, as expounded by Leo XIII and Pius XII, gives no countenance to Biblical fundamentalism. The Church's interpretation of the creation narrative in the Book of Genesis, for example, is essentially a religious one, and therefore on a level which physical science is not in a position either to refute or corroborate. That the Catholic Church has not only not discouraged, but given direct patronage to, scientific research is an historic fact too well known to call for detailed demonstration. When Poggendorf compiled his *Dictionnaire des Sciences Exactes,* from antiquity to 1863, he found that, of the 8,847 names there included, ten per cent were those of priests and religious.

On the whole the charge of trespass can be more effectively sustained against the scientists themselves than against misguided ecclesiastics. So long as science is content with its peculiar province—that of recording sense phenomena, of formulating hypotheses which can be tested by observation and embodying the results in practical inventions—no conflict with revealed religion is possible. As Professor A. E. Taylor has shrewdly pointed out: "Science in the current sense of the word is not the whole of knowledge, but a special kind of knowledge which makes up for its one-sidedness and limitations of scope by the precision and exactitude of its vision, just as the field of view under the microscope compensates its definition and wealth of detail by the narrowness of its limits." But when scientists begin to philosophize on the basis of their researches, as they have as much right as any one else to do, then a different situation arises. The conclusions drawn about the nature of man, or the originating cause of life, its meaning and purpose, lie outside the field of physical science. In these departments the value attaching to the interesting theories of Jeans and Eddington, the less impressive speculations of Einstein, or the ineptitudes of Fred Hoyle can be assessed, not by these scientific experts as such, but by the philosopher and theologian.

Unfortunately a specialist's prestige, for the uncritical mind at any rate, tends to flow over from the regions in which the scientist speaks with authority to those where he merits as much, or as little, attention as the rest of us. What adds to the resulting confusion is that mathematicians and physicists, whose proper instruments do not enable them to analyze the process whereby our minds actually acquire their knowledge, are often unaware that they have transgressed. They thus tend to approach these larger philosophical questions with the same assurance as they deal with phenomena that can be measured and observed. The true parallel to Mr. Hoyle's dogmatism on the origin of the universe is not, of course, an Aristotle discoursing on metaphysics, but a popular sportsman or film star writing in the Sunday press on "What Religion Means to Me." Not all scientists, needless to say, are so devoid of a capacity for philosophic reflection. Professor W. M. Smart, for example, in his interesting book *The Origin of the Earth* (Cambridge: University Press, 1951), shows himself in the true succession to Jeans and Eddington when he makes his own the saying of Francis Bacon: "I had rather believe all the fables in the legend, and the Talmud, and the Alcoran, than that this universal frame is without a mind."

Upon the positivism of the scientists the modern disciples of David Hume have erected their ingenious system of Logic. The Logical Positivists deny the possibility of metaphysics—that is, a reasoned, though speculative, interpretation of human experience as a whole—on the grounds that only two types of statement have real meaning.[1] These are analytical propositions ("tautologies") which serve to make explicit what is already implicit in a given assumption, and empirical propositions which can be verified by sense observation and experiment. Between them, statements of this kind exhaust the whole field of *cognitive* significant discourse. Such a proposition as "God exists," for example, since it falls into neither class, is literally and technically "nonsense," and as such meaningless. It is the product of *emotive,* not cognitive, discourse. It conveys or arouses personal emotion, but tells us nothing of which the mind can make sense. It is thus neither true nor false; it is psychologically interesting; for it reveals something of the private histories and preconceptions of those who affirm it.

The basic inconsistency of Logical Positivism has often been exposed. Its underlying postulate, that all statements (apart from definitions or tautologies) not verifiable by observation and experiment are strictly nonsense, cannot itself be verified empirically. This is not a definition arrived at by analysis (a "tautology") but a general statement put forward as meaningful, yet one that cannot be checked by reference to sense data. It conforms, therefore, to neither of the two types of statement which alone are allowed to have real meaning. Logical Positivists, like the scientists mentioned above, overlook what is involved in the simplest act of apprehension by the senses, as well as the "inter-subjective intercourse" that lies behind scientific

---

[1] These remarks are much indebted to a brief but extremely lucid critique of Logical Positivism by Greville Norburn in the *Church Quarterly Review,* Vol. CL, No. 300 (July-September, 1950).

verification. To give an account of what is delivered through our various senses implies mental processes of which the senses themselves are incapable. "The senses do not err," as Kant remarked, "not because they always judge rightly, but because they do not judge at all." Behind so seemingly self-evident an observation as "This is a man" there lie in fact two universal ideas—that of existence and that of human nature—neither of which can be reduced without remainder to sense data. As Professor Ritchie has pointed out, "the plausibility of the positivist's case rests upon his apparently appealing to actual sense data; the possibility of its being valid rests upon a concealed appeal to what is not actual sense data." We may recall Leibniz's comment on the positivism of his own day. To Locke's contention that *nihil est in intellectu quod non fuerit in sensu,* he made the unanswerable rejoinder, *excipe, nisi ipse intellectus.*[2]

Moreover, in repudiating metaphysics, the Logical Positivists remove the foundations of that actual science whose validity they are so anxious to uphold. For science lives on the assumption that nature's laws are uniform, that what happens today will under the same conditions happen tomorrow, that nature speaks a language which is intelligible, at least when deciphered by the key of applied mathematics. That Logical Positivism does not press its case against the scientists would appear to be due to an understandable reluctance to impugn a principle upon which positive science has depended since the days of Galileo. So, as Professor Collingwood dryly remarks, the Logical Positivists quietly let it pass, "and to ease their consciences drop heavily upon the proposition 'God exists,' because they think that nobody believes in God except poor miserable parsons, whose luggage enjoys no such diplomatic immunity."

Logical Positivism's fundamental mistake is an up-to-date

---

[2] There is nothing in the intellect which was not previously in the senses; *provided we make the reservation,* except the intellect itself.

version of the ancient fallacy of confusing Logic with Philosophy properly so called. Logic, as Aquinas pointed out, is the art of reasoning, and as such an indispensable preliminary to the philosophic quest. Philosophy itself is concerned with the ultimate explanation of reality. Certainly we must follow in the footsteps of Socrates and insist that scientists and philosophers, to say nothing of theologians, should tell us what they mean. It is salutary to have someone at hand who will have no truck with airy speculations, who subjects our arguments to the closest scrutiny. But an analysis of terms, combined with dialectical skill, is no substitute for the reasoned intuitions of the philosopher. Rational clarity has its place, though not as the master light of all our seeing. Socrates spent much time in exposing the "nonsense" of the Sophists, but he dies a martyr to "God, freedom and immortality."

What of the charge that Catholicism is unable "to provide the basis for a new society"? On this the Church's history has something to say. It was the Catholic Church, under the presiding genius of the Papacy, that brought a social organism to birth out of the chaos of the Dark Ages. This achievement, imperfect and short-lived, was made possible by men's common acceptance of responsibility to God and consequent obligations to each other. Within the boundaries of Western Europe a Christian commonwealth once actually existed; it provided a framework in which the lust for wealth and power could be held in check, albeit precariously. However far practice fell below the ideal, and it often fell very far, society as a whole was ordered on the assumption that the pursuit of individual self-interest was to be discouraged. Economics was regarded as a branch of ethics, and ethics of theology. The entire range of human activities was treated as falling within a single all-embracing scheme, whose character was determined by the supernatural destiny of mankind. Political and social theorists made their appeal not, as in a later age, to utility, but to natural law. The legitimacy of economic transactions was judged by reference, less to the movements of the market, than to moral standards derived from the traditional teaching of the Church. The Church itself was recognized as a society wielding theoretical, and often practical, authority in social affairs.

Post-Reformation society has changed all that. After the breakdown of the medieval synthesis we were to witness, as R. H. Tawney has shown, "the general acceptance of a scale of ethical values, which turned the desire for pecuniary gain from a perilous, if natural, frailty into the idol of philosophers and the mainspring of society." [3] The modern world is now reaping the fruits of this apostasy. But it is surely a churlish critic who would tax Catholicism with a failure to live up to its social responsibilities while repudiating the sole basis on which they can be discharged. No fair-minded observer will deny that Catholics have been infected, alike in the religious and social aspects of their lives, with the prevailing individualism. If even Newman could not escape from it, what was to be expected of lesser men? "Newman was not interested in social reform," writes a recent authority. "He owned that he had never asked himself the question whether the number of public-houses in England was excessive." [4] Not perhaps a very serious omission; a mere straw in the wind; but there are others. Which proves no more than that Catholicism is something too vast in its implications to be embraced by even its greatest exponents. The present revival of interest, stimulated by the Pope himself, in the Church as Christ's mystical Body is doing much to restore the original bal-

[3] *Religion and the Rise of Capitalism* (New York: Harcourt, Brace & Co., 1926).

[4] Humphrey J. T. Johnson, in his essay on Cardinal Newman in *The English Catholics, 1850-1950* (London: Burns, Oates & Washbourne, 1950), p. 263.

ance. It is here, as we have attempted to show, that we find the answer to the chief political and social problems of our time. Catholicism freely admits that it is vitally concerned with historical continuity. In this sense the Church will always be conservative. The Marxists should surely have taught us the dangers of being reformers in a hurry. To draw sharp distinctions between the "old" and the "new" society is the characteristic weakness of intellectuals who cling to a naïve theory of inevitable progress. The realities of the every day world, being less tractable than ideas, conform to no such watertight compartments. It is the mark of the realist, not merely of the reactionary, to be aware that civilization has been built up by a long and arduous process. Custom and tradition are its bulwarks; once these are removed, the descent to barbarism is rapid. The Church, being itself a corporate society, cannot but have a "vested interest" in social stability. No doubt there have been times and places where Catholicism has linked itself too closely with the existing regime, occasions when churchmen have blindly resisted the legitimate efforts of social reformers. Exceptional insight and detachment are required to detect the precise moment when the benefits of the *status quo* no longer compensate for its accompanying evils. There may be Catholics today who, when they advert to social questions at all, betray themselves as thinking in terms of the hierarchic structure of the comparatively static medieval society, rather than with reference to the essentially Catholic ideal of the "common good." This last is the controlling principle, as flexible as it is dynamic, which should govern politics and economics alike. Catholicism will always set its face against policies that are God-less or contrary to nature. For the rest, whatever its past history may have been, the Church's native genius is to sit loose to any and every form of temporal government.

To suggest that the Popes have failed to give a "prophetic

lead" on current social problems is a gibe unworthy of a serious controversialist. The Papal encyclicals may be couched in what, to modern ears, are less glowing phrases than the "existential" language of Karl Barth, but their message, we may be allowed to think, is likely to be more enduring. A statement of principles, which is what the Popes are concerned with, is always apt to be dismissed as "vague theorizing" by practical politicians and sociologists. Those at the executive end have little time to think about the bases of legislation. But to charge the encyclicals with being remote and in the air carries with it a like condemnation of all political theory that stems from Plato and Aristotle. Machiavelli, it is true, developed a new manner, but the careers of Hitler and Mussolini suggest that something went wrong when men took to reading Machiavelli. The last word still rests with Berkeley: "Whatever the world thinks, he who hath not much meditated on God, the human mind, and the *summum bonum,* may possibly make a thriving earthworm, but will most indubitably make a sorry patriot and a sorry statesman."

As for the actual content of the encyclicals, no one who has taken the trouble to read them—a task, one sometimes suspects, which has been carelessly omitted by their critics—can substantiate the charge that they are behind the times or out of touch with the facts of the modern world. It may be noted in passing that when an English Catholic scholar [5] came to summarize their content in a single volume, he could find no more fitting title for his work than *The Popes' New Order.* A case that can be more easily argued is not that the Popes have failed to give a lead but that large sections of the Catholic body have been reluctant to follow. The unfavorable reactions to the "advanced thinking" of Leo XIII's *Rerum Novarum,* with its insistence on the rights of the working classes, is well known. In his encyclical *Graves de Communi* (January 18, 1901) the

[5] Father Philip Hughes.

same Pope put an end to the last attempt on the part of highly placed Catholics to maintain that Catholicism and democracy are incompatible.

"It is Our will," wrote Benedict XV on March 11, 1920, "that priests consider it as one of their duties to give as much of their life as possible to social science and social action, by study, observation and work. . . . Let no member of the clergy suppose that activity of this kind is something foreign to his priestly ministry because the field in which it is exercised is economic. It is precisely in this field that the eternal salvation of souls is imperilled." Pius XI in his encyclical *Quadragesimo anno* (May 15, 1931) takes full account of the existing class war and the evils of economic individualism. "Unbridled ambition to dominate has succeeded the lust for profit; the whole economic regime has become hard, cruel and relentless to a ghastly degree." The Pope opposes to the tyranny of unmitigated State socialism the principle of subsidiary function, namely, that the State has no right to assume control over activities which can be justly and effectively carried on by subordinate voluntary bodies. But the supreme goal to be aimed at is the common good of all. The right to private property must be recognized, since it is the natural safeguard of personal liberty, but "It is rightly contended that certain forms of property must be reserved to the State, since they carry with them a power too great to be left to private individuals without injury to the community at large." The same principles have been repeatedly reaffirmed by Pius XII.

The Papal condemnation of atheistic Communism and unqualified State socialism are well known and often cited. Not so well known is Catholicism's equally forceful repudiation of monopoly capitalism as a tolerable basis for society. "Describe the modern capitalist 'system' as you will," an American priest has recently written, "we fail to see how it corresponds in any way to the concept of industrial society put forth in the encyclical, *Quadragesimo anno*." [6] And he quotes the relevant passages from Pius XI: "Free competition, though within certain limits just and productive of good results, cannot be the ruling principle of the economic world. . . . Still less can this function be exercised by the economic supremacy which within recent times has taken the place of free competition. . . . Free competition is dead; economic dictatorship has taken its place." "This accumulation of power, the characteristic note of the modern economic order, is a natural result of limitless, free competition which permits the survival of only those who are the strongest, which often means those who fight most relentlessly, who pay least heed to the dictates of conscience." The writer who quotes these words goes on to remark: "In origin, the capitalistic *status quo* defies the papal denunciation of free competition as a guiding principle for economic life"; and he asks, with regard to the situation in the United States: "Where is there any similarity between the Big Business economic set-up now prevailing in America, with its concomitant class-warfare, and the *Order* of industrial society demanded by our Catholic social doctrine." So much for the charge that Catholicism is inextricably bound up with "the fundamental institutions of the old order."

The attitude of Catholicism to modern democracy is often misunderstood, and never more completely than by Paul Blanshard in his *American Freedom and Catholic Power*. [7] The Catholic Church is not a democracy. To require that it should become so is to ask it to cease to be itself. Christianity's basic

[6] William J. Smith, S.J.: "The 'Catholic' Viewpoint on Industry Councils," *American Ecclesiastical Review*, Vol. CXXII, No. 2 (February, 1950), pp. 107-120.

[7] For a brief but penetrating critique of Mr. Blanshard's position, see the article by Father John Courtney Murray, S.J., in the *Month*, New Series Vol. V, No. 4 (April, 1951).

principle is not the sovereignty of the people, but the sovereignty of God. Mr. Blanshard, thanks to his own presuppositions, misses the whole point of the Catholic hierarchy's exercise of "power." That power is not controlled by the hierarchy itself; it is an application in given circumstances of a divine law to which all men, including the hierarchy itself, is subject. Pope Leo XIII—in a document not cited by Mr. Blanshard (*Diuturnum illud,* June 29, 1881)—has indicated far more effective checks upon any ecclesiastic's pretensions to autocracy than that of a majority vote, namely, the principles of both the divine and the natural law. Catholics have not only the right, but the duty, to refuse obedience to any order, by whomsoever given, that fails to conform to these principles. Popes and bishops may have abused or misapplied their authority, but to call their powers "irresponsible" is to forget where true sovereignty lies. They are responsible, as stewards and administrators in God's household, to the Master of the house Himself. The Catholic Church must always pronounce its verdict upon the moral content of politics and economics. Ecclesiastical authority, however, may have something yet to learn, not about its own principles, but about the virtues of taking counsel with those in close touch with the situation to which those principles apply. "It is one of the most dangerous failings of superiors," wrote St. John Chrysostom, himself a bishop, "and at the same time one of the commonest, to refuse to take account of the views of others, to have their own way as if they were absolute masters, whereas they are only stewards." [8]

The Catholic Church has no quarrel with representative institutions as such. They flourished under the Church's aegis in the Middle Ages. Political democracy, with its safeguards

---

[8] C. Spicq, O.P., *Spiritualité Sacerdotale d'après Saint Paul* ('Lectio Divina' 4, Ed. du Cerf). Quoted from *Life of the Spirit,* Vol. V, No. 58 (April, 1951).

against despotism and its principle that what touches all should be the active concern of all, is wholly congenial to the Catholic mind. What Catholicism resists is the notion that "the people" is itself the source of law. The people may elect its rulers and, should they prove unsatisfactory, replace them by others; but the rulers themselves, while they hold office, derive their authority from a higher source than the will of the people. This principle, it is interesting to note, as distinct from Rousseau's theory of the "general will," is embodied in the British Parliamentary tradition. A Member of Parliament is a *representative,* rather than a delegate, of the people. That is to say, he is no mere executive of a mandate from his constituents; while paying all due regard to their interests, he is at the same time a legislator answerable to his own conscience. In other words, he is bound to see to it that positive legislation reflects, so far as may be, the higher law of nature and of God. If Catholics have seemed in the past predisposed to favor authoritarian forms of government, that is not because of any principles in the Church's theology. Quite the contrary; since these serve chiefly to stress the limitations of all human authority. The explanation may lie in nothing more complex than the fact that Catholics, like other men, sometimes fail to see how, in new and unfamiliar contexts, what is implied in their own position may best be safeguarded. Papal infallibility is not to be confused with political sagacity, nor a vision of the things that are God's with an insight into the things that are Caesar's.

Nevertheless the Church will not cease to claim the right to judge of politics by the higher laws of religion and morality. This is not a question of exercising "power" but of testifying to what Christianity is—an all-embracing way of life. Catholicism would be false to itself if, under a democratic regime, it did not strive to organize public opinion in its favor. When, for example, in the field of education, the Church employs every lawful means to circumvent the secularists, this is not in the role of one "pressure group" among many but in virtue of its mission to preach the Gospel of Christ and thus preserve the faith of its children. In this, as in all Catholic activity in the political and social arena, it may fairly be demanded that the Church's representatives should not only be, but actually appear to be, upholding values that are authentically and manifestly Christian. The balance of emphasis in Catholic propaganda is therefore a matter for careful consideration. It may be suggested that the remoter deductions of moral casuists and canonists, whose relevance to the Gospel is not always apparent, should hold a subordinate place. If criticism of Catholic activities at the juridical level proves an occasion for bringing more prominently into the light, and imposing on us a greater fidelity to, the basic content of God's revelation—namely, the evangelical commandments of loving God and one's neighbor together with the primary precepts of the natural law—we may well learn to be grateful to our critics. To be thus obliged to discuss Catholic Christianity in the closest possible connection with its sources is a test from which we should not wish to be exempted.

We come next to the alleged failure of the Papacy "to live up to its own sublime ideals." On this only two points need be noted. First, the sixteenth-century Papacy made no attempt to deny or palliate the abuses that had arisen within its own household. Secondly, the Roman See, drawing on no other resources than those supplied by the spiritual inheritance which is never lost, by a program of self-reform to which history offers no parallel, purged and eradicated those same abuses. In the official Instruction given by Pope Adrian VI to the Nuncio Chieregati on his Mission to the Diet of Nuremburg, in 1552, is to be found the following notable passage:

You are also to say that we frankly acknowledge that God permits this persecution of His Church on account of the sins of men, and especially of prelates and clergy; of a surety the Lord's arm is not shortened that He cannot save us, but our sins separate us from Him, so that He does not hear. Holy Scripture declares aloud that the sins of the people are the outcome of the sins of the priesthood; therefore, as Chrysostom declares, when our Saviour wished to cleanse the city of Jerusalem of its sickness, He went first to the Temple to punish the sins of the priests before those of others, like a good physician who heals a disease at its roots. We know well that for many years things deserving of abhorrence have gathered round the Holy See; sacred things have been misused, ordinances transgressed, so that in everything there has been a change for the worse. Thus it is not surprising that the malady has crept down from the head to the members, from the Popes to the hierarchy.

We all, prelates and clergy, have gone astray, and for long there is none that has done good; no, not one. To God, therefore, we must give all the glory and humble ourselves before Him; each one of us must consider how he has fallen and be more ready to judge himself than to be judged by God in the day of His wrath. Therefore, in our name, give promise that we shall use all diligence to reform before all things the Roman Curia, whence, perhaps, all these evils have had their origin; thus healing will begin at the source of sickness. We deem this to be all the more our duty, as the whole world is longing for such reform. The Papal dignity was not the object of our ambition, and we would rather have closed our days in the solitude of private life; willingly would we have put aside the tiara; the fear of God alone, the validity of our election, and the dread of schism, decided us to assume the position of Chief Shepherd. We desire to wield our power not as seeking dominion or means for enriching our kindred, but in order to restore to Christ's bride, the Church, her former beauty, to give help to the oppressed, to uplift men of virtue and learning, above all, to do all that becomes a good shepherd and a successor of the blessed Peter.

Yet let no man wonder if we do not remove all abuses at one blow; for the malady is deep rooted and takes many forms. We must advance, therefore, step by step, first applying the proper remedies to the most difficult and dangerous evils, so as not by hurried reform to throw all things into greater confusion than before. Aristotle well says: "All sudden changes are dangerous to States." [9]

"It has contributed infinitely to the advantage of the Church," said Paolo Tiepolo in 1576, "that several Popes in succession have been men of irreproachable lives; hence all others are become better, or have at least assumed the appearance of being so. Cardinals and prelates attend Mass punctually; their households are studious to avoid anything that can give scandal; the whole city has put off its old recklessness and is become much more Christian-like in life and manners than formerly." Aiding the work of reform throughout the Church were such outstanding personalities as St. Charles Borromeo, St. Philip Neri and, most far-reaching in its influence, the work of St. Ignatius Loyola and his Society of Jesus. Giving permanent form to the new spirit of austerity were the decrees of the Council of Trent. "Out of that Council the Church emerged with its doctrine defined, its discipline strengthened, and its services enriched by the exquisite music of Palestrina." [10] "It is one of the most remarkable facts in Christian history," write the authors of the Anglican report *Catholicity,* "that the Papacy of the sixteenth century first cleansed itself of its vile and most notorious Renaissance scandals, and then itself directed and impelled the cleansing of the Renaissance Church." Catholicism had suffered grievously, both from internal disease and the violent amputation of its members, but the sickness was not to prove mortal. The gates of hell could not prevail against Christ's Church.

[9] Quoted in L. Pastor, *History of the Popes,* English translation ed. R. F. Kerr, C.O., Vol. IX, pp. 134-5.
[10] H. A. L. Fisher, *A History of Europe* (London: Edward Arnold & Co., 1936), p. 556.

PROTESTANT CHRISTIANITY

The Catholic reply to Protestantism must always take the form of a countercriticism, a protest against the protesters. To propound the thesis, as is now the fashion, that Protestantism protested not against but *for* the Church, may not be disingenuous but it is certainly naïve. It is the fallacy known as begging the question. Christianity, by definition, protests a doctrine of the Church against those who would deny or pervert it. In this sense Catholicism has been "protestant" since the day of its birth. But Protestantism as a creed is something quite other. To affirm Christian doctrine as isolated from its context within the whole, to concentrate attention upon certain aspects of God's revelation while repudiating or neglecting others, is to produce the distorted picture which is the inevitable result of arbitrary selection. The correct term to describe this insistence on making a personal choice—in its etymological, as well as historical, significance—is "heresy." We may eliminate the unpleasing emotional associations from this word, but it is always better to call things by their right names. Barth and Brunner, given their basic assumptions, are theologians of genius; their sincerity is not in question; but their position vis-à-vis Catholic Christendom, as they would be the first to acknowledge, is essentially one with that of Luther.

We need not linger over Luther's equivocal personality. For his courage, at any rate, he deserves full credit. Nor shall we exploit the vast field of *tu quoque* arguments which open before the defenders of Catholicism. What it is essential to remember about the Reformers is that, in withdrawing allegiance from the successor of St. Peter or in deliberately incurring his excommunication, they broke away from the Church as it had been constituted by Christ. They had their pretext in the existing scandalous abuses. Nor are they necessarily to be blamed for failure to foresee the horrifying results which followed, once the political, social, and economic sanctions of the Church were no longer acknowledged. But whatever the possibilities of personal good faith, the thing itself was inexcusable. The message of the Gospel on this point could not be plainer: those who sat in Moses' chair, worthless though they might be, were to be obeyed when interpreting the Law. Popes and bishops may be rebuked for their infidelity to their own teaching, but their God-given authority is not to be challenged. St. Catherine of Siena, for example, spoke out fearlessly against scandals at the Papal court. She wept over the wounds being inflicted upon Christ's mystical Body; yet she dedicated her life to the cause of preserving its unity. For a group of Christians to withdraw from the community of Christendom and set up a rival altar is immeasurably more scandalous, in the literal sense of that word, than any amount of corruption in ecclesiastical high places. These can be, and have been, purged from within; but schism is a lethal weapon, not a cure. To condone its use, as modern apologists for the Reformation are logically compelled to do—"in certain circumstances schism may seem to be the least of a number of evils." [11]—only shows how far they have departed from the central Christian tradition. "Among the sins against our neighbor," wrote St. Thomas, "schism is the greatest of all, since it is an attack upon the spiritual well-being of the community": *"inter peccata quae sunt in proximum, peccatum schismatis videtur esse maximum; quia est contra spirituale bonum multitudinis."* [12]

The Protestant suppression of reason and natural law, in the supposed interests of evangelical faith and grace, must always appear to a Catholic thinker as a disastrous simplification. The motives may have been admirable: to focus attention on the

[11] Daniel T. Jenkins, *The Nature of Catholicity*, p. 128.
[12] *Summa Theologica*, II-II, 39, 2, 3.

all-sufficiency of Christ, on the supremacy of the word of God, on the paramount need for faith; but good intentions do not atone for intellectual mistakes. Protestantism appears as a transposition into voluntarist terms of the Gnostic and Manichaean dualism with which the Church had to contend from its beginnings. Among the basic doctrines of Christianity is the truth that the God who redeemed the world is the God who originally created it. God the Creator and God the Redeemer are one and the same. Once this is accepted—and it took centuries of strenuous controversy to get it understood—the notion that there is anything positively and radically evil in nature becomes untenable. The devil does not stand over against Christ the Redeemer, disputing the mastery of the universe with Him on equal terms. The world, throughout its length and breadth, lies under God's almighty hand, the devil being allowed his role of tempter only in so far as it pleases God and accords with His designs. Sin is the greatest of evils, but it is a moral, not an ontological, disorder. It is a deviation in the human will, bringing in its train incalculable harm to God's creatures, but the damage lies in a misuse, and not the total extinction, of what is essentially good. To refuse to acknowledge the fundamental goodness of nature, even of fallen human nature, reflects by implication on the goodness of the Creator.

The specifically Lutheran doctrines concerning the manner in which man is justified and the nature of faith are both of them, let it be frankly admitted, deeply religious in their content. They are an overstatement of Biblical truths which, it may be, Catholic theologians tend to understate. Man, even when made righteous by grace, is still held in the grip of *concupiscence;* and this is a far more deep-seated disorder than some would have us believe. It is more than a tendency to carnal sin, with which it is predominantly associated, to be kept more or less adequately in check by self-discipline, prayer, and the sacraments. It is a weakness so affecting man's spirit that, until holiness has reached its consummated state, even our best actions may be infected with unconscious willfullness and pride. That we are so often unaware of this condition is due to our insensitiveness to what God demands of us, a certain hardness of the heart, which is itself the most radical symptom of the disease. Moral theologians might profitably reflect whether there is any point in the criticism that they are too much preoccupied with sins, too little with sin. Luther would have found few to quarrel with him had he been content to remind his contemporaries that, even when justified, they had nothing of which to boast. What he failed to understand is that God does not treat His children *as if* they were lovable in His sight; He makes them so by infusing His own regenerative love into them. The terms of this transaction are indeed the divine mercy on the one hand and human wretchedness on the other; its effect is to make the creature not less, but more, dependent on God. Nevertheless it gives us a new status: we are not only called, we actually are, the children of God (I John 3:1); not simply His servants, but His friends.

If Catholicism proclaims the Christian community as the Church of saints, it is no less certainly, we may agree with Barth, "the Church of sinners." Equally, including saints and sinners, it is "the Church of the pity of God." As St. Thomas taught, long before Luther, mercy is God's supreme attribute with respect to His creatures; it not only permeates all His dealings with them, it is their sole foundation. Again, if Catholicism stresses the intellectual content of faith, on the grounds that it gives us a sure insight into things unseen (Heb. 11:1), this is to provide a basis for, not to exclude, a humble trust in God's mercy. More than right belief, it is the faith that works by love which marks the Christian man. Catholics have little interest in a God who is an "It," a "Neuter." "Thou and I" is the only acceptable expression of the relationship between the members of God's family and their Heavenly Father. But if we may speak of a "nature" that is human, so also, by analogy, can we do so of one that is divine, a "super-nature." In being given a mysterious created participation in the divine nature (II Pet. 1:4), which makes us true brethren of Christ, we are not on that account anything more than God's creatures, or He anything less than the transcendent Lord of creation, without whose sustaining love we are but dust and ashes.

In according absolute supremacy to the word of God, again the Protestant instinct is sound, but it fails to give any satisfactory, or indeed intelligible, account of what this implies. God's word, embodied in Christ, is also unquestionably in the Bible; but how is the Biblical message mediated to each individual Christian? Subjective assurance, the fact that one *feels* that one has the truth, is no guarantee. In contrasting the proclamation of God's word, through the pronouncements of the ecclesiastical hierarchy, with the word in all its purity, Protestantism is correct up to a point. The teaching of Pope and bishops, since it is not, like the Bible, inspired by the Holy Spirit, is the word, not of God but of man. The Church's hierarchy are as much "under" God's word as the least member of the faithful. They do not control the word; the word controls them. The hierarchy's function is not to substitute their message for God's, but, as commissioned and guided by Christ, to state what that message is. What Barth and Brunner overlook is that when the Catholic Church affirms that she "possesses" God's word—or, in Catholic terminology, the *depositum fidei*—she does not claim any rights over it, other than those of declaring and keeping faithful to it. The Lutheran voluntarism combined with Kant's denial that we can know things in themselves—and the Kantian epistemology underlies much of the "theology of crisis"—together explain how men of great learning and sagacity are blind to the simple fact that we can, at one and the same time, know God's truth and remain in complete submission to it. Divine revelation is indeed the irreplaceable word of God; but, once more, the "articles of faith," as formulated by the Church, are the word of man responding in faith to the word of God. That is why they are called articles, not of revelation, but, precisely, of faith—a faith that is controlled by the Spirit of Truth.

Catholics do not, as Brunner apparently thinks, believe the mysteries of the Trinity and Incarnation on ecclesiastical authority. Thomist theologians point out that the proclamation of the credenda by the Church does not enter into the "formal object" of faith; [13] it is a condition, not a cause, of belief. A Catholic does not believe that Jesus Christ is the Son of God *because* the Church teaches this. The Church "proposes" this article of faith, but the individual surrenders his mind and heart to it from the same motive that St. Peter did: because "it is my Father in heaven that has revealed this to thee" (Matt. 16:17). Divine revelation, in the last analysis, is both the object of, and motive for, the faith that brings salvation. No theological thesis is more firmly upheld by the disciples of St. Thomas than this one, since it protects the central Christian mystery, not only from desecration by rationalistic unbelievers, but also from misrepresentation by well-meaning apologists who attempt to "prove" what cannot in fact be proved. The preliminaries to the act of faith, what are called the "motives of credibility," have a more important part to play than Protestantism, with its disparagement of human reason, is ready to concede. On this point, however, Brunner is substantially at one with St. Thomas: "Either faith or proof; you cannot have both."

In his *Commentary on St. John's Gospel,* St. Thomas dis-

---

[13] For a further discussion of this point, see pp. 208 ff.

cusses the incident of the Samaritan woman (in particular, John
4:42: "It is not through thy report . . .") and observes as follows: "We have right faith when we give obedience to truth for
no other reason than because it is truth. In this passage it is
related that 'they told the woman' that they now believed 'not
through thy report' but on account of truth itself. Three things
lead us to faith in Christ. First, the natural reason, as is shown
in Rom. 1:20: '. . . men have caught sight of his invisible nature,
his eternal power and his divineness, as they are known through
his creatures.' Secondly, the witness of the Law and the
Prophets. 'But, in these days, God's way of justification has at
last been brought to light; one which was attested by the law
and the prophets, but stands apart from the law' (Rom. 3:21).
Thirdly, the preaching of the Apostles and others: 'How can
they listen without a preacher?' (Rom. 10:14). But when a
man is led to belief along these paths, then still can he say that
not on account of any of these things does he believe. Not
because of natural reason, nor through the Law's witness, nor
on account of any one's preaching, but as moved by truth alone.
So we find it in Gen. 15:6: 'And he [Abraham] believed in
the Lord; and it was accounted to him for righteousness.' " [14]
Protestants should reflect on this characteristic teaching of St.
Thomas before taxing Catholicism with an un-Biblical notion
of faith, one which substitutes a human rationalism for the *pistis*
of the New Testament.

For the Catholic theologian, no more than for the Lutheran,
is faith merely a question of intellectual understanding. Faith
not only transcends rational knowledge, it is imperfect, dead,
without charity. For the whole man, mind and heart, to be surrendered to God the light of the intelligence needs as its complement the love which informs the will. "Charity is said to be

[14] *Comm. in Joan.,* cap. iv, lect. v, 2 (Parma edit., p. 374).

the *form* of faith, inasmuch as it is through charity that the act of faith is perfected and receives its form." [15] St. Thomas's technical language is less eloquent, though in reality more exact, than the existential description of Brunner, with its insistence on "personal decision" and the part played by the will; but there is no difference of view about what is involved. With every word of the following passage a Catholic theologian may cordially agree: "Faith means being gripped by the Word of God; it means that the person submits in the very centre of his being, in his heart, to Him to whom he belongs, because He has created him for Himself. To be actually surrendered like this is very different from knowing *about* it. . . . But this does not mean an intellectual understanding, but a personal encounter. Here, and here alone, lies the gulf between this world and the world beyond, between reason and revelation. That is why a person who has long ago given up faith can still go on for a long time teaching correct theology. It is always at his disposal. But there is one thing that he can no longer do: he can no longer pray from his heart. For in prayer we are concerned with Thyself and myself. The twofold self—which is still reflected in the theological idea but is no longer there as a self—that is the secret of the Holy Spirit and of faith, and here theology ceases." [16]

Catholicism furthermore is well able "to distinguish between the action of Christ and the action of the hierarchy." Christ alone is the Lord of the Church. Christ alone gives it life through His Spirit. Christ alone is the author of grace. Christ alone can institute the Church's sacraments. Christ alone, as coequal with the Father and the Holy Spirit, can effectively answer the Church's prayers. Peter and the Apostles could perform none of these functions; no more can the Pope and the bishops. The episcopate are ministers of the word and the sac-

---

[15] *Summa Theologica,* II-II, 4, 3.
[16] Brunner, *Revelation and Reason,* pp. 421-2.

raments in complete subordination to Christ. Their jurisdiction concerns the external structure of the Church; that of Christ controls its inner life. [17] The Pope is the successor, not of Christ, who is in need of none since He is the Church's everlasting Lord, but of St. Peter. The hierarchy's authority is divinely given, for it is Christ's own ordinance, but its exercise is hedged about with human limitations. Christ Himself and His Holy Spirit are present within the Church, guiding and assisting its counsels, preserving its faith intact. God's gifts, however, are not bestowed *in vacuo;* the measure in which they are received is conditioned by the capacity of the recipients. The treasure is carried in earthen vessels.

If Catholicism is not normally prone to stress the human imperfections in the Church, this should not be hard to understand. Whatever the personal shortcomings of its members, the Body of Christ is a holy community. Being such, it both challenges and offers salvation to a sinful world. As the living temple of God's Spirit, the Church would betray its mission if it ever ceased to think of and proclaim itself as holy. It is humble before God, not obsequious towards men. The Church on earth has still to become, as St. Augustine and St. Thomas were at pains to point out, a "glorious church, not having spot or wrinkle" (Eph. 5:27), but it bears within itself even now the seeds of this final state. Nor has Catholicism been guilty of the "absolutizing of relative human language about God." The use of analogical predications, which steer a middle course between the Scylla of anthropomorphism and the Charybdis of agnosticism, have been much too carefully thought out by Catholic theologians to merit this description. By the same token, it is unfair to label the conservative attitude of the Church towards Holy Scripture as "timid and prosaic."

[17] See St. Thomas: "Utrum esse caput Ecclesiae sit proprium Christo" (*Summa Theologica,* III, 8, 6).

When the theories of Scripture scholars appear to conflict with the Church's traditional teaching, ecclesiastical authority is naturally anxious that they should not be confused with the Catholic doctrine or taught to students who are ill-equipped to deal with them. But full encouragement has been expressly given to the researches of modern Biblical scholarship. "It is therefore a mistake to maintain, as do some who fail to appreciate the conditions of Biblical study," writes Pius XII, "that nothing remains for the modern Catholic exegete to add to the achievements of Christian antiquity. On the contrary, these times of ours have raised many problems which call for further examination and serve as a powerful stimulus to unremitting study by the interpreter of today." [18]

The recent infallible pronouncement of the dogma of the Assumption again brought to light the oversimplified Christology of Protestantism. The parallelism between Christ, the new Adam, and Mary, the second Eve, has always been implicit in the sources of revelation. It was inevitable that the Church should one day make explicit its conviction that our Lady shared in Christ's victory over the devil, sin, and finally, death. The truth had found its expression in the Catholic liturgy for centuries. Nor is the Church embarrassed by the fact that explicit Biblical evidence is lacking. The Bible as the sole rule of faith is an invention of the sixteenth-century Reformers. The matter is well summarized, after a lengthy discussion based on the sources, by the distinguished Anglican scholar, Dr. B. J. Kidd.

Books, therefore, or the writings of Christian Apostles and Prophets would, at first, be of less account; and, in any case, they never have been regarded by the Catholic Church as the sole, or even the primary, source of Christian truth. There is no book in the New

[18] *Divino afflante Spiritu* (*Acta Apostolicae Sedis*, Vol. XXXV, No. 10—October 20, 1943—p. 313).

Testament but implies that it was written for those who had already been instructed in the truth. Christians, therefore, and the Christian Church, might conceivably have gone on indefinitely without Christian Scriptures. They were not disposed to write them, without occasion; nor, when written, to collect them. Indeed, they lost Q; and nearly left our second Gospel to perish on the shelf. [19]

The word of God was thus preserved in the apostolic tradition quite independently of the Church's inspired writings. There is written evidence for the recognition of our Lady as the "Second Eve" from at least the date of St. Justin Martyr (who died *circa* A.D. 163). Moreover the attention of the early Fathers, preoccupied as they were with the Trinitarian and Christological controversies of the first four centuries, was not fully focused upon her rôle until the Council of Ephesus (A.D. 431). It is not, then, surprising that the tradition with regard to the Assumption should not come clearly to light until after that date. This glorification of Mary, Catholic theologians now see to be intimately connected with the facts of the Redemption and Resurrection—man's victory, in Christ, over sin and death—and with the part assigned to her whose co-operation at the Annunciation was instrumental to these triumphs. Protestantism, in registering its objections to all this, is, it must be confessed, being no more than consistent with its original repudiation of the Christian tradition of both East and West. It is interesting to note, with regard to the dogma of the Assumption, that a representative of the Eastern Orthodox Church [20] has lately admitted that, "after the clarifications given by the texts of the Preamble and of the Bull which accompanied the actual definition, he was convinced that not only did it con-

[19] *A History of the Church to A.D. 461*, Vol. I, p. 269.
[20] Professor Pierre Kovalevsky, Secretary-General of the Inter-Orthodox Oecumenical Action Committee. See the *Tablet* for May 5, 1951, p. 364.

tain nothing contrary to Eastern Orthodox tradition, but the text
of the promulgation entirely agreed with this tradition."

Nevertheless the controversy to which the Papal definition
gave rise may have proved instructive. It cannot be historically
accurate to say that it was no more than a repetition of what
happened when the Immaculate Conception was defined in 1854
and Papal Infallibility in 1870. Neither the popular press nor
the radio was in existence at that time. A cherished article of
Catholic faith could not then have been wrested from its
appropriate setting, in the liturgical and devotional life of
believers, and exposed to the rude unfriendly blasts of quasi-
theological journalism. No doctrine is more harmonious with
Catholic theology than the Assumption; none more difficult to
present as reasonable to the historian who questions the Catholic premises. Whether the stimulus given to devotion to Mary,
and the splendid spectacle of the Holy Father exercising his
rightful authority, compensated for the hostility and even open
derision to which the act was exposed in full view of the faithful
—on whom the burden of sustaining the Catholic side in an
abstruse theological controversy chiefly rested—can be known
only to Him who reads the secrets of men's hearts.

An observer, jealous for the prestige of the Church, sensitive
to what St. Thomas calls the *irrisiones infidelium,* in reflecting
on the Pauline principle that what is lawful is not always
expedient, may merely show himself too much influenced by
the counsels of worldly prudence. If he is wise, he will acknowledge that the question of expediency had been fully weighed
by those most competent to judge. The Church's first care is
for its own members; if at times it appears to be wanting in a
sense of responsibility to the world at large, appearances are
often deceptive. It was no small thing challengingly to remind
mankind of the fact of the bodily resurrection—for that is what
underlies our Lady's Assumption—at a time when the worth

of the body is in practice widely denied and human hopes grow dim. But this chapter would fail of its purpose if some more general principles affecting the Catholic position were not kept clearly in view.

First, it should be borne in mind that, as with the world, so with the Church, what occupies popular attention at any given moment is not necessarily in itself the most important thing to be considered. The wholeness and balance of Catholicism are not manifested everywhere and always. It is permissible to think, even to hope, that now the final exaltation of Mary has been assigned its due place in the Catholic *corpus doctrinae,* the attention of the faithful will be directed once more to the unique position held by Christ the Redeemer, no less the Saviour of Mary than of ourselves. There is perhaps nothing presumptuous in the thought that the time occupied by certain theologians in drawing yet further deductions from the revealed data concerning our Lady could be more profitably devoted to illuminating, from the inspired Scripture, those theandric acts of her Son which were His alone, constituting Him the one Mediator between God and man (I Tim. 2:5). Eloquent tributes to Mary, which reflect neither the proportions of the New Testament nor the balanced theology of the Incarnation, may gratify the emotions but can give little satisfaction to the Catholic mind. Signs are not wanting that the Church's *magisterium* has been disturbed at certain enthusiastic excesses of uninstructed devotion. An Assessor of the Holy Office has written to the point:

A good Catholic knows from his cathechism that the true religion rests in the true Faith, in Revelation, which ended with the death of the last Apostle and has been entrusted to the Church, its interpreter and custodian. Nothing else necessary to our salvation can be revealed to us. There is nothing more for which we must look. We have everything, if we wish to make use of it. Even the most accredited visions can furnish us with new motives for fervour but not with new elements of life or doctrine. True religion abides essentially, apart from in the conscience, in the love of God and the consequent love of our neighbour. And, more than in acts of worship and rite, the love of God consists in doing the will of God, obeying His commandments. This is true religion. [21]

Nor is he heedless of how non-Catholics regard the Church:

Why should we offer the spectacle of fatuousness or unhealthy exaltation before those who oppose and despise us? "Christians, be more prudent," wrote Dante in his day. "Do not be like feathers that bend to any wind." The great poet urged the very same reasons that we give today: "You have the Old and New Testament, and the Shepherd of the Church to guide you." Dante's conclusion is the same as ours: "This is sufficient for your salvation" (Canto V, vv, 73-77).

Needless to say, the extravagances here alluded to take nothing from the Church's essential doctrine. Protestants will remain impoverished in their understanding of the Incarnation until they can lend imaginative sympathy to such verses as the following, evoked by the thought of Mary.

> If I have understood,
> She holds high motherhood
> Towards all our ghostly good
> And plays in grace her part
> About man's beating heart...
> Yet no part but what will
> Be Christ our Saviour still...
> Be thou then, O thou dear
> Mother, my atmosphere;
> My happier world wherein
> To wend and meet no sin... [22]

---

[21] Monsignor Alfredo Ottaviani. Quoted from the *Tablet*, February 24, 1951, p. 145.

[22] Gerard Manley Hopkins, "The Blessed Virgin compared to the Air we Breathe."

Those who decry the celebrated definition of Papal Infallibility should scrutinize carefully their motives. They may find
that what gives rise to their protests is not so much a disinterested
attachment to the Biblical revelation as a reluctance to acknowledge any concrete expression of divine authority apart from the
private conscience. To be "under the word of God" is the only
possible position for the Christian; but that position need be
neither difficult nor particularly religious, when modified by a
liberalism which allows each individual to interpret the word
as he thinks best. Given the two premises of the presence within
the Church of the truth-giving Spirit (John 15:26) and the
place held by St. Peter, the conclusion that final doctrinal authority in Christ's Church rests with Peter's successor is surely
inescapable. The Vatican Council defined that the Pope enjoys
"that infallibility with which the Divine Redeemer willed *His
Church* to be endowed when defining doctrine concerning faith
or morals." When the Pope speaks *ex cathedra,* therefore, it is
not by an arbitrary and merely personal *ipse dixit;* he acts as the
organ of the Spirit-guided Church. So far from countenancing a
"Papal despotism," this pronouncement is at once so comprehensive and yet so guarded in its terms that many theologians
consider it to have raised more problems than it has solved.
Apart from such obvious examples as the dogmatic definitions
of the Immaculate Conception and the Assumption, the experts
are not agreed as to what Papal pronouncements actually fall
within its scope. Bernard Shaw, who after all claimed no more
than to perform by divination what others achieved by scholarship, was not so wide of the mark in the well-known passage
from *Saint Joan.* "Perhaps I had better inform my Protestant
readers that the famous Dogma of Papal Infallibility is by far
the most modest pretension of its kind in existence." A simple
question remains to be answered by those Christians who would
challenge the Catholic Church at this point: Is there in this

world a living voice which is qualified to state, on Christ's authority, what is contained in God's saving revelation?

With regard to the Council of Trent, it may be admitted that, like every Oecumenical Council, its work was conditioned by the circumstances of its time. The positive content of the doctrine there defined is, of course, permanently incorporated in Catholic belief, but there is no need to suppose that aspects of the Church's teaching thrown into sharp relief by the Tridentine theologians may not be complemented at some future Council by an insistence on other aspects which were not then in need of definition. The way in which the Chalcedonian Christology enlarged and completed what had been laid down at the earlier Councils of Nicaea and Ephesus is a pointed illustration of what can happen. Thus it was a matter for regret that the Fathers at the Vatican Council were obliged to conclude their deliberations before they could formulate the doctrine of the Church as Christ's mystical Body, so to balance the emphasis that had been laid since Trent on the Church's juridical structure. In general it may be allowed that Conciliar definitions, being concerned with particular Catholic doctrines under attack, are occasioned by a "defense reaction" which largely controls both their choice and the form of their expression. Theological syntheses normally emerge from the minds of speculative theologians, not from those of bishops assembled in a General Council, whose urgent deliberations have for their chief purpose the extirpation of heresy. Modern Catholicism, it has been suggested, has learned its catechism—or rather, it might have been added, its theological textbooks—too much against Luther, against Baius, or even against Loisy. We may agree with Maritain that among the present needs of the Church is another St. Thomas to perform for the twentieth century, with the same fidelity to Catholic tradition, the work of synthesis which he achieved so successfully from the resources at his disposal in the thirteenth.

Whether in the day to day practice of the Church, canon law is kept in its rightful place, in subordination to all that is implied in the Catholic faith and the supreme science of theology, remains perhaps an open question. Only an antinomian irresponsibility would disparage the virtues of administrative efficiency; without an accepted legal code ecclesiastical discipline, and with it religious observance, inevitably grows lax. The Church's saving mission to the world is closely conditioned by nicely balanced arrangements and instrumentalities which would break down without regulative sanctions; genuine spiritual freedom, as St. Paul pointed out (I Cor. 14:40), is in no way curtailed by things being done decently and in order. But when all this is allowed for, the unprejudiced observer may still feel dissatisfied.

There is a tendency in human affairs for the technical experts to have their way at the expense of the men of vision. Even in the Church a capacity to produce practical results may often be more highly valued than gifts of spiritual insight. Again, the close historical connection between the Roman Law—"the godly approved laws of Justinian the Emperor"—and the canon law is not without its lessons. The "know how" of running the ecclesiastical machine was largely derived from its political counterpart. Nor are the mental habits engendered by these studies so very dissimilar. Henry VIII, it will be remembered, discovered the bureaucrats with the requisite technical knowledge for executing the royal plans among the ranks of the episcopate; admittedly his own appointees. Here he could find men, not troubled by the principles upon which positive law depends, but adept at making the existing law work; not theologians prone to ask themselves how it all squared with the Gospel, but compliant instruments content to exercise their skill in drawing up and interpreting legal documents. True, there was a notable exception, a bishop not a canonist but a theologian— John Fisher of Rochester. The legist, needless to say, may have a profound understanding of the spirit, as well as the letter, of the law, as can be gathered from the career of Henry's one-time Lord Chancelor, Thomas More. But when we look, not at those who have held high ecclesiastical office, but for the men who have been the Church's outstanding spiritual leaders, we do not, with rare exceptions, find them among the Doctors of Canon Law.

Catholic moral theology is possibly in need of some revision in its methods. It has been pointed out how the ground plan of a coherent system of Christian ethics, worked out in great detail by St. Thomas, later became overlaid with merely legal conceptions.[23] In the sixteenth century this synthesis, based on the high virtue of prudence, wherein all human actions were co-ordinated with reference to man's final end, was for the most part replaced by a juridical doctrine of conscience. This had the double effect of substituting a subjective for an objective rule of conduct and opening the door to that kind of moral casuistry so bitterly satirized in the "immortal libel" of Pascal. Even today the moral textbooks have a way of conveying the impression, to the casual student at least, that the chief preoccupation of the Christian should be, not so much with leading the good life, as with the conscientious avoidance of sin. Those who have seen technical tractates on the Sixth Commandment on sale alongside less reputable matter on Paris bookstalls may wonder how it has come about that the queen of the sciences should have fallen so low. Minute discussions of possible and, one would

---

[23] See T. H. Deman, *La Prudence* (being a commentary on the *Summa Theologica,* II-II, 47-56. Éditions de la Revue des Jeunes); also the same author's article, *"Probablisme"* in *Dictionnaire de Théologie Catholique,* Tome 13.

have thought, impossible contingencies cover pages that could have been more profitably devoted, in line with St. Thomas, to an exposition of the cardinal virtue of temperance. Here, surely, is a legitimate field for the exercise of that self-criticism in which, according to outside observers, we Catholics are so reluctant to indulge.

Catholic moral theologians and canonists, however, are fully aware of the misunderstanding to which their professional activities are exposed. The ablest among them are the first to concede primacy in order of importance to the Church's positive and speculative theology. Their sole aim is to discover how the implications of the Catholic faith can best be realized in the details of everyday life, to find a solution to new and often urgent problems in the light of unchanging principles. How far the sedulous application of canon law has furthered the centralization of the Church cannot easily be determined. It has certainly helped. But may not those who protest at this be unconsciously seeking a convenient pretext for overlooking the fact that Rome has been the center of Christendom since the days of St. Peter? It was only to be expected that the process of centralization should gather momentum after the onslaught of the Reformation. *"Cet animal est très méchant, quand on l'attaque il se défend."* When the physical body is wounded it instinctively recoils, gathering itself together to protect its most vital organs. The same law holds good for the mystical Body of Christ. When at length those wounds are healed the lifeblood may again flow freely through all its members. Until then, a certain outward awkwardness and constraint may be the necessary price to be paid for preserving life itself.

Thus we have tried honestly to face—and, let it be added, in all loyalty and with sincere diffidence—the apparent defects in contemporary Catholicism. The Church, as Pius XII has reminded us, "prays daily to God 'Forgive us our trespasses.'"

Though of divine institution, the Church is not without those blemishes due to "the infirmity of our condition." [24] What then remains? Substantially, everything remains. Even those who put forward the criticism just considered are magnanimous enough to admit that this is so. The Catholic Church, they say, "has never wavered in its adherence to the central Christian truths of the Trinity, the Incarnation, and the Redemption: for its mighty witness to these all orthodox Christians of the nineteenth and twentieth centuries have had cause to be deeply grateful." "... the Papacy can still command the attention and to a large extent secure the following of all Christians, and ... it is the only Christian institution which can do so." [25]

Catholicism, before the reign of the Emperor Constantine, performed its essential function in very different conditions from those we now know. It may well be called upon to do so again. But the seeming rigidity of the Church's outward structure is in fact infinitely adaptable, since all is subservient to the supreme task: that of proclaiming God's word and administering Christ's sacraments. By these means the great work—"to bring together into one all God's children, scattered far and wide" (John 11:52)—is going forward. The Church, drawing its vital energy from the truth-giving Spirit, lives calmly in the assurance of its Lord—that He will be with it "through all the days that are coming, until the consummation of the world" (Matt. 28:20).

[24] Encyclical *Mystici Corporis Christi* (*Acta Apostolicae Sedis,* Vol. XXXV, No. 7—July 20, 1943—p. 225).
[25] *Catholicity*, p. 40.

8

The Debate Continues

PRELIMINARIES

A WRITER in a recent number of the *Hibbert Journal* supplies a convenient text for our final reflections. "... the Roman Church, *tam antiqua et tam nova,* haunted by many recurring conflicts and crises, skilled in statesmanship, enriched by an unfathomable memory, is a vigilant Mother-Confessor and a wise Director of Souls. A candid Protestant or an honest humanist will find himself at last asking —what, in a world rocking in helpless indecision and revealing ominous cracks of threatened collapse, will become of our Christian heritage and traditional culture should that Church compromise its sense of divine commission, or if, bribed or tortured by lust of power, it should tremble to impose its own discipline, lose its nerve and snap under breaking strain?" [1] What indeed?

From the fall of the Roman Empire until the sixteenth century the Catholic Church was the chief formative influence in our Western civilization. For the past four hundred years the

[1] J. M. Lloyd Thomas, *Hibbert Journal;* Vol. XLIX, April, 1951, p. 306.

Church, broadly speaking, has been preoccupied with the task of recovery from the catastrophe of the Reformation. When a community is in a state of siege, those who are responsible for its welfare can have eyes for little else but the needs of defense and the possibilities of a counteroffensive. The numerical strength and internal vigor of modern Catholicism suggest that it has emerged successfully from an unprecedented ordeal. Not, however, without suffering grievous loss; it still carries the wounds inflicted by the severance of former members. The Church has preserved its life, but it no longer influences society as once it did. Whether the present situation is no more than the inevitable consequence of a general rejection of ecclesiastical authority, or whether to this capital difficulty have been added others arising from Catholicism's apparent incapacity to rise to the level of its opportunities, are questions we may leave to historians. Our concern is with the present and the future.

Certainly not even the most hostile critic can tax the nineteenth- and twentieth-century Papacy with failing to put first things first. During the past hundred years, Leo XIII regained for the Chair of St. Peter something of the intellectual prestige which, in the common estimation at least, it had forfeited during the previous reign. The world's attention has lately been focused upon the personal holiness of Pius X. Benedict XV, perhaps the ablest and most distinguished of twentieth-century Popes, and Pius XI were men, if we may presume to judge, of hardly less stature than Leo. The Roman See remains true to its ancient role, not that of being in the vanguard of Christian scholarship or providing a nursery for theological genius, but of upholding the traditional Creeds. Loyalty to St. Peter's successor will not forbid Catholics from reflecting how much now depends on the personality and natural endowments of the occupant of that supreme office. Final decisions in matters of doctrine and the giving of authoritative guidance have always been the prerogatives of the Pope. But when so much of the effective administration of the Church has passed from the hands of the diocesan bishops into those of the Roman Congregations, it would seem that only a mastermind in control can make the realities of Christian wisdom dominate the appearances of an impersonal bureaucracy.

The inspiring leadership that is looked for from the Vatican demands, reciprocally, that reliable information should flow from the circumference to the center. Such information has not only to be received; it requires enlightened interpretation based upon an accurate assessment of the facts. It is perhaps not so much the statement of Catholic teaching, safeguarded as this is by the Spirit of Truth, as the form it shall take, its timing, how it will survive in newspaper headlines and radio summaries, the response evoked in minds unversed in theological technicalities but critical of conventional rhetoric and vague generalities, which together make necessary that almost superhuman discrimination and prudence, a finger on the world's pulse, for Papal pronouncements to prove effective. Catholics have good reason to join earnestly in the Church's often repeated prayers for the Holy Father, that he may be given the insight and strength to keep the bark of Peter on its course through the troubled waters that lie ahead. We know that it is divinely protected against shipwreck, but the gifts of steady and far-reaching vision are called for if it is to be preserved from harm.

Questions of high policy, however, may safely be left to those authorized to deal with them. What is now to be discussed is something much more modest, namely, the climate of thought in which Catholicism confronts the world of today. The importance of a correct appraisal of this need not be labored. It is an indispensable condition of any attempt to reconstruct a civilization in imminent danger of collapse. The preceding chapters may have thrown a little light on the question which here concerns us; that is to say, What helps can Catholics bring to the society in which they live? Their contribution will be in terms of intellectual enlightenment and creative good will. The call to generous unself-regarding charity was never more urgent. Not the least impressive form this can take will be that of re-educating our contemporaries, with no pretence at superiority, in their lost traditions. The necessity for this will hardly be questioned, but in practice good intentions can be largely frustrated by our taking for granted Catholic principles that are not in fact admitted and therefore need to be discussed. Here, as so often, it is not what people say, but the assumptions behind what they say, which is the real point at issue. In the great debate between the Church and the world, whether on the basis of reason or on that of faith, we are prone to talk at, rather than to, the majority of our non-Catholic neighbors.

ON THE BASIS OF REASON

Catholicism, at the merely rational level, makes its appeal to the world in general on the basis of *natural law* and *personal freedom.* Yet neither of these ideas is understood by the moderns in the manner in which they are expounded by Catholic philosophers. A divergence of view at this point may explain why, among other things, the Papal encyclicals elaborating these themes are apt to be impatiently dismissed as nebulous documents having little relation to actual realities. A serious ambiguity, particularly with reference to natural law, underlies a common use of apparently identical terms. As the whole conception of natural law touches closely upon our present inquiry, we must give it our careful attention.

The Catholic theory of natural law has its most lucid exponent in St. Thomas Aquinas.[2] St. Thomas's doctrine is independent

[2] See especially *Summa Theologica,* I-II, 91, 1 and 2.

of any supernatural elements deriving from faith and revelation, but it presupposes both the existence of God as rationally known and the fact of divine providence. God's guidance of created things in harmony with reason is the "eternal law." By this law all that falls under God's providence is measured and regulated. From the eternal law everything receives its inclination to act in a manner appropriate to it. Man especially, since he controls his own actions, has a certain share in the divine reason itself. *"This participation in the eternal law by rational creatures is called the natural law."* The light of reason, by which we discern good from evil, is a kind of reflection of the divine light in our minds. The first dictate of the natural law is "Do good and avoid evil." This can be particularized in a concrete order of precepts. Man, for example, shares with all created things the desire for self-preservation. Whence follows a first group of natural law precepts which include all that makes for the preservation of human life. Man also has in common with other animals a tendency to more specific ends. Hence it may be said that "that which nature has taught all animals" pertains to natural law—such as sexual relationships, the rearing of offspring and the like. Finally, "there is in man an inclination to ascertain the truth about God and to live in society. From this point of view the natural law includes all activities connected with such inclinations."

Natural law as so conceived provides the ultimate basis for morality. Man's nature and his reason may have been weakened by sin, but in principle they remain sound. We can know the laws by which life is governed, even if, in default of grace, we cannot continually act in accordance with them. "Grace does not abolish, it perfects, nature." There is continuity, rather than a radical cleavage, between nature and grace. Thus Catholicism is more than a doctrine of sin and redemption; it is a Christian humanism, a crowning of nature by grace. Sin has calamitously weakened our capacity to follow the dictates of reason, but it does not prevent us from knowing what they are. Sin, that is to say, does not invalidate the existence of purely rational, in other words, *natural* values. And it is in the light of these values that the character of all human activities must, in the first place, be judged.

It cannot be too strongly emphasized, in view of later developments, that the Thomist doctrine of natural law is not so much a legal as an ethical conception. It does not merely envisage juridical relationships in an already constituted society; it bears upon the foundations of human conduct and of society itself. Natural law, therefore, is not only the basis of morality and of all political and social institutions; it is the criterion by which these institutions are to be examined. Hence allegiance to the State is conditional upon its positive laws being in conformity with justice as disclosed to man in the precepts of natural law. Unjust laws are not properly speaking laws at all. "They do not, in consequence, bind in conscience."

The subjection of all positive law to the higher sanctions of the eternal law is not, needless to say, a discovery of St. Thomas Aquinas. He simply worked out what was implied in man's innate conviction that earthly rulership must be kept within bounds. The same principle had been given classical expression by Sophocles. Antigone, in performing her act of piety despite Creon's prohibition, stumbled against "law enthroned," but has all the world with her in that tragic conflict.

CREON: Now tell me, in as few words as you can, Did you know
    the order forbidding such an act?

ANTIGONE: I knew it, naturally. It was plain enough.

CREON: And yet you dared to contravene it?

ANTIGONE: Yes.
    That order did not come from God. Justice,
    That dwells with the gods below, knows no such law.

I did not think your edicts strong enough
To overrule the unwritten unalterable laws
Of God and heaven, you being only a man.
They are not of yesterday or today, but everlasting,
Though where they came from, none of us can tell.
Guilty of their transgression before God
I cannot be, for any man on earth. [3]

There is thus nothing particularly "medieval" about the Catholic conception of natural law. Lord Acton, impressed by St. Thomas's doctrine, conferred upon him the title which Dr. Johnson, at an earlier date, had ascribed to the devil—that of being the first Whig. Clearly we have here the necessary premises for a radical criticism of existing institutions. Disobedience to unjust authority may even be a duty. The State, in given circumstances, can rightly be resisted. The final decision, however, does not rest solely with the individual. Many factors come into play and the resulting problems are a legitimate field for the exercise of complex casuistry based on the virtue of prudence. A speculative theory of resistance must not be confused with a practical program for revolution. Moreover despite the immutable character of natural law, the application of its principles is flexible and adaptable. Positive laws are not required to conform to it in any rigid pattern. Natural law is subject to "addition" and "subtraction." For example, we may speak of a "common possession of all things," or of an "equal liberty of all men." Neither private property nor forced service was imposed by nature. Natural law was not altered but simply added to by their adoption.[4]

Deductions from natural law may be incorrectly drawn, its principles erroneously applied, or applied with a rigidity which bears little relation to the complexity of the facts. To do good

---

[3] *Antigone*, 446-460. Trans. E. F. Watling (Harmondsworth, England: Penguin Books, Ltd., 1947).

[4] *Summa Theologica*, I-II, 94 and 95.

and avoid evil is an axiom of unchanging validity; but what is good and what evil in this case and that, in these circumstances and those, is not so easy to determine. This should suggest caution to those who are apt to regard natural law as a ready-made solution to all our problems. In the hands of intellecuals and doctrinaires it can be a dangerous weapon; it may even be bent a little out of shape in the hands of canonists. The basic position, however, remains untouched. Alluding to the contemporary attitude to natural law, Professor D'Entrèves shrewdly remarks: "We tend to consider the very notion of natural law as a typical form of unhistorical thinking. The assertion of absolute and immutable values seems to imply the denial of evolution and development. A correct appraisal of St. Thomas's notion of natural law may lead us to modify these conclusions. However different it may be from our own, a deep feeling for history pervades his legal philosophy. The largest possible allowance is made for historical circumstances, the largest compatible with belief in truth and in justice. History is not the last resort, nor can it provide man with the ultimate standard. 'The Lord has said *I am the Truth*, not *I am Custom or Constitution.*' " [5]

It should further be noted that although the Catholic conception of natural law indicates the fundamental harmony between reason and faith, nature and grace, human and Christian values, it offers no basis for a rationalist system of ethics. What is absent from it is the self-sufficiency of modern secularist rationalism. It is, if you like, progressive, in that it points to the perfectibility of man; it recognizes the power of dignity of his reason, but it says nothing of his inherent perfection. The rights of the human person—the person being, for St. Thomas, "the most

[5] A. P. d'Entrèves, *Natural Law* (London: Hutchinson & Co., 1951), p. 44. This is an admirable account, to which the present exposition is much indebted.

perfect thing in nature"—are something quite different from the "rights of man" as commonly understood. Natural law is not in the first place a vindication of "natural rights"; it provides no sanction to the autonomy of the individual as the primary source of all laws and all standards. What is stressed, by implication, is the duty of the State rather than the abstract rights of individuals. It supplies an imperative to restore the true order of things rather than an invitation to the perilous experiment of revolution. Natural law starts not from the individual but from the cosmos, from the idea of a world ordered and guided by the eternal law, of which natural law is the expression. Thus natural law has its limitations; it is not a self-contained system. Rather it has an upward reference and is open to the further light of revelation. If grace does not abolish nature, neither can nature dispense with grace. Reason and faith walk hand in hand, but reason is the handmaid. When all is said, it is faith alone which can lead man to his "end of eternal blessedness." The gradual approach of the soul towards God is symbolized in Dante's long and hazardous journey. The words which the poet attributes to Virgil can fairly be applied to St. Thomas's notion of natural law:

> . . . So far as reason plead
> Can I instruct thee; beyond that point, wait
> For Beatrice; for faith is here thy need. [6]

What has just been outlined is the notion of natural law expounded or implied in the Papal encyclicals and manuals of Catholic social teaching. But it is an error to suppose that it provides an accepted common ground between the Catholic Church and twentieth-century liberalism. Much has happened in the sphere of legal philosophy between St. Thomas's day and our own. Professor D'Entrèves has convincingly shown that,

---

[6] *Purgatorio,* xviii, 46-48, trans. Laurence Binyon (London: Macmillan & Co., 1938).

despite the efforts of certain neo-Scholastics to prove the contrary, the view that Hugo Grotius, a Dutchman (1583-1645), is the originator of the specifically modern theory of natural law is in essentials correct. It is a misreading of his thought to say that it is "a direct continuation of the great Natural Law tradition which stretches from St. Augustine to Suarez, and which culminated in St. Thomas." Grotius's doctrine of natural law breaks away from medieval scholasticism not so much in content as in method. His famous dictum that natural law would retain its validity even on the supposition that God did not exist (*etiamsi daremus non esse Deum*), though it can be traced back to earlier writers, is in fact a turning point in the history of thought. Grotius himself, being imbued with the Christian spirit, did not of course exclude God's governance from human affairs, but he erected a system of law upon a hypothesis that was essentially rationalist and secularist. This hypothesis was to become a thesis with Grotius's successors. They sharply divided what St. Thomas had been at pains to reconcile.

A further complicating factor in the history of natural law was the appearance in an accentuated form, at the time of the Reformation, of a nominalist theory of ethics. Mention must be made of this since it forms the background to Grotius's thought. Nominalism has also entered deeply into the spirit of Protestantism and is plainly evident in the writings of such modern exponents as Barth and Brunner. Essentially nominalism is a rejection of the validity of abstract, universal, ideas and a concentration upon the concrete and particular. Such notions as "man" and "human nature" are mere words, say the nominalists; all that we really know is this particular man. It may be remarked in passing that what underlies the thought of the contemporary Existentialists is a kind of dynamic nominalism. Nominalism attaches no significant meaning to natural law; it regards law as a manifestation not of reason but of *will*. Hence natural law can no longer be considered as a link between God and man; it provides no indication of the existence of an immutable and eternal order, or of man's capacity to participate in that order. God's control of the universe is thought of as the exercise of unlimited and arbitrary power. Good and evil are grounded, not on the character of God's reason, but simply on His will. Murder, for example, could become a good deed if God willed it so, as conceivably He could. Law is made known to us only through the divine decrees; it has no foundation in the essential nature of things.

This subordination of intelligence to will, issuing in a voluntarist theory of ethics, is already apparent in Duns Scotus (1266-1308) and its implications are fully drawn out by William of Ockham (1300-1350), the chief exponent of nominalism. From these sources the notion of the moral law as the expression of the divine will was inherited by Wyclif, and later on by Luther and Calvin. Calvin's theology and ethics depend, not on God's nature or truth or reason, but precisely on His "sovereignty." God is above the law, *legibus solutus*. If it is true to say that many of the basic concepts of modern political theory are no more than secularized versions of their theological counterparts, it is interesting to reflect how much the underlying assumptions of the "divine right of kings"—a typical product of the Reformation era—owed to this doctrine. In the Roman Law, with its glorification of the power of the prince, combined with the ethical supremacy of the will, we are furnished with all the elements necessary to justify political despotism. The Thomist theory of natural law, on the other hand, stands four-square against any pretensions to State absolutism. The voluntarist emphasis in Protestant ethics and the disparagement of natural law in favor of the divine law as discerned in the Bible—the word of God "striking vertically downwards," as Barth phrases it—may explain how the positive law of the State came to be looked upon as ultimately grounded upon the will of God. By this disregard of natural law the basis for a rational criticism of State action was removed. The way lay open both to theological Erastianism, that is, the subordination of ecclesiastical to secular power, and, as was later to be vindicated by Hegel, the political totalitarianism, by whatever name described, which today threatens to destroy Western civilization.

But we must beware of oversimplification. Grotius did succeed in preserving for the West, while subjecting to a radical transformation, a doctrine of natural law. He was a Protestant, but, as a follower of Arminius, he repudiated the excesses of Calvinist theology. As a jurist he was also successful in vindicating natural law in opposition to the new and dangerous challenge of State absolutism. But the embryonic rationalism of Grotius, the postulate that his theory would be valid even if God did not exist, reached its logical development in the Age of Reason. The doctrine of natural law expounded in the great treatises of the seventeenth and eighteenth centuries shows men as increasingly withdrawn from God. Such natural law theory as is embodied in the American *Declaration of Independence* of 1776 and the French *Déclaration des Droits de l'Homme et du Citoyen* of 1789 is a purely rational construction having no intrinsic relation to God. As Professor D'Entrèves observes: "The laws of nature are to Jefferson the Laws of Nature's God. The French legislators solemnly put themselves 'in the presence and under the auspices of the Supreme Being.' But Nature's God or the Supreme Being are no more akin to the God Omnipotent of the Creed than Deism is to Christianity. What Grotius had set forth as a hypothesis had become a thesis. The self-evidence of natural law had made the existence of God perfectly superfluous." [7]

Liberalism had thus removed the vertical dimension from

[7] *Op. cit.,* pp. 52-3.

the traditional Catholic conception of natural law and left it only with its horizontal, manward, reference. In consequence the center of interest had shifted from the cosmos to the individual, from a graded system of law, to which all alike are subject, to the *rights* of each individual man. Hence arose an entirely modern individualistic theory in politics, namely, the doctrine of social contract. Political philosophy, as Maitland pointed out, borrowed from the lawyers the notion of contract, "that greediest of legal categories," and made it the basis of the State. The first principle of natural law is no longer an ethical precept: "good must be done, evil avoided," but a legal enactment: "contracts must be observed": *"pacta sunt servanda."* The idea of contract, as Kant acutely perceived, was necessary to preserve the rights of the individual within the framework of an all-powerful State.

We are now well on the way to the all but completely secularized democracy of our own day. In default of a sound theory of natural law, "government of the people by the people for the people" has no safeguard against the opposing dangers of anarchic individualism and tyranny by the majority in power. When the source of law is looked upon as coming from below, from the people, instead of from above, with the people claiming no more than to act as its intermediaries and responsible ministers, democracy tends either to dissolve into chaos or harden into a party despotism. Rousseau, with his theory of the "general will," presents the situation plainly enough, though its inherent inconsistency appears to have escaped him. He is responsible for the doctrine that "whoever refuses to obey the General Will shall be compelled to do so by the whole body"—for "this means nothing else than that he will be forced to be free."

Natural law, then, as it was conceived by St. Thomas had undergone a double modification. First, an ethical imperative of universal application was transformed by the seventeenth- and eighteenth-century jurists, preoccupied as they were with the merits of rational clarity and logical coherence, into a system of contractual relationships. Secondly, the idea of law as the expression of will, introduced by the nominalists, had provoked a reaction by which natural law was yet further discredited. This was legal positivism, a type of empirical thinking which assumed that all that gave validity to law was its actual enactment. There is no law but positive law. The final and complete break with natural law was to be achieved in the nineteenth century by the German philosopher Hegel. Hegel attacked the whole tradition of thought which had centered on the natural law. He pointed out, not without a measure of truth, that the upholders of natural law were merely generalizing from existing institutions which they were anxious to justify. Hegel devoted himself to removing the tension between the ideal and the real which underlay traditional natural law thinking. His doctrine of the "ethical State," that the State is the incarnation of God in history, completely reverses the relationship between the ideal and the real which is the necessary presupposition for a philosophy of natural law. For Hegel the antithesis between "what ought to be and what is" is an illusion; it has prevented man from reconciling himself to the historical world of his own creation. "The great thing is," writes Hegel in the Preface to his *Philosophy of Right,* "to apprehend in the show of the temporal and transient the substance which is immanent and the eternal which is present."

Behind Hegel stood, not Thomas Aquinas, but Machiavelli and Rousseau. Machiavelli, with his doctrine of *raison d'état* to explain, if not to justify, the subjection of ethical conduct to the needs of the State. Rousseau, with his theory of the "general will" to bring recalcitrant individuals into line with the demands of the majority. If moralists have criticized politicians, Hegel suggests, may not this be due to their "superficial ideas about morality"? For the welfare of the State is to be considered in terms "totally different from those of the welfare of the individual." It is no longer the abstract principles of natural law—"the many universal thoughts supposed to be universal commands"—but the "concrete existence" of the State which should determine its policies. If the State acts with apparent injustice, the only appeal is to history, since "the history of the World is the World's court of judgment." The vain harangues of ethical theorists will be put to silence by the "solemn cycles of history." The higher morality may well reveal itself, not in the vague generalizations of natural law, but "in the form of hussars with shining sabres."

The modern world has but lately reaped the fruits of this doctrine. Mussolini and Hitler were both disciples of Hegel. At a deeper level the Communism of Karl Marx is in direct line with Hegelianism. Marx may or may not have "turned Hegel upside down." What he unquestionably did take over from Hegel was the denial of any antithesis between the real and the ideal. For the Marxist there is no standard of right and wrong other than that immanent within the historical process; which means, in Communist terminology, the development of the class war. Catholics, in their polemic against Communism, have always to keep the implications of this fact in mind. Appeals to the Marxist on a basis of natural law are for him, if we may borrow the phrase from the Logical Positivists, "non-sense propositions"; they beg the whole question; it is natural law itself which demands vindication. There is, of course, plenty of room for a radical criticism of the Marxist philosophy, leading to a *reductio ad absurdum* of its chief tenet, dialectical materialism; but there are signs that the only argument he will accept is a refutation within the actual process of history. This can be nothing other than a Christian way of life as true to its principles, that is, as concrete and realistic, as Marxism itself.

We have dwelt at length on the question of natural law because it is the key to the whole structure of Catholic ethics. The Church's teaching, for example, on marriage, birth prevention, and the use of contraceptives is, for the most part, an application of the pre-Reformation doctrine of natural law. That these particular points give rise to so much controversy and misunderstanding may be accounted for by the fact that they are conclusions drawn from premises which are no longer accepted. Further, it is within the framework of natural law that personal freedom must be defined and its problems resolved. All except anarchists will now admit that without law there can be no effective liberty. But as you conceive law, so will you understand liberty. Even the Communists, it should be noted, are not without a theory of freedom. A modern liberal and a Catholic theologian would both accept the phrase "liberty within the law," but they would not mean the same thing by it, for they differ in their notions of law. "Liberty is not a means to a higher political end," wrote Acton. "It is itself the highest political end." According to a British Prime Minister (Sir Henry Campbell-Bannerman), "Self-Government is better than good government." We need quarrel with neither of these sayings; they can be interpreted in a Christian sense; but their stress is on the rights of the individual, not on his responsibilities. Secular liberalism performs for personal freedom the same service that it has rendered to natural law: it removes its heart.

Beneath the modern individualistic conception of liberty there lies no positive purpose other than that of resisting oppression, whether from the State or from rival individuals. It is with reference to the rights of man that we speak of the price of liberty being eternal vigilance. These are indeed real, though negative, aspects of liberty; but the imminent breakdown of Western liberalism suggests the need for re-examining its foundations. They can be shown to be little more substantial than a series of contractual relations, taken for granted or explicitly formulated, between man and man, group and group. If liberalism attempts to clothe its bare bones with living flesh, in the shape of eloquent tributes to the dignity of the human person and even a passing acknowledgment of God, these are but rhetorical embellishments disguising an inner poverty. The human person of a de-Christianized liberalism is the autonomous individual,[8] an isolated human atom; its God has no greater significance than the "Supreme Being" of the Deists. Thus liberalism's loudly proclaimed defense of man's freedom falls upon ears that have become increasingly deaf to its appeal. It seems destined to share the fate of every ideology that offers itself as a substitute for religion. Secular liberalism has no solution to the two capital problems of our time: that of supplying Western society with the necessary element of cohesion, and that of providing mankind as a whole with a worth-while objective for its endeavors.

When, on the other hand, the Catholic Christian thinks of personal freedom he has something quite definite in view. Free will is a faculty of the human spirit by which the mind, presented with an object seen to be a mixture of the good and not so good, is able to choose or not to choose it. So jejune a description compares unfavorably with the lyrical encomiums of liberty which are the stock in trade of platform oratory. On examination, however, it proves to be pregnant with meaning. First, we note that liberty as so conceived is not a condition of society, a vague cultural atmosphere; it is an attribute of the human person, a power rooted in the spirit. Secondly, it presupposes rational deliberation, a capacity to weigh the pros and cons. In this sense man was not born free; he becomes free when he uses his reason. Thirdly, and most important of all, it is not a legal or political but a moral notion; it has to do with *the good*. Whatever we apprehend by the mind presents itself to the will as having

---

[8] We may here recall our earlier discussion on individuality and personality. See pp. 44 ff.

some element of goodness; not necessarily in explicitly ethical terms, nor as always demanding a choice, but as having some aspect that is qualitatively good. If we choose mistakenly or wrongly, we do so because we have elected to follow the apparent rather than the genuine good.

The basis of this conception of liberty is that the will is of its nature ordered to the ultimate Good in the same way as the mind is ordered to ultimate Truth. Now just as no given embodiment of truth realizes completely the mind's potentialities, so neither does any particular good impose itself irresistibly on the will. The difference between what can finally satisfy desire and what here and now entices our choice is the measure of our freedom. It will be obvious that this view of human liberty—a view that is represented in moral philosophy from Plato to St. Thomas and still discoverable in Kant—carries us back to the earlier doctrine of natural law. No intelligible account of freedom can be worked out on the horizontal plane of reciprocal relations between man and man. We must seek our explanation by rising vertically to the source of the human will, namely its Creator. God, as the *summum bonum,* alone satisfies man's desire. Confronted with the supreme good, the will is drawn into freely given surrender; confronted with anything less, it remains master in its own house. Here we are at once presented with an idea of freedom that is no longer negative and static, but positive and dynamic. Man is not left simply with the privilege of standing up for his rights, which is all that secularist liberalism can offer him; his mind is focused upon an objective in harmony with its nature and informed by a larger purpose.

Freedom is essentially a question of choice. We may be forced to do this or that; we cannot be compelled to choose it. The area of possible choices determines the extent of our freedom. But choice centers upon means and subordinate ends, not upon the human will's final end, namely the Good. If the will is deflected from this end, as its freedom allows it to be, then disorder enters into each of its choices, just as we fumble in the dark when our eyes are deprived of light. A will rightly ordered to its end is precisely a *good* will. Once more, a true notion of good will can be arrived at only on a basis of natural law; whose first principle, it will be remembered, is "Good must be done, evil avoided." No one denies the ever-present need for good will, but our secularized Western culture has lost its secret. Good will cannot be achieved simply by well-meaning intentions and the desire to promote agreeable relations, whether between individuals or sovereign States. It presupposes the sharing of accepted aims and ends, the framework of a common purpose. As with individuals, so with societies, a satisfactory relationship comes into being, not merely through a mutual recognition by each party of the interests and susceptibilities of the other—for the limits of this kind of preoccupation are soon reached—but by a parallel endeavor to further a cause more absorbing than the restricted concerns of either party. This cause, stated in its most general terms, is to fulfill the laws of our being, to make actual our potentialities for freedom. Politics and morality meet, not by identifying might with right—as in the monstrous perversity of Hegel's "ethical State," now materialized in Marxian Communism—but by the fidelity with which the laws of the State embody the precepts of a natural law which has God for its acknowledged author.

The Catholic notion of freedom is essentially progressive; it aims at an end not yet realized, that is to say, the good life for man "in widest commonality spread." Natural law, as we have seen, provides a basis as much for the criticism, as for the support, of existing institutions, since each of these exhibits a characteristic tension between what is and what ought to be. It rises above any juristic conception of liberty founded on contractual relations. As Burke pointed out, "It is not what a lawyer tells me I *may* do, but what humanity, reason and justice tell me I ought to do." But as nature does not proceed by leaps, Catholicism will favor progress by evolution rather than revolution. Indeed the final goal, where the human will is at one with the law which it obeys, when freedom comes to fruition in the *beata necessitas non peccandi,* lies beyond nature's powers: it demands the perfecting of nature by grace. As Kant correctly perceived, the imperatives of law may be looked upon merely as formulas for expressing the relation of objective laws of willing to the subjective imperfections of the human will. "A perfectly good will... [cannot]... be conceived as *necessitated* to act in conformity with law, since of itself, in accordance with its subjective constitution, it can be determined only by the concept of the good. Hence for the *divine* will, and in general for a *holy* will there are no imperatives: *'I ought'* is here out of place, because *'I will'* is already of itself necessarily in harmony with the law." [9]

We may conclude this section by summarizing what appear to be the terms of the debate, at the rational level, between Catholicism and those who no longer accept its traditions. They are reducible to nominalism in philosophy and empiricism in ethics. The first concerns the nature of knowledge: How does the mind get to know truth? What is the relation between our mental concepts and the facts they claim to represent? It will be noted that these questions are not only philosophical; they affect our understanding of the Church's dogmatic formulas. If general ideas and universal principles are regarded as no more than collective names, having no foundation in reality, then much of the Church's official language becomes unintelligible, or at most, vague and platitudinous. Nominalism as a philosophy was refuted in advance by Aristotle, but the nominalist habit of

[9] Kant, *The Moral Law,* trans. H. J. Paton. Quoted from D'Entrèves, *op. cit.,* p. 122.

mind is always with us. It has been especially fostered by the positivist bias in post-Renaissance education. Our national distaste for pure ideas and an incapacity to deal with abstractions, a preference for the concrete and factual, a literature which feeds the imagination rather than the mind, all point in the same direction. Did not Keats, a typical Anglo-Saxon in this respect, complain that philosophy would clip an angel's wings, take the very colors out of the rainbow?

This situation should give thought to those who have it in view, not simply to announce the Church's teaching, but to get it understood. Helps to understanding, it may be added, are needed almost as much by the Catholic faithful as by their non-Catholic neighbors, for they breathe together the same cultural atmosphere. To produce an English translation of the average Papal encyclical, for example, is to begin, not to end, the task of elucidating the Church's mind on the points in question. It might be revealing to discover, if the computation could be made, how many, even among the educated Catholic laity, have summoned up the energy to read, to say nothing of appreciate and find a lively interest in, Pope Pius XII's lengthy and formidable treatises on the Church as Christ's mystical Body and on the Christian Liturgy. If our contemporaries are being invited to think the thoughts of the Church, there is something to be said for meeting them half way: not by modifying the thoughts, but by re-expressing them in the idiom of today. This requirement, it may be suggested in passing, is as little met by transliterations of sonorous Latin periods and theological terminology as it is by elegant paraphrases which leave the original meaning in doubt. What is called for is the capacity to re-think the Church's teaching accurately at its source and to express the results in natural English. The educational task incumbent upon responsible Catholics carries with it an obvious corresponding duty: that of acquiring both the requisite knowledge and a suitable technique.

Finally, a word remains to be said about what we have described as empiricism in ethics. This means, in other words, a judgment of moral conduct in terms of what is here and now possible and workable, rather than with reference to an immutable law. It might be thought that the characteristically English distrust of logic combined with a genius for compromise, a reluctance to push a principle to its ultimate conclusion, our aversion from written constitutions and irrevocable commitments, present an insurmountable obstacle to the acceptance of Catholic moral and social teaching. Certainly these prejudices have always to be reckoned with. The utilitarianism of Jeremy Bentham and John Stuart Mill, still perhaps the classical exponent of whatever theory may be said to underlie English representative democracy, has entered deeply into our political tradition, bringing with it evident repercussions in the sphere of morals. Yet against this lies the unshakable conviction, shared from his own point of view by Mill himself, that Government is subject to law. What has been called the *damnosa hereditas* of Roman Law which seemed, with its doctrine of absolute sovereignty, to uphold the contrary was always resisted by our ancestors. The dangerous principle *"Quod principi placuit, legis habet vigorem"* was in fact circumscribed by the Roman lawyers within precise and well-defined limits; but those limits were only such as might be formulated by positive law. The history of the Tudor despotism illustrates how easily they could be circumvented.

But the emphasis on personal freedom in the English common law not only served to express, it was explicitly combined with, the traditional Catholic notion of natural law. To the Anglican divine, Richard Hooker, is due the chief credit for this. Hooker was here a faithful disciple of St. Thomas. Indeed he showed a deeper insight into the Thomist doctrine of natural law than Suarez, who found St. Thomas's theory "to be too broad and general." Hooker had the secret, which has still to be recovered, of putting St. Thomas into good vernacular English: "The being of God is a kind of law to His working"; "Of law there can be no less acknowledged, than that her seat is in the bosom of God, her voice the harmony of the world." Hooker made good use of this doctrine against the extreme Augustinianism of the Puritans. It was to be employed also as a basis for the defense of the Church of England. However little the fact be recognized, the Catholic conception of natural law has been among the chief formative influences in the English way of life. Those of our contemporaries who no longer read St. Thomas may perhaps lend a more sympathetic ear to the words of the judicious Hooker. "These School-implements are acknowledged by grave and wise men not unprofitable to have been invented."

ON THE BASIS OF CHRISTIAN FAITH

Before embarking on the final section of this book some preliminary remarks will be in place. The scope and purpose of our inquiry have not demanded that we should engage in an objective exposition of the Catholic faith, with an eye for nothing but the principles of the Church's dogmatic theology. That theology has been assumed throughout, but it has of set purpose been left to emerge from the background rather than placed in the center of the picture. The aim in view has been to explore that region of thought where Catholicism impinges upon modern civilization, influences it, and is in turn acted on by it. This has required a candid facing of difficulties, an attempt to remove misunderstandings, and a throwing into relief of those aspects of the Catholic position which seem to provide the most satisfying answer to the needs of the human spirit. Whatever success may have attended these efforts, their object has been to elucidate the differences between Catholics and others and only incidentally to suggest how they might in some degree be resolved. It will not, however, have escaped the reader's notice that the whole theme of this essay touches closely on a difficult and delicate problem, all the more difficult and delicate for being of paramount importance—that of Christian "reunion." On this a word must now be said.

Two highly relevant Catholic documents have lain on the author's desk throughout the writing of these pages: the Holy Office *Instruction on the Oecumenical Movement* (December 20, 1949) and, still more authoritative, the encyclical of Pope Pius XII *Humani Generis* (August 12, 1950). Their contents, as part of the Church's official teaching, have not only been accepted *ex animo;* I have striven, with the framework of an investigation for which there are few precedents to serve as guide, to observe them to the letter. Far from applying a brake to original thought and constructive criticism, as some have imagined, these carefully balanced pronouncements are a positive encouragement to examine, by making use of all available resources, the as yet unrealized implications of Catholicism. What they forbid is what is likewise precluded by the terms of this study, that is to say, an exposition of Catholic doctrine which is not in line with the traditional rule of faith as expounded by the Church's living magisterium. To what extent I have been able to "clothe our philosophy in a more suitable and richer dress," to "make it more vigorous with a more effective terminology," to "enrich it with the fruits of progress of the human mind," must be left to the judgment of others. These words of Pius XII, at any rate, have furnished the ideal.

Good intentions, however, do not necessarily beget good deeds. It should be remembered that a Catholic theologian is, by definition, a student, not an official teacher, in the Church. He has the advantages of a professional equipment and the duty to employ it responsibly, but his individual word carries essentially no more weight than that of any other member of the faithful. This qualification applies to all that has so far been said. It applies with even greater force to the tentative reflections which are now offered, in all deference, simply for what they may be worth. They are submitted without reserve to the Church's divinely constituted authority. Again, any practical implications they may contain are subject to those prudential considerations of policy which are the affair, not of theologians, but of those appointed to rule the Church of God. The Catholic Church, says the Holy Office Instruction already mentioned, "has never ceased, nor ever will, from following with deepest interest and furthering with fervent prayers every attempt to attain the end which Christ our Lord had so much at heart, namely, that all who believe in Him 'may be perfectly made one' (John 17:23)." It is in the spirit and intention of these words that what follows should be considered by Catholic and non-Catholic readers alike.

"May our blessing be also upon those who, though not belonging to the visible body of the Catholic Church, are near to us by their faith in God and in Jesus Christ. . . ." So spoke Pope Pius XII in his Christmas Eve allocution in 1941. We may take as our text this expression of fatherly good will from the one who is universally acknowledged as the chief Bishop in Christendom. What makes non-Catholic Christians near to us of the Catholic Church is not simply that common brotherhood in a human nature which we all share alike, but something much more significant, a "faith in God and in Jesus Christ." They are nearer to us than agnostics and secularists, nearer than "good pagans" and humanitarians, nearer than mystical-minded intellectuals in search of the Absolute or romanticists communing with Nature, nearer than the devotees of the Eastern religions who know nothing of the Incarnation. In this sense we may agree with William Temple, that "The difference between

Catholic and Protestant is very small as compared with the difference between Christian and non-Christian, between those who do and those who do not believe that in Jesus Christ, God hath visited and redeemed His people."

A line of thought on this grave matter which both Catholic and Protestant thinkers may find it helpful to pursue is that set out in St. Augustine's treatise *On the City of God.* St. Augustine has influenced Western Christianity more powerfully than any other writer since St. Paul. St. Thomas Aquinas is unintelligible without Augustine. He systematized Augustinianism, demarcated the boundaries between nature and grace with a sureness of touch lacking to St. Augustine, but such was his respect for this prince of theologians that he was careful to interpret and never to contradict him. The Reformers, too, claimed to be Augustinian. With what justification we need not here consider. But if we disregard in the *De Civitate Dei* its author's extreme views on predestination, which the Catholic Church has never made her own, we are left with a Christian world view as valid today as when it was first thought out.

St. Augustine's central thesis can be summed up in the single sentence: "Two loves made two cities—the earthly, built up by the love of self to the contempt of God, and the heavenly, built up by the love of God to the contempt of self." The *De Civitate Dei* as a whole has often been regarded as an elaborate tractate on Church and State. That this is a misconception can be shown by the fact that, for St. Augustine, the heavenly city is not identical *sans phrase* with the Church, nor the earthly city with the State. The heavenly city is a "mystical" entity comprising all those who stand for God, the earthly all those who stand against Him. What makes the *De Civitate Dei* peculiarly relevant to our time is that it amounts to the most devastating critique of secularism ever penned. It provides a masterly series of variations on the theme that politics and economics are not enough. It embodies Catholicism's fundamental axiom: man must lead the God-centered life or perish. St. Augustine's object, as a recent expositor has well said, "is not to discuss the Christian state, but to give a glimpse of that fellowship which began before any state and which will endure beyond any and is beyond the reach of any, but whose lineaments must be copied, so far as may be, by any state which aspires to be Christian." [10]

The heavenly city is a community existing on earth whose members adhere to God by faith and love. They are joined together in fellowship not by the slender ties of a common interest, which are not strong enough to keep the individual's self-centeredness in check, but by the strong links of grace binding each to God and each to each. St. Augustine's characteristic thought is summarized in a letter, anticipating the *De Civitate Dei,* written in reply to a question that might be asked by any Christian today. How do the ethics of the Sermon on the Mount apply to ordinary social and political life? Here is St. Augustine's treatment of the problem:

"Thou shalt love the Lord thy God with thy whole heart and with thy whole soul and with thy whole mind" and "thou shalt love thy neighbour as thyself." Herein is contained all physics, for all the causes of all natural things reside in God their Creator. Herein is all ethics, since a good and upright life cannot be moulded unless the objects of its love are the right objects and they are loved as they should be loved—namely God and one's neighbour. Herein is all logic, since the truth and the light of the reasonable soul can be only God. Herein is the welfare of every state worthy of praise, for a state cannot be founded nor preserved to the best advantage unless it rests upon and is held together by faith and lasting concord —unless the object of its love is the good of all, which at its highest and truest is God—unless men love one another in Him with all sincerity, basing their love for one another on their love for Him from whom they cannot conceal the motive of their love.[11]

What occupies the mind of St. Augustine is not directly and in the first place the outer framework of an ecclesiastical structure. His thought is focused on the living heart of religion, which can be described in the single phrase "clinging to God" (*adhaerere Deo*). Men in the last resort are to be judged not by what they think or say, not even by what they do, but by what they love. "A people is a gathering of a multitude of rational beings united in fellowship by sharing a common love of the same things." To see the character of each people you have to examine what it loves. " 'Happy is the people which has the Lord as its God' (Ps. 144:15). Miserable, therefore, is the people which is estranged from that God." Those who have the Lord as their God are members of His city. Their righteousness consists in this, "that God should rule man who owes Him his obedience, that the mind should control the body and the reason our evil desires, either by subduing or resisting them, that God should be asked for grace that we may merit, pardon for our sins, and that He should be thanked for all His benefits." The peace of God's city, its ordered tranquillity, depends upon its members' acknowledgment of His rule. The city lives by faith. Through the virtues of faith, hope, and charity, the city grows in strength, prepares itself for that state of eternal blessedness which will be realized hereafter. The privilege of citizenship is now granted only to those who receive the divine revelation that is in Jesus Christ, the one Mediator between God and man. He came in the flesh "in order that through one and the same faith granted to us through Christ all who are destined for the city of God, for God's house and God's temple, may be led towards God. . . ."

[11] *Letter* cxxxvii (17). Trans. R. H. Barrow, *op. cit.*, p. 143.

It will surely be agreed that these thoughts from St. Augustine are rooted in the basic principles of the Christian religion. If they present the matter in a somewhat different dimension from that in which Catholic theologians habitually consider the structure of the Church, they may still provide food for reflection to Catholics as well as Protestants. The *De Civitate Dei* places before us the one fundamental antithesis: between those who give their allegiance to God as He is revealed in Christ and those who do not. All who sincerely pay their vows to God, who think of Him as *"Our* Father," and together may call Him so, can lay claim to membership of the heavenly city, "built up by the love of God to the contempt of self." From this point of view, the lines of their activities are not simply parallel; they converge. But if the Catholic Church is not seen by St. Augustine in the same perspective as the "city," the Church is the one institution which, precisely as such, works for its construction. The Church is expressly willed, founded and assisted by God to recruit the elect for the heavenly Kingdom. From which it follows that, in principle, the Church's members will be the future citizens of that Kingdom.

The heavenly *civitas* and the Church alike live by faith in God's revelation as perfected in Christ. This last is a point at which we must pause. There is perhaps no matter in which Catholicism is more misunderstood by its critics than on the nature of the Christian revelation. Revelation, we are told, does not consist in verbal propositions; it cannot be reduced to credal statements, much less to the narrow categories of a theological system. Revelation has to do with *facts*: it is made known in the long history of God's chosen people, in the vital personality of Christ, in the presence of the Holy Spirit. Revelation is a living reality, not a static dogma. The Catholic Church replies to this criticism by pointing out an important distinction: It is true that revelation bears essentially upon facts; it is concerned with things, not words; it is the manifestation of some *reality* hitherto hidden or at least obscure: *"Revelatio igitur significat manifestationem REI antea occultae vel saltem obscurae."* [12] But what Catholicism equally insists upon is that the content of divine revelation, so far as its transcendent and mysterious nature permits, can be apprehended in rational concepts and hence accurately expressed in words. If this were not so, men would have no assurance of what God requires them to believe. The Church has no control over the revelation; she is controlled by it. But she is empowered, in virtue of the truth-giving Spirit's presence within her, to state truthfully what that revelation is.

Thus, in the last analysis, it is not the statements of Catholic dogma, infallibly preserved from error though they be, which constitute the *revelata,* but the realities to which they give expression. This is why St. Thomas asserts that what terminates the believer's act of faith is not the words of the credal formulary but the thing they represent: *"actus autem credentis non terminatur ad enuntiabile sed ad rem."* [13] If Protestant theologians are unhappy about this position, it may be suggested to them that the difficulty arises, not from anything in the nature of revelation itself but from their own inadequate epistemology. If you hold, with Kant, that we cannot know things in themselves, or that the classification of such knowledge as we have is based upon subjective *a priori* categories, then you are forced either into a vague agnosticism: "I don't quite know what I believe," or an irrational fideism: "I believe because I believe." How much of non-Catholic Christianity exhibits an uneasy vacillation between just these two positions! Catholicism resists as strongly as Barth and Brunner any attempt to "rationalize" the word of God. To express divine revelation truly in rational terms

[12] R. Garrigou-Lagrange, *De Revelatione per Ecclesiam Catholicam proposita* (Paris: Lethielleux, 1926), p. 57.
[13] *Summa Theologica,* II-II, 1, 2, 2.

is to leave the substance of that revelation completely untouched. What it does do is to equip the human intelligence with the means to make sense of what God has revealed. The change thus effected is not in the word of God but in the mind of man. The Bible, we agree, contains the word of God; its whole contents is inspired by Him; but not all of it is revealed. The distinction between inspiration and revelation, which qualifies the whole manner in which the Bible is to be interpreted, is a point which contemporary Protestant theologians would do well to consider.

We have already examined some of the consequence of the Reformation break with the perennial philosophy: that way of thinking which holds together in a single vision the witness of common sense and the abstractions of metaphysics. It did service as early as the Council of Nicaea and proves a no less useful instrument for theology today. Whatever may be owed to the intellectual genius of Descartes and Kant, the taint of subjectivism in their systems is what Catholicism regards as suspect when applied to the content of revelation. If the Church still appeals to the *Summa Theologica* of St. Thomas, this is not on account of any reactionary medievalism but because, by mastering the problems involved in the subtle interplay between revelation and reason, he succeeded in articulating a synthesis whose clarity and comprehensiveness has not yet been surpassed. Needless to say, neither St. Thomas nor any other theologian is a "source" for the revelation committed to the Church. That is comprised solely, as the Vatican Council affirms, in "the word of God written or handed down." A further reason why Thomism retains its relevance is because it transcends the dichotomies between nature and grace, reason and revelation, latent in St. Augustine and emphasized by the Reformers. This notwithstanding, the Church is committed to no philosophical or theological system. Catholic orthodoxy is wholly compatible with a difference of viewpoint from that of St. Thomas. In any case Thomism is not so much a "system" as a living organism of thought; it is patient of developments and applications undreamed of by its author. As St. Thomas was reaching the final sections of his *Summa,* he laid down his pen wearily and left it unfinished. He confessed that, compared to his personal experience of the content of God's word revealed to him in faith, all that he had written seemed so much straw. Ecclesiastical authority, however, not unreasonably looks for similar qualifications to those of Aquinas before encouraging others to subscribe to his verdict.

Among the corollaries that follow from the Catholic defense of the rights of reason is the fact that, prior to the gift of faith being received, the mind, given the requisite good will, can be led to see the credibility of the Christian religion. The remarkable history and mysterious vitality of the Church, made visibly manifest in its external structure, are themselves a compelling witness to the truth of its claims. Anyone who has presented the broad simple lines of the traditional Catholic apologetic to an unprejudiced listener can testify to their forcefulness. But there are signs that, within their ample framework, there is room for considerable elaboration. Many Protestant scholars are quite familiar with the apparatus of learning and argument set out in the standard Catholic manuals; yet somehow they do not find the total effect persuasive. Those who would hasten to dismiss this reaction as due to either a failure in understanding or in good will should pause before passing so summary a judgment. An elementary psychological insight, to say nothing of the obligations of charity, may lead us to another explanation.

As has already been suggested, the educated Western mind, conditioned by its preoccupation with vast stores of positive knowledge, can no longer approach the Christian revelation on a purely intellectual basis. Arguments that are lucidly simple to a Catholic appear a little too lucid and much too simple to a Protestant. Where a Catholic is concerned with principles, a Protestant is concerned with facts. What a Catholic is content to affirm, a Protestant is anxious to discuss. A Catholic lays down premises and points to their conclusion; a Protestant questions the premises and doubts the validity of the conclusion. Positions that to a Catholic seem necessary and self-evident strike a Protestant as authoritarian and doctrinaire. These antitheses are doubtless too sharply drawn, but it can hardly be denied that they embody a substantial element of truth. Discussions between Catholic and non-Catholic theologians, as distinct from catechetical instructions to the public at large, are now countenanced by the Holy See. That they should be fruitful may be presumed to be the wish of the authority which gives them its sanction.

Let us attempt to elucidate the relevant theological principles. Catholic theologians, in their tractates *"de Fide"* draw a distinction, following St. Thomas, between what they call the *formal object* of faith and its *material object*. This is an application of Aristotelean-Thomistic terminology. By "formal object" is meant that which is in the first place apprehended; by "material object" all that falls within the scope of the original act of apprehension. For example, the formal object of sight is light or color, its material object illuminated or colored things. Or again, the formal object of hearing is sound, its material object whatever is heard: speech, music, thunder and so forth. Thus these technical terms represent a common-sense, and at the same time scientific and philosophical, approach to reality. That they indicate the way in which our minds actually work can be seen by substituting for formal object "point of view" or "frame of reference," for material object all that comes within a given point of view or frame of reference. We can deal with nothing scientifically unless we consider it from a specific point of view; and further, the point of view is itself determined by something in the nature of the objects dealt with. These principles are stressed because, until they are appreciated, the manner in which Catholic theologians habitually think of, and discuss, the content of divine revelation cannot be understood.

To return to the matter in hand. The *formal object* of Catholic faith is the ultimate extra-mental ground for the first of the theological virtues, providing the basic *ratio* for the whole content of our belief. This *formal object* is none other than God, the First Truth, making himself known to us by revelation: *veritas prima in dicendo*. Faith's *material object* is the variety of truths actually revealed, which are made significant by being seen through the medium of God's primordial revelation (i.e. the *formal object*).

Accordingly, if we consider, in faith, *the formal aspect of the object,* it is nothing else than the First Truth. For the faith of which we are speaking does not assent to anything unless it is revealed by God. Hence the medium through which faith is reached is Divine Truth. If, however, we consider *materially the things to which faith assents,* they include not only God, but also many other things, which, nevertheless, do not fall under the assent of faith except as bearing some relation to God; that is to say, in as much as through certain effects of the Divine activity man is helped on his journey towards the enjoyment of God. [14]

St. Thomas's view of the matter, as here expressed, anticipates what was later to be laid down by the Vatican Council. For the

[14] "Sic igitur in fide, si consideremus *formalem rationem objecti,* nihil est aliud quam veritas prima: non enim fides de qua loquimur assentit alicui nisi quia est a Deo revelatum; unde ipsi veritati divinae innititur tamquam medio. Si vero consideremus *materialiter ea quibus fides assentit,* non solum est ipse Deus, sed etiam multa alia. Quae tamen sub assensu fidei non cadunt nisi secundum quod habent aliquem ordinem ad Deum; prout scilicet per aliquos divinitatis effectus homo adjuvatur ad tendendum in divinam fruitionem." *Summa Theologica,* II-II, 1, 1.

technical phrase *formal object* we find "the authority of God revealing":

The Catholic Church professes that the faith which is the beginning of man's salvation is a supernatural virtue. By this same faith, with God's inspiring and helping grace, we believe those things to be true which God has revealed. We believe them, not in virtue of their intrinsic truth as perceived by the natural light of reason, but *in virtue of the authority of the God who reveals them,* the God who can neither be deceived nor himself deceive. For faith, as is said in the Epistle to the Hebrews, *"is that which gives substance to our hopes, which convinces us of things we cannot see"* (Heb. 11:1). [15]

Now it must be evident that the integrity of Catholic faith presupposes the complete fusion in the mind of these two elements, of *what* we believe and *why* we believe it. But there is a third integrating element: the acceptance of the various articles of belief (the *credenda*) *as these are proposed by the Church;* for the infallible Church is alone the divinely appointed instrument for mediating God's revelation to us. It should be remarked, however—and this is important as touching the position of those outside the Church—that the proposition by the Church does not enter into the formal object of faith. The Church's declaration of what God reveals is not the cause, but only the condition, of our acceptance of it through faith. "... the proposition [of what is to be believed] in no way pertains to the formal motive of faith, *but only conditions it. For the proposing of what is to be believed does not formally*

[15] "Hanc vero fidem, quae humanae salutis initium est, Ecclesia catholica profitetur, virtutem esse supernaturalem, qua, Dei aspirante et adiuvante gratia, ab eo revelata vera esse credimus, non propter intrinsecam rerum veritatem naturali rationis lumine perspectam, sed propter auctoritatem ipsius Dei revelantis, qui nec falli nec fallere potest. *'Est* enim *fides,* testante Apostolo, *sperandarum substantia rerum, argumentum non apparentium'* (Hebr. 11:1)." *Constitutio dogmatica de fide catholica, cap.* 3. Denzinger: 1789 (Freiburg: Herder & Co.).

influence the believer's mind and will; *it simply focuses upon us the Revelation* which already exists, and what moves the believer is solely the authority of God in His very act of revelation." [16]

The question which concerns us may now be formulated as follows: How is this grace-given state of mind—accepting the content of God's revelation as proposed by the Church precisely *because* it is God's revelation—to be brought to birth among those outside the Church? In what sense can we be instruments in this process? It will be noticed that the more usual presentation of Catholic doctrine takes account of two elements of fundamental importance in the act of faith, viz., faith's *formal object* ("the authority of God revealing") and the *condition* (the proposition by the Church) whereby divine revelation is made known to us. It summarizes, but seldom examines on their merits, the contents of faith's *material object*— the *credenda*. Here we are confronted with the difference of standpoint between Catholics and Protestants already alluded to. While Catholics start with divine authority and work downwards to its teaching, Protestants start with the teaching and work upwards to divine authority. Can these two characteristic ways of approach be brought to meet?

The fatal weakness in the Protestant case is its refusal to consider seriously the problem of God's authority. Protestations of submission to the word of God as it is in the Bible, however eloquent and sincere, can provide no answer to the charge that, on this view, the ultimate court of appeal is in fact the individual's private judgment. But Catholics cannot insist too

[16] "... propositio Ecclesiae nullo modo pertinet ad formale motivum fidei, sed *est solum conditio. Nam haec propositio non formaliter influit* in intellectum et voluntatem credentis, *sed solum nobis applicat Revelationem* iam existentem, et id quod movet credentem est unice auctoritas Dei actu revelantis". R. Garrigou-Lagrange: *De Revelatione per Ecclesiam proposita,* cap. 14, p. 239. (Italics the author's).

strongly, more especially at the present time, that the Church does not proclaim her teaching by an arbitrary *ipse dixit*. She is concerned only with announcing what is contained "in the word of God written or handed down" [17] and, while abating nothing of her authority to pronounce a final decision, invites men to examine her credentials for themselves and to discover, in the light of reason and historical research, how in fact God has revealed Himself. We recall the well-known teaching of Pius IX:

> Human reason, lest in a matter so momentous it should fall into error and be deceived, ought diligently to enquire into the fact of divine revelation, so that it may be assured that God has spoken, and thus give to Him, as the Apostle most wisely teaches (Rom. 12:1) a "reasonable service." [18]

It appears, then, that to insist only upon the authority of the Church when appealing to those outside is to oversimplify a practical problem of great complexity. For we have to remember that many non-Catholic Christians are "near to us by their faith in God and in Jesus Christ"; they adhere to a part of what God has revealed. Is there any reason to doubt that a large number of sincere Anglicans, for example (who do not knowingly and willingly reject the Catholic *regula fidei*) believe *with supernatural faith* the revealed mysteries of the Holy Trinity and the Incarnation? Their belief is indeed highly precarious because this revelation is mediated to them not, as by Christ's ordinance it should be, through the infallible magisterium of the

[17] "Porro fide divina et catholica ea omnia credenda sunt, quae *in verbo Dei scripto vel tradito continentur* et ab Ecclesia sive solemni iudicio sive ordinario et universali magisterio tanquam divinitus revelata credenda proponuntur." *Vatican Council* (Denzinger: 1792).

[18] "Humana quidem ratio, ne in tanti momenti negotio decipiatur et erret, divinae relevationis factum diligenter inquirat oportet, ut certo sibi constet, Deum esse locutum, ac eidem, quemadmodum sapietissime docet Apostolus, *rationabile obsequium exhibeat*." (Rom. 12:1) (Denzinger: 1637).

Church, but through a defective ecclesiastical organization which has no authority to speak in God's name. Moreover, having no more reliable guide as to what is in fact contained in the deposit of faith than fallible human opinion, there is an ever-present danger of their losing grip upon such truths as they do hold. Nevertheless since, as we have seen, the proposition by the Church is the *condition,* and not the *cause,* of our belief, the possibility is not to be excluded of genuine faith in a portion of the credenda on the part of those Christians who are guiltless of the sin of formal heresy.

This should give us grounds for thought in our approach to them, and theirs to us. At no point can there by any whittling away of what is required for membership of Christ's Church. But there remains the question of method. Are we to begin with the fact of revelation and the Church's authority and thence proceed to faith's actual content? This, as has been said, is the way the Catholic mind tends to work. It has the logic of speculative theology in its favor, with the added advantage of making less demands upon such stores of positive learning as we possess. But there are occasions when logic, without detriment to truth, may yield place to psychology. Are there not circumstances when it is better to reverse the above procedure: to start with the credenda and, passing upwards from what is clear to what is less clear, show how all holds together in the light of God's revelation and the Church's office with respect to it? Let me attempt to illustrate the problem by means of a parable, fanciful and inexact, but perhaps serviceable enough for the purpose. We might call it the *Myth of the House of Light*:

There stands on the earth's surface a building, vast and magnificent, upon which, and upon which alone, the Sun's rays are directly focused. The roof and walls of this building have just such a degree of transparency as allows the sunlight to reach unimpaired the eyes of the house dwellers in a manner perfectly adapted to their sight. This house is called the House of Light, its inhabitants are the "enlightened ones." They see, or at least, are able to see, whatever is before them in exact proportion and perspective; their vision extends to all the sunlight reveals. The variety of color in the objects that meet their gaze, the fall of light and shade, are perceived to owe their reality to the Sun's originating splendor. With this illumination the enlightened ones find their way purposefully about; they know the final goal to which they bend their steps; their task is to live in accordance with their knowledge and to bring into the House those who do not yet share their blessings.

Outside the House of Light are the "unenlightened ones." Some of these live in houses of their own, much overcast with cloud, so that only a little of the sunlight pierces through, which in any case is not directly focused on them. Others have no houses at all; living in almost perpetual fog, they hardly know of the existence of the Sun, and fancy that what they do see is illumined only by their native power of vision. Still, unenlightened as they are, they have not been deprived of the faculty of sight; within a limited range they often see with startling penetration. Numbers of them—those especially who live in the little cloud-covered houses—actually see one or two very precious things in the clear rays of the Sun, caught here and there obliquely and uncertainly as they are refracted from the walls of the great House. But all the unenlightened have this in common: they lack the balanced, comprehensive view of things needful to find their way through life—the wider, deeper, surer vision which can be found only within the House of Light.

What can the enlightened ones do to help their unenlightened brethren? They can and must tell them that the source of all light, and all their seeing, is the Sun; if they do not recognize this their case is hopeless. That so it is many of the unenlightened will agree, for they have themselves enjoyed a little of the sunlight. It must further be impressed upon them that only within the House of Light, into which they are warmly invited, can they perceive things as man is meant to see them. But, alas, the outer walls of the House do not appear to the unenlightened as they do to those within! Not a few are fascinated by what they see; others, misled by defective vision, are repelled; others, again, are discouraged by the lack of interest shown in them by so many of the enlightened ones. What more will the inhabitants of the House do for those without? They will surely engage them in friendly conversation—not first obtruding their own superior insight, but inquiring what it is in fact that they for their part see. The enlightened ones may sometimes be surprised at discovering how far the unenlightened have reached along the line of vision open to them. Little by little, while paying full respect to every element of truth held by those outside, the inhabitants of the House will strive to piece together the broken lights, the partial views, until the unenlightened ones begin to find themselves bathed in the living radiance which comes from the House of Light. Moving onwards *ex umbris et imaginibus in veritatem* they too, at last, are able to say: "Now, indeed, I see."

If this somewhat obviously contrived flight of fancy has any significant lesson, it points to the need for giving attention to what we have seen to be the "material object" of faith, the credenda. There is a widespread, and not unfair, demand that we should deal with the content of Catholic faith, not merely as so many instances of the Church's infallible authority, but in the closest possible connection with the positive sources from which it derives. How otherwise is the criticism to be met that the Catholic Church acts inconsistently with its own position, taking refuge, when hard pressed, in an irrational and unhistorical fideism? "The rejection of the appeal to history," Dr. Cyril

Garbett has recently written, "and the substitution of an appeal to faith, appears to come dangerously near the distinction between the truth of history' and the 'truth of faith' for which Loisy and the modernists were condemned by the Pope early in the century." That Catholic theologians must always return to the sources of divine revelation is explicitly laid down by Pope Pius XII in his encyclical *Humani Generis.* [19] The implications of this requirement in terms of Scriptural and Patristic study need no stressing. Inquirers have always to be reminded that the proximate rule of Catholic faith is the Church's living magisterium, but they are entitled to every possible assistance from us in showing them how in fact any given article of belief is contained "in the word of God written or handed down."

From this point we are led to a further aspect of our question which a preoccupation with the all-important authoritarian element in faith may cause us to overlook—what St. Thomas calls "the correct order in speaking about the Faith": *"ordo dicendorum circa fidem."* In this context, having spoken of faith as a foretaste of that beatifying knowledge which is to be ours hereafter, he continues:

The Lord taught that this beatifying knowledge is focused upon two realities, namely, the divineness of the Trinity and the humanity of Christ. Thus, when praying to His Father, He says, "This is eternal life, that they should know thee, the only true God, and Jesus Christ whom thou hast sent" (John 17:3). The entire knowledge of faith, therefore, is centred upon these two truths, namely, the divineness of the Trinity and the humanity of Christ. [20]

---

[19] *Acta Apostolicae Sedis,* Vol. XXXII, No. 11 (September 2, 1950), p. 568.

[20] "Illam autem beatificantem cognitionem circa duo cognita Dominus consistere docuit: scilicet circa Divinitatem Trinitatis, et humanitatem Christi: unde ad Patrem loquens, dicit (Joan. 17:3) 'Haec est vita aeterna, ut cognoscant te Deum verum, et quem misisti Jesum Christum.' Circa haec ergo duo tota fidei cognitio versatur: scilicet circa Divinitatem Trinitatis, et humanitatem Christi." *Compendium Theologiae,* Cap. 2.

While we rightly insist that Catholics believe, let us say, in the Immaculate Conception or Papal Infallibility, with the same faith as they believe in the Trinity or the Incarnation (the reason being that all these truths alike fall under faith's "formal object," *the authority of God revealing*), we must not forget that these recently defined doctrines are ontologically subordinate to the yet deeper truths on which they depend. There is no distinction to be drawn in Catholic dogma between what is "essential" and what is "inessential"—as if the "faith once delivered to the saints" consisted of certain basic truths in which belief is obligatory and others whose acceptance may be regarded as optional—but we may justly distinguish, within the framework of the Faith, between what is primary and what is consequent and to that extent secondary. The order of the traditional Creeds, the liturgical regulations concerning the administration of Baptism—where prebaptismal instruction, in the case of those in danger of death, may be wholly concentrated on the mysteries of the Trinity and Incarnation—as well as the expositions of the theologians, all serve to emphasize the existence of a hierarchic structure in the Catholic doctrinal *corpus*. Thus, with regard to the two dogmas mentioned above, it is not irrelevant to notice that the Immaculate Conception is a consequence of the mystery of the Redemption, and not vice versa; that Papal Infallibility depends upon the Holy Spirit's presence within the Church, but again, not vice versa.

To keep clearly in view, with St. Thomas, "the correct order in speaking about the Faith" is of some moment in the lifelong personal endeavor to bring our own minds into full harmony with that of the Church. We, too, in our thinking and devotional practice should strive to see, and give the appropriate response to, all the elements of Catholic doctrine as these radiate outwards from the central mysteries of the Holy Trinity, the

Incarnation, and of the Church herself—which in Bossuet's words, is "Jesus Christ spread abroad and communicated." But whatever be the results of our own failure in achieving a rightly ordered understanding of Catholic doctrine, such failure is fatal to any effective presentation of the Faith to those outside the fold. If we are correct in our diagnosis of the Protestant mind: that it does not grasp, as we do, the all-embracing character of faith's *formal object*—"the authority of God revealing"—it still remains true that non-Catholics often perceive clearly that some aspects of the Christian revelation have a deeper religious content than others. When, therefore, they see us preoccupied with what appears to them, at best, peripheral doctrine, to the neglect of what is central, they are bewildered and even repelled. It is worth recalling that a witness so well-qualified as Cardinal Manning set down his views on this particular matter. Among the "Hindrances" which stand in the way of the spread of Catholicism in England, he enumerated the fact that

We do not sufficiently ascertain before we begin to teach what those who hear us already believe... I have said before that we ought to play at dominoes with the English people. Where is the good of preaching on the Immaculate Conception to people who do not believe in the Incarnation? Or on the Church to those who do not believe in Christianity? Surely a procession through the streets would do better to sing or say the litany of the Holy Name than the litany of Loreto. Give the English people what they can understand, and they will listen, and listen gravely.... [21]

These remarks perhaps still have their relevance not only to England but to the Anglo-Saxon world viewed as a whole.

The point may be further illustrated by a pertinent example. How careful are we, in presenting the Church's teaching to the world at large, to relate the position held by the Pope, Christ's

[21] Edmund Sheridan Purcell, *Life of Cardinal Manning* (London & New York: Macmillan & Co., 1895).

Vicar on earth, to the traditional Catholic Christology? [22] The average Protestant is in no doubt that we preach the Pope. Is he quite so convinced that we preach Christ? Has he not been taught that we are in fact the "Papal Communion"?—even that we indulge in "Papolatory"? If a much respected and normally well-informed Anglican theologian can bring himself to write such a passage as the following, what are we to expect from the non-Catholic rank and file?

For many centuries those who accepted the papacy did so because they saw in the solidity of that institution, and in its challenging witness to supernatural religion, a great defence and support of the Catholic faith. The faith came first, while the Pope was venerated as a bulwark of the faith. In the last hundred and fifty years a subtle change has taken place. The Pope has become, by inference, the first article of faith, including all others. The Creeds, it would seem, are to be believed because the Pope says so. What then happens? There is no limit to the number of articles, however devoid of historical support, which might be imposed as *de fide*.[23]

It should have emerged from the present inquiry that in these six sentences there are almost as many errors of fact. But if such

[22] With what exemplary precision is this done in the Church's official teaching! In the Vatican Council's *Constitutio dogmatica de Ecclesia Christi* defining the Roman Pontiff's prerogatives, before any mention is made of the Primacy given to St. Peter, the following preliminary doctrine is set out: (a) that Christ Himself is "the shepherd and bishop of our souls" (I Pet. 2:25); (b) that He wished to make permanent the work of the Redemption; (c) that for this purpose He founded the Church, *"in qua veluti in domo Dei viventis fideles omnes unius fidei et caritatis vinculo continerentur";* (d) that He prayed for His apostles and for those who through their word should come to believe in Him, that they all might be one (John 17:20 ff.); (e) that He sent His chosen apostles to preach the Gospel, even as He had been sent by the Father; (f) that He decreed that there should be shepherds and teachers in His Church "until the consummation of the world" (Matt. 28:20). Not until the ground has been thus prepared—and then in its full Scriptural setting —is the place held by Peter and his successors, *"in quo totius Ecclesiae vis ac soliditas consistit,"* definitively laid down. See Denzinger: 1821-2.

[23] The Dean of Chichester in the *Church Times,* September 29, 1950.

serious misunderstanding can arise, the fault is not necessarily always on the side of our critics. Even apart from the "psychology" and mental background of those whom we seek to unite with ourselves, is the "correct order in speaking about the Faith" in this context, first to focus attention upon Christ's Vicar, demanding the preliminary acceptance of his position as the way of approach to Christ Himself and to His Church? Or is it, broadly speaking, the reverse of this: an invitation to inquire into the deeper significance of Christ, and the nature of His Church, thence to pass on the divinely sanctioned prerogatives of Peter and his successors?

With reference to the situation in England, and the point is doubtless equally applicable to America, a Catholic publicist has humorously remarked that the English people are as likely to submit to the Dalai Lama as they are to the Pope. Certainly, if there is one method calculated to bring to life centuries of ingrained prejudice, it is to present Catholicism in terms of "submission to the Pope." Nor is there any necessity to do so. The Holy Office *Instruction on the Oecumenical Movement* nowhere directs non-Catholics to be told that they must submit to the Pope. It uses language that is much more satisfactory because, as we should expect, more theologically exact. It insists on the acceptance of the truth of "the Roman Pontiff's primacy of jurisdiction": *"de primatu iurisdictionis Romani Pontificis."* The Pope holds an authoritative primacy with respect to the Church's *juridical structure* which, though an essential part of Christ's mystical Body, is, as Pius XII has emphasized, "something of a completely lower order by comparison with the spiritual gifts which enrich it and give it life." [24] On these spiritual

---

[24] "Siquidem, quemadmodum mortalis nostri corporis compages mirificum utique est Creatoris opus, sed quam longissime distat ab excelsa animi nostri dignitate: *sic socialis christianae reipublicae structura,* quamvis divini Architecti sui sapientiam praedicet, *aliquid tamen inferioris*

gifts the Pope himself is as much dependent as any member of the faithful. The interior grace of salvation comes to believers from Christ alone, who is uniquely and in His own right the Church's Head. The Pope, as Christ's vicegerent, the "servant of the servants of God," controls only the external government of the Church.[25] When Christians stand in the divinely intended relationship to God and His Christ, they will *ipso facto* own a rightful submission to the Pope. To the simple catechism question asked of all Catholic children: "Who is the Head of the Catholic Church?" will be found the only possible reply: "The Head of the Catholic Church is Jesus Christ Our Lord."

Bearing upon the whole topic now being considered, there is an instructive parallel to be drawn from the supreme authority. The central proclamation of the New Testament is that "God was in Christ, reconciling the world to himself" (II Cor. 5:19). Or, in the thought of St. John, that Christ Our Lord is the unique Son of God, coequal to the Father, and that only through a living faith in Him can men achieve salvation. "God so loved the world, that he gave up his only-begotten Son, so that those who believe in him may not perish, but have eternal life" (John 3:16). Such was the "dogma" which marked off the primitive Church from the surrounding cults, including Judaism—all men must own their submission to Christ, recognize Him as Lord and Saviour. Yet this is not the message that we find Our Lord preaching in the early stages of His ministry. There was a preparatory work to be done. "Repent," He tells His hearers, "the kingdom of heaven is at hand" (Matt. 4:17). He speaks day in, day out, of the "Kingdom of God"—

---

omnino ordinis est, ubi cum spiritualibus donis comparatur, quibus eadem ornatur ac vivit, cum eorumque fonte." Encyclical *Mystici Corporis Christi* (*Acta Apostolicae Sedis,* Vol. XXXV, No. 7—July 20, 1943—p. 223).

[25] See *Summa Theologica,* III, 8, 6.

the "Kingdom" which His hearers had been confidently await-
ing, the "God" (of their fathers, "of Abraham, Isaac and
Jacob") in whom for centuries they had steadfastly believed.
"Do thou reign over us, Yahweh, thou alone," was the daily
prayer of the Palestinian Jews. Not until they are in some
measure made ready does He reveal what are the full implications of these truths—that God's Kingdom is *His* Kingdom
also, that He stands in so intimate a relationship to the Father
that only through acceptance of Him can they count themselves
God's children. "My Father has entrusted everything into my
hands; none knows the Son truly except the Father, and none
knows the Father truly except the Son, and those to whom it is
the Son's good pleasure to reveal him" (Matt. 11:27). Only
towards the end does He enhearten His disciples with the
assurance that the trust they give so unreservedly to God they
can place with no less confidence in Him. "Do not let your
heart be distressed; as you have faith in God, have faith in me"
(John 14:1). In proclaiming divine truth to the world we have
perhaps something yet to learn from the pedagogy of the greatest of teachers.

Let me end these reflections with some remarks on the subject
of *conversion*—a word that comes so naturally to our lips when
considering the case of those outside the Catholic Church, yet
one so ill-sounding in the ears of the persons to whom we apply
it. To those who have no interest in wishful thinking, the
possibilities of a large-scale return of the English-speaking
peoples to their ancestral faith look exceedingly bleak. It has
been said that Catholics themselves do not consider the prospect
as seriously as they did even thirty years ago. They pray for
the conversion of mankind and, for the most part, leave it at
that. It may be that there is a need for some readjustment of
outlook. The grounds of the debate have shifted, from par-

ticular doctrinal points to those larger issues which it has been the purpose of this book, however inadequately fulfilled, to throw into relief.

In former times the dominant religion of a country was established by authority, both spiritual and temporal. Doubt was impious, dissent was penalised. One creed was given a monopoly; all others were deliberately discouraged or even forcibly suppressed. This is generally no longer the case. The creeds must now stand on their own merits. Their claims to truth have to be defended in open debate.[26]

What, then, is being asked for in our prayers for the world's conversion? Is it to be supposed that the God who deals with men as they are, who leads them gradually to self-realization by graces adapted to their nature, will suddenly transform Himself into a *Deus ex machina,* with the result that whole sections of the population will suddenly be found acknowledging the supremacy of Rome? It seems unlikely.

It may be that we do not sufficiently consider what is implied in the theology of conversion. When Our Lord called upon men to be converted, as in Matthew 4:17—which the Douay Bible incorrectly translates as "Do penance"—He was not urging them to unwonted austerities; He was inviting them to a change of heart. They were to turn away from secular preoccupations, from the trivialities of formalized religion, and center their lives upon God. Let them place their confidence in the Almighty Father, whose providence controls the world, whose loving-kindness meeting with man's response is what gives reality to religion. The final term of all conversion is that men should cling consciously to God (*adhaerere Deo*). The proclamation of this truth can still dominate the party cries, the ubiquitous

[26] Viscount Samuel, "What is Happening to Religion To-day," *Hibbert Journal,* Vol. 49, April, 1951, p. 212.

propaganda, the hawkers of social, political, and even religious panaceas based on any level but the highest. It can do so because, though our contemporaries have grown cynical and a little weary of being mobilized for a cause, the human heart remains unchanged: *"quia fecisti nos ad Te, et inquietem est cor nostrum, donec requiescat in Te."* Whatever lends support or brings some degree of fulfillment to this ineradicable longing which only God can satisfy helps to establish man where he belongs. Thus it is not doctrinal instruction merely—which presupposes much that often is simply not there—but a positive concern for "all that rings true, all that commands reverence, and all that makes for right; all that is pure, all that is lovely, all that is gracious in the telling; virtue and merit, wherever virtue and merit are found" (Phil. 4:8), that will promote the conversion of our own people and the world.

A distinguished historian has brought a remarkable series of lectures to a modest, though significant, conclusion: "There are times when we can never meet the future with sufficient elasticity of mind, especially if we are locked in the contemporary systems of thought. We can do worse than remember a principle which both gives us a firm Rock and leaves us the maximum elasticity for our minds: the principle: Hold to Christ, and for the rest be totally uncommitted." [27] This is to oversimplify, but it touches the root of the matter. To hold to Christ is to hold to His mystical Body, the Church; nor can a Catholic Christian ever lose sight of the conditions for membership of that Church, the universal fellowship with which Christ identified Himself. What he can do, however, is to keep clearly before his own mind the profound meaning of "being converted," as this emerges from the pages of the New Testament. Our Lord demanded of

[27] Herbert Butterfield, *Christianity and History* (London: G. Bell & Sons, 1949), p. 146.

His disciples, not merely that they should acquire a right view about the nature of the Kingdom, but that they should turn away from sin and self-will and all that alienates man from God. There can be no genuine Christian "conversion" if either of these complementary elements is lacking. Seeing the matter thus, we become aware that we ourselves need to be converted—not, it is true, from heresy to orthodoxy, but from proneness to evil, from egoism and overconfidence, from the moral and intellectual shortcomings that mar the Christian integrity even of the best, and so make us, in thought and speech and action, as yet so *un*-Catholic.

In taking this deeper view, Catholics will be freed from the wrong kind of proselytizing zeal: the impression we sometimes give that those we talk with are regarded, not as *persons* whose sincerity and private conscience we are bound to respect, but as so many objects for a recruiting campaign. They will be spared the underlying suspicion that somehow they are being "got at," that, when it comes to understanding Christianity, we, as individuals, are confident that we have nothing more to learn. There can be no concealment of the fact that Catholicism, by definition, embodies the wholeness of truth. Our object, however, is not to capture them for a cause but, as its sadly imperfect instruments, to mediate that truth to them. Fundamentally we are concerned to do for them what, in another sense, we need to do for ourselves—bring them, and ourselves along with them, more effectively under the *"Rule* (the Kingship) of God." They lack the light that is centered only upon the Catholic Church, though they may well be living up to such light as they have with greater fidelity than we. We have all the illumination we need; even so, the Church's liturgy puts daily on our lips the words "Converte *nos,* Deus, salutaris noster." Together we stand before God; they are still, alas, our "separated brethren," but the accent now is upon the noun rather than the adjective.

Following some such lines as these, in no spirit of compromise or unworthy conciliation, with unswerving loyalty to the Church's authority and every article of her creeds, may we not hope to bring a little nearer to fulfillment the petition of Christ's priestly prayer—"that they may all be one"?

Index